The Russian Research Center was established February 1, 1948. It is supported by the Carnegie Corporation on a grant covering the period until July 1, 1958. The major objective of the Research Center is the study of Russian institutions and behavior in an effort to make for better understanding of international actions and policy of the Soviet Union. The participating scholars represent all of the social sciences. In accord with the expressed wish of the Carnegie Corporation, the fields of anthropology, psychology, and sociology, which have hitherto played little part in Russian studies in this country, are strongly represented. The staff of the Center are grateful to the Carnegie Corporation not only for the opportunity to carry out their studies under favorable circumstances, but also for the moral encouragement and intellectual stimulation which have been provided by contact with individual officers and trustees of the Corporation.

4. **Chinese Communism and the Rise of Mao**
by Benjamin I. Schwartz

5. **Titoism and the Cominform**
by Adam Ulam

6. **Documentary History of Chinese Communism**
by Conrad Brandt, Benjamin Schwartz, and John K. Fairbank

7. **The New Man in Soviet Psychology**
by Raymond A. Bauer

Russian Research Center Studies

1. **Public Opinion in Soviet Russia**: A Study in Mass Persuasion
by Alex Inkeles

2. **Soviet Politics — The Dilemma of Power**: The Role of Ideas in Social Change
by Barrington Moore, Jr.

3. **Justice in Russia**: An Interpretation of Soviet Law
by Harold J. Berman

BY
GEORGE FISCHER

# SOVIET OPPOSITION TO STALIN

## a case study in world war II

HARVARD UNIVERSITY PRESS
CAMBRIDGE, MASS., 1952

Distributed in Great Britain by
GEOFFREY CUMBERLEGE
Oxford University Press
London

This volume was prepared, in part, under a grant from the Carnegie Corporation of New York. That Corporation is not, however, the author, owner, publisher, or proprietor of this publication and is not to be understood as approving by virtue of its grant any of the statements made or views expressed therein.

Library of Congress Catalog Card Number 52–9387
Printed in the United States of America

Contrary to most journalists, exiled na-
tives, and other eyewitnesses, American
scholars have tended to portray the Soviet world almost exclusively in terms
of what its leaders had said, thought,
and done. The impact of the leaders and
their actions on the population at large
has remained a neglected topic. For this
neglect at least three weighty explanations may be offered. First of all, the
leaders' acts are particularly significant
for any authoritarian form of government. Secondly, detailed documentation of conclusions — a near-absolute
requirement in the academic profession
— is attainable with least difficulty in
that segment of Soviet official activity
which is accompanied by publication
of speeches, decrees, statistics, reports.
Lastly, scholars appear to have been even
less successful in overcoming the travel
restrictions of the Soviet world than
journalists, government officials, and the
business community — and yet system-
atic observation of mass phenomena almost by definition needs be more extensive than that of a circumscribed group
of leaders or institutions.

That the point of departure has indeed been the top layer of the Soviet
world is perhaps best illustrated by the
fact that the studies published to date by
the Harvard Russian Research Center
and the Rand Corporation, the two major postwar undertakings in American
research on the USSR, have all adhered to this pattern. Yet the desirability
of extending analysis to mass behavior
and attitudes requires no elaboration.
The Russian Research Center, for one,

**Preface**

☆

is already engaged on a large-scale Project on the Soviet Social System which aims at such a broadening. And it is into this scholar's *terra incognita* that I have been moved to venture with my own first work. I do so in the hope that its obvious grave hazards — the more than usually incomplete documentation, the untried interpretations and conjectures, the specific subject selected for investigation — may, in the eyes of the reader and the specialist, be lessened somewhat by the venturing itself into an ever more important *terra incognita*.

This book contains two component parts. One is the little-known story of one of the most dramatic episodes of World War II. The other is a general dissent from prevailing American interpretations of the Soviet regime.

The book's component parts are closely interconnected. It is the specific episode in World War II that furnishes the raw material for the general conclusions. In their present form, many of these general conclusions emerged only after the historical research had been completed. Hence it is only partly, as a means to an end, the aim of this book to present one specific case study of Soviet opposition to Stalin. This case study is of the Vlasov Movement, a unique wartime grouping of Soviet citizens on German territory under the leadership of ex-Red Army Lieutenant General Andrei A. Vlasov. Part I and Part II of the book are devoted to the Vlasov Movement. The end itself of the book is to explore the larger problem of Soviet opposition — organized resistance, passive disaffection, active individual defection — and the resulting insights into the functioning of the Soviet system as a whole. This is attempted principally in Part III. There the problem's major aspects are discussed under the headings of "Likelihood of Opposition," "Forms of Opposition," and "Aspirations of Opposition," and in the concluding chapter, "The United States and Soviet Opposition." To augment the study, the Appendixes reproduce in full the English translations of four wartime documents of special interest. And to maintain the continuity of the narrative a number of detailed descriptions have been placed in various portions of the section on References and Notes, at the end of the book.

While the Vlasov Movement differs in a number of ways from anti-Stalin opposition within the USSR itself, it is richly suggestive for this endlessly complex topic. Nor is the possibility excluded that future Soviet opposition will, like the Vlasov Movement, arise in wartime and — at least partly — on foreign soil. And exactly because it took place abroad, far more data are available on the Vlasov Movement than on any comparable manifestation inside the USSR.

In gathering material for this book, revealing eyewitness information and close-ups of key figures grew out of extensive interviews. Of the thirty interviewed eyewitnesses listed in the section on Sources on the Vlasov Movement, fifteen occupied prominent posts in the wartime Vlasov Movement — including ten as members of the Committee for the Liberation of the Peoples of Russia (KONR). Six of the eyewitnesses were members (four of them chairmen) of other Soviet-area National Committees sponsored by Germany in World War II. The four German eyewitnesses dealt with these movements throughout the war, as key officials of the *Wehrmacht*, the Foreign Office, and the *Ostministerium*. But in the end even more valuable than the eyewitness interviews were my numerous other contacts with the two centers of former Soviet citizens, Munich and New York. These contacts grew out of organizational activities for the Harvard Russian Research Center (1948, 1950) and the Ford Foundation's East European Fund (1951) and from personal associations as a Junior Fellow of the Society of Fellows, Harvard University (1949–1952). In seeking a true-to-life picture, I also drew upon my own years in the USSR and Germany, the two countries on which the study focuses. The testimony of eyewitnesses, and my observations of them as well as their native and exile habitats, were used as supplements to the available wartime documents.

The wartime documentary material has been sorely limited by the physical ravages and the research restrictions of the past decade. It was drawn principally from two sources: the fifty-two massive volumes published for the Nuremberg Trial in two series (*Trial of Major War Criminals Before the International Military Tribunal, Nazi Conspiracy and Aggression*) and nearly complete sets of the Vlasovite organs (*Zaria, Dobrovolets, Volia Naroda*) and of the two other outstanding German-sponsored newspapers in Russian (*Novoe Slovo, Parizhskii Vestnik*). Another important source of wartime material was official German documents dealing most immediately with Soviet defections in World War II. Their publication in the Nuremberg Trial series was discouraged by the status of the USSR as one of the Trial's four sponsors. But a portion of these revealing documents found its way into accessible America depositories such as the Hoover Institute and Library of Stanford University and the Columbia University Library. It is the variety and the volume of evidence gathered over the years which explain why the interpretation presented in this study differs considerably from my initial analysis of Soviet opposition, in 1948–1949.

The completion and publication of the book were made possible by the exceptional generosity of two Harvard institutions: the Society of Fellows and the Russian Research Center. Work on the present study was not formally associated with either the Russian Research Center or its Refugee Interview Project — the latter sponsored and financed, as part of the Russian Research Center's Project on the Soviet Social System, by the Human Resources Research Institute of Air University, U. S. Air Force, Contract 33–(038)–12909. But the Harvard and Air Force organizations involved facilitated greatly my travel and interview arrangements in Europe. Indispensable technical and material aid was given by the journals *Der Monat* (Berlin) and *Possev* (Frankfurt, formerly Limburg), the Institute for the Study of the History and Institutions of the USSR in Munich, the B. I. Nicolaevsky Collection in New York, the Bibliothèque de Documentation Internationale Contemporaine of the University of Paris, the Archive of Russian and East European History and Culture of Columbia University, and, above all, the Ford Foundation and its East European Fund. To all of these organizations, and to each and every individual who helped me, I express deep gratitude.

GEORGE FISCHER

*Cambridge, Massachusetts*
*May 5, 1952*

# I

THE VLASOV MOVEMENT:
PHANTOM STAGE

Contents

☆

# II

THE VLASOV MOVEMENT:
HIMMLER STAGE

# III

SOVIET OPPOSITION AND
THE SOVIET SYSTEM

APPENDIXES

# The Vlasov Movement:
# Phantom Stage

How much opposition to Stalin is there within the USSR? What are its characteristics? its sources? its implications for the West?

These are questions of primary importance, and also of a peculiar fascination and perplexity. For not only are no direct answers possible today; direct methods of tackling the problem are also unavailable. Instead, we must improvise, search for sidelong means by which we may approach the problem area. The particular approach undertaken in this book has been to examine in some detail the most notable recent instance of organized opposition to Stalin — the Vlasov Movement — in which a group of Soviet nationals, during World War II, allied themselves with Hitler Germany in the struggle against their native regime. From a study of this Movement we have attempted to derive, when possible, certain broader implications regarding Soviet opposition in general. Though the Vlasov Movement flowered and died in the alien environment of Hitler Germany, no meaningful analysis of it would be possible if we did not first look at its context: the native soil from which this opposition sprang and its wartime German habitat.

The Soviet context of opposition to the Stalin regime potentially embraces everything within the USSR. Thus, considering the scope and the elusive difficulties of the subject, it is hardly surprising that American interpretations of this Soviet context have been both strikingly varied and relatively slight in substance. Rather than attempt at this point to analyze or improve upon earlier American discussions of the problem, however, let us first turn to a concrete occurrence in recent Soviet history, an occurrence of the greatest significance to this entire study. This is the reaction of the USSR, and particularly of its armed forces, to the initial German attack of June 22, 1941.

## 1. 1941

What followed the German invasion was a dramatic and far-flung retreat which augured a repetition of the German blitzkrieg victories in Poland in 1939, in France in 1940, and in the Balkans in the spring of 1941. Just how drastic the outlook was for the USSR was later summarized by Stalin. At a Kremlin victory reception, in May 1945, Stalin said: "In 1941–1942 we were at times in desperate straits. Our army was retreating, it was leaving our native villages and cities in the Ukraine, Byelorussia, Moldavia, the Leningrad Province, the Baltic, the Karelo-Finnish Republic. The army was abandoning them because there was no other way out." [1]

Of greatest direct interest to this study is the vast number of Soviet soldiers that fell into German hands. No complete tabulation of the numbers of Soviet prisoners taken during this early period of World War II appears to be available. However, we do have German statistics on the prisoners taken during major battles before November 1, 1941.[2] As these are military statistics prepared for use within the German general staff, and classified "Secret" at the time, their authenticity appears unquestionable. We also have a total figure cited in a "Top Secret" letter of Alfred Rosenberg, dated February 28, 1942.[3] The figures are: 2,053,000 prisoners taken in major battles before November 1, 1941; 3,600,000 total prior to March 1, 1942. These figures are certainly suggestive of the enormousness of Soviet losses during this initial period.

The vast Soviet retreats, which within a few months brought the Wehrmacht to the gates of Moscow and Leningrad, to the Volga, and into the Crimea and the Caucasus, together with these millions of Soviet war prisoners, have led to various interpretations and explanations in the United States of their over-all significance.

One of the major interpretations is that of the "surprise attack" school of thought. An example of it is Frederick L. Schuman's *Soviet Politics at Home and Abroad*.[4] This interpretation emphasizes the element of surprise in Hitler's attack, and also the Red Army's rapid recuperation from the initial shock. Much of the reasoning behind this interpretation was first enunciated by Stalin in his remarkable appeal of July 1941 to the Soviet population. He strongly defended the wisdom of the Soviet-German Nonaggression Treaty of 1939 as having given the USSR a year and a half of peace "and an opportunity to prepare its forces to repel a blow, should fascist Germany risk attacking our country despite the pact." But at the same time he admitted that whereas Germany, the aggressor, had fully mobilized the 170 divisions intended for its attack on the USSR and stationed them at the border, "the Soviet troops had to be alerted and moved to the border." [5] In effect, Stalin implied that surprise was the basic explanation of German successes. Though apparently unwilling to state this outright in his public wartime announcements, at the time he admitted privately that his government had in fact beeen caught off guard by the German onslaught. As early as July 1941, Harry Hopkins, President Roosevelt's first personal emissary to Stalin, recorded that "Stalin said that the Russian Army had been confronted with a surprise attack; he himself had believed that Hitler would not strike." Churchill tells the same story.[6]

The second point of the "surprise attack" school also derives from Stalin. In 1945, in reference to that earlier period, he said: "Our government made not a few mistakes . . . Another people might have told the Government: you did not justify our expectations, go away and we will install another government, which will conclude peace with Germany and assure us rest. But the Russian people did not take this course, for it believed in the correctness of the policy of its Government." [7]

In essence, the "surprise attack" interpretation is a twofold one. It stresses the element of surprise. Then, minimizing the extent of the initial defeats, it emphasizes the remarkable later recovery, ascribing it to the unprecedented and unmatched loyalty of the Soviet people to the government of the USSR.

The other, the "revolt" school of thought on the causes of early Soviet defeats prevails in America. It anticipates revolt within the USSR, given favorable circumstances. Representative of this interpretation is Wallace Carroll, an American editor and journalist, who has served as European director of the Office of War Information and, more recently, as consultant to the U. S. Departments of Defense and State. In his much-discussed article in *Life*, Carroll wrote: "Although Soviet propaganda had denounced the Germans all through the 1930's, Soviet soldiers, peasants, and townspeople, particularly those of the minority races, welcomed the Germans as liberators from a hated regime." [8]

Among the many others, like Hanson W. Baldwin and Drew Pearson, who have voiced essentially the same view,[9] perhaps the most extensive American presentation has been made in a recent book by Boris Shub. Shub is a young, Russian-speaking journalist who spent much of the Cold War in Berlin as political advisor to the American radio station RIAS. In his book, *The Choice*, Shub said: "If one finally puts aside the Soviet propaganda version of what happened during the first few months of fighting, it becomes plain that the main reason Hitler's armies were able to sweep across so much of Russia was that millions of Russian soldiers, equipped with all the weapons of modern war, were unwilling to fight for Stalin and looked forward to a quick debacle that would destroy his regime." [10]

It is clear that the question raised by these two divergent interpretations is of central importance to this study, not only because it is essential to the understanding of what caused the early Soviet defeats, but more especially because, without these first great numbers of Soviet prisoners of war, there would probably have been no wartime opposition movement. It was from their ranks that the movement drew its members. What, then, was the crucial factor — uncommon loyalty or uncommon disloyalty? Or was it something else altogether?

To comment first on the "surprise attack" school, one truth that we must borrow from this school is rather obvious: the Soviets did fight on and, after the initial disastrous reverses, the government of the USSR did appear to enjoy more support than could have been expected if one wholeheartedly accepts the "revolt" interpretation. Much of the subsequent internal strength of the Soviet government must be traced to external causes, however. One of these was the impact on the population of the Western democracies' allying themselves firmly with Stalin, the impact being perhaps as great in moral as in material terms. The other, and probably still more decisive, outside factor in strengthening Stalin was the German policy toward the USSR.

Regarding the other, the prevailing American interpretation, it is quite probable that in 1941 many Soviet citizens felt only lukewarm loyalty toward their government, and that there did exist considerable potential disaffection. But having gone this far, we can go no further with this "revolt" interpretation. It is our contention that the vastness of the early Soviet defeats cannot be satisfactorily explained without the inclusion of an entirely different concept, that of Inertness.

The term itself is derived from the adjective "inert," whose dictionary definition is "inactive, slow, sluggish." The concept of Inertness may be defined as a state of mind and emotions that reduces individual initiative to a minimum. The concept thus embodies the accommodation made by the individual that had existed for decades under Soviet totalitarianism. Under the pressure of this huge totalitarian structure, the individual becomes extraordinarily dependent in his every action on continuous and usually minute directions from above. This is as likely to be true of rather highly placed figures in Soviet officialdom as it is of the man in the street. If the average person's Inertness tends more toward outright apathy and passivity, that of the official takes the external form of opportunism and careerism. But here, too, the decisive ingredient is inert dependence on outside direction, and the dividing line between these two facets of Inertness is too blurred and flexible to allow for a clear-cut distinction.

If Soviet Inertness is marked by this passive dependence, its concomitant is a unique skill. This is the nearly perfect ability of the Soviet citizen to adjust instantaneously to what he guesses instinctively, through senses perfected to the $n$th degree for this pathetic yet all-important task, to be the "party line," the policy, or the official wish, of the moment. That individual spontaneity must petrify in such circumstances seems sadly inevitable. Understandably, this is particularly operative in anything pertaining to the State or to "big politics." Therefore, if Inertness minimizes individual initiative, it must be recognized as a basic obstacle to political opposition. And it is a widespread obstacle. For Inertness has become the single most characteristic political feature of Soviet society. It means that the individual has become apolitical. He has excluded politics from the areas in which he is far from inert, such as personal and technological matters. To all these the political ingredient must be added continuously by the state.

A chapter in Part III will detail the concept of Inertness. But the primacy of Inertness stands. What remains central in explaining the response to the German invasion is the extreme and universal dependence, induced by Inertness, on minute guidance from the top leaders. When a lapse in this guidance occurred after the surprise German attack, the reaction of the Soviet officialdom and mass was to surrender to a vast chaos. This was a chaos more swift and more absolute than could have occurred if either the military factor alone had been involved, or a similar situation had developed in a nontotalitarian power, a power not so affected by mass Inertness. The indescribable chaos in turn led to the military debacles of the Red Army. And it was these debacles that engendered the nearly universal conviction in the frontal area, embraced *regardless* of political attitudes, that German victory was imminent. The debacles, together with the general mood of hopelessness, then resulted in the capture of millions of Soviet soldiers.

In fact, the tide on the Eastern front turned not only with the Battle of Stalingrad in 1943, but as early as the beginning of 1942, in the Battle of Moscow. This decisive change occurred before new or outside *military* factors entered into the Soviet picture. It occurred also before either the Soviet propaganda stress on nationalism or the German invaders' atrocities could affect basically the Soviet population's *political* attitude toward the regime. What did happen in the intervening months was that after a dramatic lapse the Soviet leaders regained control of the reins over officialdom and population. Thus in 1941 the *decisive* factor in the behavior of the Soviet *majority* was not political conviction, whether pro-Stalin or anti-Stalin, nor even objective military factors. Instead, it was Inertness.

Inertness is the outstanding trait of the Soviet individual. It is this highly complex accommodation to decades of totalitarianism that is, above all else, the context of all Soviet opposition to Stalin. In the specific instance of the Vlasov Movement, the picture is endlessly complicated because alongside a Soviet context its every action took place in the context of wartime Germany. The different policies and currents inside Hitler Germany shaped, constricted, and distorted the course of the wartime anti-Stalin movement as minutely as only a totalitarian system could. This is the German context.

## 2. *Ostpolitik*

In World War II, Germany often used the prefix *Ost* (East) as an equivalent for Soviet, or Russian. Thus the term *Ostpolitik* refers to German policy toward the USSR, and, more particularly in this study, German policy toward the Soviet areas occupied by the *Wehrmacht* and toward the Soviet citizens under German control. This *Ostpolitik*, like so much else of Hitler's regime, must be traced back to the bible of German fascism — *Mein Kampf*.

At the root of Hitler's long-range *Ostpolitik* lies his well-known obsession with adequate living space (*Lebensraum*) for his adopted fatherland. Where and how this space is to be obtained he spells out unmistakably. "For Germany, therefore, the only possibility of carrying out a sound territorial policy was to be found in the acquisition of new soil in Europe proper . . . If one wanted land and soil in Europe, then by and large, this could have been done only at Russia's expense." [11]

Looking back into the development of the Russian nation, Hitler reached the conclusion that "the organization of a Russian state structure was not the result of Russian Slavdom's state-political capacity, but rather a wonderful example of the state-building activity of the German element in an inferior race." [12] But today this element has been obliterated, almost without a trace, and "in Russian Bolshevism we must see Jewry's twentieth-century effort to take world dominion unto itself." [13]

Here, then, more than a dozen years before the outbreak of World War II, Hitler set forth four basic attitudes with immediate bearing on Russia. One feels at a loss to find among them even one on which Hitler might have relented, become less intransigent in time. They are the four most fundamental dogmas of German National Socialism itself: *Lebensraum, Drang nach Osten*, racism, and anti-Semitism. And the policy of Nazi Germany became ever more dependent on this one man, the Führer. Thus in November 1939 he told his top generals: "As a last factor I must name, in all modesty, my own person; irreplaceable . . . The destiny of the Reich depends only on me." [14]

As the attack on Russia grew imminent, Hitler's basic *Ostpolitik* was presented in still more specific terms. A document dispatched three weeks before the invasion to some of the German personnel slated for occupation duty recommends "the harshest and most ruthless measures"; it appeals: "Above all, do not become soft and sentimental"; it admonishes: "Maintain a distance from the Russians — they are not Germans, but Slavs"; and it explains, most explicitly: "We do not want to convert the Russians to National Socialism, but to make them into our tools." [15]

These sentiments were echoed, and reinforced, by other resounding voices of German officialdom. Goering, in supreme command of the economic field, issued "Top Secret" instructions: "All measures are to be taken which are required to bring about the *immediate and greatest possible exploitation of the occupied areas* for Germany's benefit." [16] And, perhaps most influential of all, because it provided ethical sanction for this official *Ostpolitik*, was Himmler's bitter, primitive, and virulent propaganda pamphlet, *Untermensch* (Subhuman Being), which was published in 1942 by the SS and distributed in millions of copies all over the Hitler empire. Its basic principle was that the population of the USSR was the present-day embodiment of everything in man's history that had been murderous, barbarous, rapacious, "oriental." It reiterates again and again the dichotomy between the beautiful, Aryan-led Europe and the barbarous *Unter-menschen* from the East, the USSR, ruled by Jews. This Nazi message of hate was directed not only against Jews and the Soviet system but against every inhabitant of the nation. And to drive this home, the crudest atrocity photographs and distorted ugly images of every Soviet national type dominate its pages. Its closing words are: "The *Unter-mensch* has risen to conquer the world . . . Defend yourself, Europe!" [17]

Backed by such an ideology, Nazi Germany's official *Ostpolitik* could hardly be other than a policy characterized by extreme grossness, narrowness, and cruelty — a harshness far more severe than that imposed by the always harsh imperatives of war. That it was so is amply demonstrated by even the most abbreviated examination of two of the areas in which it operated: the administration of occupied territory, and the treatment of the *Ostarbeiter* — the millions of Soviet civilians drawn from occupied territory to work for Germany through-out Nazi-controlled Europe. This examination [18] sums up the myopic perspective and cruel values that were inherent and unchangeable in the official *Ostpolitik* of Nazi Germany. It was a policy that conceived of the USSR solely in terms of narrow economic, demographic, and strategic profits for the Greater Germany, colored through and through by the ideological concept of the Soviet citizen as an inferior, a subhuman being.

## 3. *Dissents from* Ostpolitik

It would be hard to conceive of a policy less likely to encourage Soviet nationals to collaborate with their captors than the almost incredibly harsh and narrow official *Ostpolitik* of Hitler Germany. Indeed, there were those high in Nazi officialdom who were neither blind to nor silent upon this fact. Thus we find Rosenberg, in a "Top Secret" letter addressed to Field Marshal Keitel, protesting that "it was apparently completely ignored, in the treatment of prisoners of war, that Germany found, in contrast to the West, a people who went through all the terror of Bolshevism, and who now, happy about their liberation, put themselves willingly at the disposal of Germany . . . But instead of accepting this gift, the people of the East are being treated more contemptibly and worse than the people of the West, who do not hide their enmity . . . All propaganda will be useless if there is more fear of captivity than of death and wounds on the battlefield." [19]

Goebbels, too, so often in disagreement with Rosenberg, shared this view, and, in a 1942 entry in his diary, wrote: "The inhabitants of the Ukraine were more than inclined to regard the Fuehrer as the savior of Europe and to welcome the German Wehrmacht most cordially. This attitude has changed completely in the course of months. We have hit the Russians, and especially the Ukrainians, too hard on the head in our manner of dealing with them. A clout on the head is not always a convincing argument." [20]

These quotations suggest what was indeed the case: that there was dissent from the official *Ostpolitik;* that even in so totalitarian a state as Nazi Germany, even on a subject to which the Führer reacted so obsessively and inflexibly, there were opinions that deviated, to a greater or lesser degree, from the official view.

It is interesting, and somewhat paradoxical, that one of the men most intimately concerned with *Ostpolitik* consistently favored a policy that diverged rather sharply from the official version. This was Alfred Rosenberg, official ideologist of the Nazi regime and long head of the party's Office for Foreign Policy and Ideology. In 1941 he was given the post of Reich Minister for the Occupied Eastern Territories. At no time did Rosenberg doubt the Nazi doctrines that he himself had promoted so vigorously. More specifically, Rosenberg accepted the basic assumption of Hitler's *Ostpolitik*: that the USSR was to be exploited, and exploited solely for the benefit of the German state. What, then, are the specific deviations of the "Rosenberg Conception"? What was the position that brought about the frequent clashes between the views advanced by Rosenberg and his *Ostministerium*, as his ministry was generally called, and those held by Hitler and other top German leaders?

The adherents to Hitler's own *Untermensch* theory were so intent upon the exploitation of Russia and its population that they were wholly unwilling to think in political terms of any post-Stalin organization of the USSR. To Rosenberg, however, these "political considerations" were crucial, and it was his insistence on their importance that chiefly accounts for his various deviations from the official *Ostpolitik*.

Rosenberg's political theory was clearly and explicitly formulated. Its aim was "to free Germany forever from the political pressure of the East." Obsessed by a dread of the Soviet colossus, Rosenberg was diametrically opposed to the establishment of a united Russia, insisting that "Russia was never a national state; instead it was always a state of different nationalities." Therefore, Rosenberg advocated "seizing upon the independent aspirations of all these peoples in an intelligent and purposeful way . . . to transform them into state forms . . . and to build them up against Moscow." For this visionary design, Rosenberg provided a specific blueprint. "There are four great blocs which are a shield to us, and at the same time will push far into the East the concept and the reality of the West: (1) Greater Finland, (2) Baltica, (3) Ukraine, (4) Caucasus." As for "Great" Russia itself, Rosenberg would "lead these original Muscovites back to their tradition and turn their faces again to the East."[21] Foster the separatist tendencies of the borderlands of the USSR, build up these regions into independent satellites subservient to Germany, and let a truncated, no longer dynamic Russia seek its *Lebensraum* eastward — that, in brief, is the Rosenberg Conception.

Fully dedicated to this concept, Rosenberg consistently pressed those measures which would foster and opposed those which would obstruct the realization of his dream of a *cordon sanitaire* of border satellites. From this major theoretical deviation arose various particular dissents from Hitler's *Ostpolitik*. Rosenberg recommended preferential treatment for the inhabitants of the border areas; he encouraged the many organizations of the political leaders or would-be leaders of these areas. And continually he pleaded, remonstrated, warned against the excesses of the official policy for the damage that they did to his cause. Sometimes, since Rosenberg was something of a weakling among Nazi leaders, he compromised, and urged that Hitler and the others merely *disguise* their intentions toward the USSR.[22] Yet the fact remains that much of the severest contemporary criticism of official *Ostpolitik* that has survived stems from Rosenberg or his closest *Ostministerium* associates.

Inevitably, a program so at variance with that of Hitler was doomed to frustration. Rosenberg's record is far more one of protestation and complaint than of achievement. His ministry pleaded that "the treatment of Ukrainians and other Eastern peoples within the Reich must be fair and human . . . the populace must sincerely feel that Germany is its friend and liberator."[23] Koch, whose appointment as Gauleiter of the Ukraine Rosenberg had unsuccessfully opposed, continued his policy of not spreading bliss. Thus Koch cynically inquired, "What is more important, that I teach the Ukrainian to repair boots, or that I send him to the University so that they can build up the Ukrainian state."[24] Occasionally Rosenberg did win a point, as in the case of a directive issued in September 1941. It directed that Soviet prisoners of war of ethnic German, Ukrainian, Byelo Russian, Baltic, Rumanian, or Finnish origin "be speedily sent home."[25] But it is typical that a scant two months later the order was countermanded, and a statement issued by Goering that "Ukrainians have no special privileges. The Fuehrer has ordered that in the future they should not be released from war captivity." [26]

Nevertheless, Rosenberg cannot be dismissed as having been completely ineffectual. He not only continued to plead and protest. He remained in a position of power, and the Rosenberg Conception continued to play a part in the German context within which the Soviet opposition to Stalin arose and developed.

If the deviation represented by the Rosenberg Conception was theoretically motivated and precisely defined, the same cannot be said of the second major current of dissent from official *Ostpolitik*. Here we find the men whose dissent might best be termed Utilitarian, who criticized the official *Ostpolitik* more because of pragmatic considerations directed toward insuring German victory than because of any genuine ideological objections. A far more diverse group than those who espoused either *Untermensch* or Rosenberg theories, the Utilitarians included both Nazis and non-Nazis. In the scope, degree, and chronology of dissent, they revealed innumerable variations. Yet all these varying shades of dissent were based less on opposition to Nazi aims than to Nazi methods of achieving them. This essential difference is underscored by the fact that the Utilitarian deviation apparently did not exist in the early days when victory seemed assured. It evolved only as the German war machine began to bog down and the disastrous impact of the *Untermensch* policy on Soviet troops and civilians became increasingly obvious.

Outstanding among the Nazi Utilitarians was Joseph Goebbels, Minister of Propaganda and Enlightenment. That Goebbels had no fundamental quarrel with the *Untermensch* theory is clearly shown in one of the early notations in his famous *Diaries*. "They [the Russians] are not a people but a conglomeration of animals. The greatest danger threatening us in the East is the stolid dullness of this mass." [27] It is doubtful whether anyone committed to so "racist" an opinion could ever entirely abandon it. But Goebbels was astute enough to recognize that, even with *Untermenschen*, "a clout on the head is not always a convincing argument," and he soon began to question the actions of official *Ostpolitik*. How thoroughly Utilitarian Goebbels' attitude was, however, is shown unmistakably by the specific criticisms and recommendations he offered.

One of the measures favored by Goebbels was a system of local governments in the occupied territories. But they would be even more limited in independence than the satellites that Rosenberg envisioned; Goebbels foresaw "sham governments in the various sectors which would then have to be responsible for unpleasant and unpopular measures. Undoubtedly it would be easy to set up such sham governments, and we would then always have a façade behind which to camouflage our policies."[28] Citing the example of an ally, Goebbels continued: "The Japanese . . . have everywhere installed territorial governments which naturally are tied to the apron strings of the Japanese military commander, but which nevertheless keep up the semblance of national liberty."[29]

After his question, "Why don't we do that in the East?" was answered by Hitler's flat rejection of the scheme, Goebbels concentrated his efforts on another idea — a grandiose *Ostproklamation*, a policy address by the German government to the Soviet population. "Germany neglected to take advantage of political means of waging war in the East," Goebbels thought; "the very absence of a proclamation for the East was having a most deleterious effect on the whole conduct of the war. We would certainly be able to stir up many of the peoples of the USSR against Stalin if we knew how to wage war solely against Bolshevism but not against the Russian people. Therein lay our only opportunity for bringing the war in the East to a satisfactory conclusion."[30]

Goebbels also consistently recommended a more moderate occupation policy. A notation in his *Diaries* stated: "Personally, I believe we must change our policies essentially as regards the peoples of the East. We could reduce the danger of the Partisans considerably if we succeeded in at least winning a certain measure of confidence with these people."[31] And another entry noted: "Our administrative and policy-directing offices there have not succeeded in spurring the Ukrainian people on to collaborate with us. Accordingly the harvest will be poor. We shall barely be able to feed our soldiers from the grain surpluses there. There can be no thought of transporting food to Germany."[32]

But these very protests serve to point up the essential limitations of the Nazi Utilitarian position. Not only were Goebbels' local governments to be shams, his *Ostproklamation* was to consist primarily of promises signifying little or nothing. His advocacy of more humane treatment was likewise plainly on the practical grounds of less military resistance, more food exportable for the German war effort. Nevertheless, despite the paucity and meanness of its content, the

Goebbels type of deviation cannot be considered inconsequential. Goebbels was critical, often severely so, and he was persistent. Though he acknowledged, regarding his *Ostproklamation* proposal, that "for the present I can't start on the subject again with the Führer, as he has taken such a positive stand," he immediately went on to say, "I do believe, however, that sometime in the near future the moment for broaching the subject again will be more favorable." [33] These Utilitarian protests, constantly reiterated and coming from high within the Nazi party, were bound to have their effect on the total *Ostpolitik*.

Goebbels provides outstanding evidence that, particularly among the Nazis, dissent also took the form of personal feuds. The record is replete with references like this notation from Goebbels' *Diaries*: "How badly we are doing our political job in the East can be seen from the fact that Rosenberg has still not carried out the Führer's order to transfer the propaganda there to us. He is doing everything he can to sabotage and to torpedo it. I can't understand how the Führer can leave such an obstreperous nincompoop in his job." [34] As this quotation indicates, friction was frequent and acrimonious between Rosenberg and Goebbels. Even worse were the relations between Rosenberg and Koch, who was in turn backed by the powerful Bormann and Goering. Thus Koch's drastic measures in the Ukraine against the Ukrainian separatist groups, which enjoyed the special friendliness of Rosenberg, must be traced at least in part to this fiery quarrel.

The Utilitarian approach, it has been stated, was also to be found among the non-Nazi elements in Germany. Here the most prominent figures were those of the German military, the higher staff and field commanders of OKW (Supreme Command of the Armed Forces) and of OKH (Supreme Command of the Army). [35] Considerable controversy has raged ever since World War II over the question of the extent to which the German *Wehrmacht* can be identified with the Nazi ideology. A minority, exemplified by Field Marshal Keitel, Chief of Staff of OKW, became totally subservient to Hitler. But in general the officer corps of the *Wehrmacht* cannot be said to have become Nazi, in spite of its apolitical passivity and its willingness to let Hitler further its own nationalist dreams. But it also appears that *Untermensch* sentiments within the military group were rather widespread early in the war. [36] Opposition to them became operative only when the German blitz in the East began to slow down in 1942. Then, still loyally concerned with winning the war for Hitler, some German officers turned to the Utilitarian approach as a better means of accomplishing this.

Just as Goebbels' Utilitarianism derived from his preoccupation with propaganda, with "psychological warfare," the military Utilitarians centered their attention on the area of *Ostpolitik* most directly related to their practical, professional interest. This was the particular nature of the deviation taken by Field Marshal von Kluge, OKH Quartermaster General Wagner, and other top commanders who agreed. They insisted that greater, more effective use be made of the enormous numbers of Soviet prisoners of war. This, in turn, took various forms — for example, their use behind German lines to relieve *Wehrmacht* personnel for combat duty. Colonel General Lindemann was quoted at a major conference with Hitler: "We have now managed to release our soldiers for the front through the fact that I alone in my harvesting districts have 47,000 *Hilfswillige* (ex-Soviet 'Volunteer Helpers'). These, for example, handle my whole railroad for me; and this in return for food and lodging." [37] But the program most consistently advocated by these *Wehrmacht* Utilitarians, and the one of most central interest to this study, was the use of ex-Soviet soldiers in the ranks of the German army — a subject discussed in greater detail in a following chapter.

In the very course of furthering their pragmatic military program, these Utilitarians were led to a concern with the broader political aspects of *Ostpolitik*. There was, after all, the morale of the ex-Soviet volunteers to be taken into account. It is not surprising, therefore, to find in Goebbels' *Diaries* the entry: "Major Balzer reported to me about his visit to the headquarters of Field Marshal General Kluge. They are placing great hopes in me and expect me to persuade the Führer to issue a proclamation for the East." [38] But this interest was usually in *Ostpolitik* as a means, seldom as an end. The non-Nazi, like the Nazi, Utilitarians were essentially indifferent, if not actually hostile, to any ventures and postwar plans not clearly for German benefit or under German control.

In contrast to the various currents of dissent that either adhered to Nazi ideology or were essentially lacking in a positive creed, there is a third major deviation from official *Ostpolitik*. This deviation favored promoting independent anti-Stalin movements among Soviet nationals not solely, perhaps not even primarily, to help Hitler win the war. We may call this the Other Germany group, borrowing the name from the memoirs of a prominent German resistance figure, Ulrich von Hassell.

To the Soviet defectors, the Other Germany was not only the anti-*Ostpolitik* grouping. Part of the Other Germany is the material well-being — vast in comparison with that of the USSR — that Soviet citizens now observed. This is an aspect that on the whole has been both exaggerated and oversimplified in the United States. The Soviet citizen came sufficiently schooled from the USSR to have his admiration for material riches muted by less tangible shortcomings, or what seemed to him as such. Moreover, the craving to return to a long-familiar habitat, together with elementary patriotism, was apt to have cut further into this admiration for "life in the West." It remains completely valid, nevertheless, to suggest that the impact of this affluent existence outside the USSR must have been considerable in many instances. This impact, moreover, was undoubtedly magnified not only by the vastly distorted picture of the outside world presented by Soviet propaganda; equally important were the Soviets' traditionally great awe of German technical superiority and — last but not least — the technical and often the moral impressiveness of the German front-line troops that were seen first by the Soviet populace, before Himmler's police units entered the country in 1942.

In terms of the Vlasov Movement, it was the anti-*Ostpolitik* grouping, however, that was the outstanding element of the non-Nazi Other Germany. The exact size and composition of the group advocating this position, so drastically divergent from the official one, is not known, nor can its influence be fully estimated. It is, however, clear that its effect upon the actual course of the Soviet opposition movement was of great and immediate importance. For this Other Germany policy was put forth, chiefly, by a group of German officers and diplomats who were either Old Russia Hands or of Russian and Baltic birth, or, at times, both. Knowing the country, speaking the language, it was inevitable that they should be assigned duties that would bring them into direct contact with Soviet nationals under German control, particularly the higher-ranking ones.

As is true of any group, these men differed in the intensity and clarity of their views, and in their readiness to translate these views into action. Nevertheless, the entire Other Germany category was characterized by a belief in a nonauthoritarian successor to the Stalin regime. Many of them also believed in a nonauthoritarian Germany and a free, civilized world. This may be inferred from the same fact that has deprived us of much vital information regarding this group; many of them were executed after the July 20, 1944 *Putsch* against Hitler.

Though our knowledge of its key figures is limited for this tragic reason, two famous adherents to the Other Germany policy have been identified: Colonel Claus von Stauffenberg, the hero of the Twentieth of July, and Count Friedrich Werner von der Schulenberg, until 1941 German Ambassador to Moscow. Both of them lost their lives after the *Putsch*. In World War II Schulenburg became chairman of the German Foreign Office's largely dormant rival to the *Ostministerium* (*Russland-Gremium*). Early in the war he was among those who urged an Other Germany *Ostpolitik* on the Hitler government. He advised that Germany proclaim that it had no territorial claims on the USSR, allow the population of the occupied areas to establish local governments of their own, and encourage these governments, as its allies, to join in an anti-Soviet government.[1] Such a recommendation highlights the enormous disparity between the Other Germany and the official views of *Ostpolitik*.

There is another adherent to the Other Germany position, as little known as Stauffenberg and Schulenburg are famous, who was to play a role rivaled by no other German in the Soviet opposition movement. This is Wilfried Strik-Strikfeldt. Born and educated in pre-1917 Russia in a Russianized German merchant family, he left the country after having fought as a "White" officer against the Red Army. Following relief and business activities throughout Europe from his center in Riga, Strikfeldt was called into the German army in World War II. He served through most of it as a captain in an obscure position. But it was also a strategic position, a position that kept him in close touch with most of the ex-Soviet citizens who were to lead the opposition against Stalin, and particularly with General Vlasov.

From even so brief a consideration of the aims and actions of the various schools of German *Ostpolitik*, it is immediately apparent that only the Other Germany category could purposively and consistently champion anti-Stalin activity among ex-Soviet personnel. Indeed, it was in large measure owing to the efforts of these German believers in a nonauthoritarian Russia, though with frequent backing by the military Utilitarians, that an organized opposition movement was actually launched, channeled, and kept afloat during World War II.

Another part of the non-Nazi Other Germany must be mentioned if wartime Soviet opposition to Stalin is to be seen within its total context. Not another version of German dissent, indeed not German at all, this is the group of post-1917 old émigrés from various parts of the USSR. As is true today of the old and recent exiles from the USSR, the old émigrés prior to World War II were almost wholly isolated in a jungle of émigré passions,[2] personal and political, and forgetting how little influence on their homeland returned exiles have had in past history. As now, many were pressing for an early military venture to overthrow the Soviet regime[3] and accusing Western opponents of such a policy as utterly naïve or as Soviet stooges.[4] And again as in the present situation, the West knew little of this émigré world[5] and tended to lend its ear and support to the sensationalist and reactionary émigré leader more than the sadly few statesmanlike and libertarian figures who, like Thomas G. Masaryk after World War I and Ernst Reuter after World War II, might return from exile as a small "third force" against — rather than for — either a bloody and chaotic Time of Troubles or a new dictatorship.[6]

Throughout Europe, as World War II approached, the old emigration became increasingly divided into three camps: those who adopted a pro-Soviet position, those who were both anti-Stalin and anti-Hitler, and those who in varying degrees sided with Germany. The last group, which is the one that concerns us here, also falls into two divisions. One consisted of actual Russian fascists, mostly Tsarist monarchists who can be speedily dismissed from any account of the Other Germany. They tended to serve directly in German agencies, and had little but loathing for the Soviet collaborators, believing them to be deep-dyed reds or Stalinist agents. It is the other group, the non-Nazis among the old émigré collaborators, that became intimately associated with the Soviet opposition movement. They too had entered into a "marriage of convenience" with Nazi Germany, and they too sought organizational forms of some, even if only relative, independence. To the newly-arrived Soviet defectors, this type of old émigré appeared as an important part of the Other Germany.

It can well be said, regarding their collaboration, that the old émigrés had long enjoyed the advantage of free European thought and institutions; for them the issues should have been clearer than for the Soviet collaborators, and their political standards more sophisticated and operative. Nevertheless, many of them succumbed, under the pressure of their burning anti-Stalinism, to the opportunity of perhaps at last realizing their dreams of overthrowing and replacing the Soviet regime. And after so many years of barren exile, it seemed a distinct possibility in 1941–1942. Just how ecstatic many an old-émigré *Wehrmacht* officer on the Eastern Front felt at the chance of actively fighting the Soviets is reflected in a letter printed in a Russian-language newspaper in Paris. "I do absolutely nothing against my conscience . . . This war is not terrible for us, Russian patriots, but only joyous; for the Bolshevik yoke over our motherland will be ended . . . I consider myself a warrior of Christ." [7]

However joyfully the old émigrés may have sought to serve against Stalin, their proffered service was not received with equal enthusiasm; their nationalist aspirations were far too fervent to be acceptable to the official *Ostpolitik*. Moreover, Hitler was suspicious of their loyalty, believing that "each country thinks of itself and of nothing else. All these émigrés and advisors only want to occupy positions for later." [8] Completely negative at first, the Nazi attitude toward the old émigrés soon became, and remained, equivocal. Though Hitler and his closest associates retained their distrust to the end, the magnitude of the personnel problem forced the Germans to use old émigrés as interpreters, administrators, and analysts in most agencies dealing with the USSR and the war against it.

One of the spots where old émigrés were first put to use was the Wustrau center for the selection and training, from among Soviet prisoners, of propagandists and administrators, chiefly for German-occupied areas of the USSR. Here, somewhat ironically, since the center was set up by Rosenberg's *Ostministerium*, the actual course of instruction came to be controlled largely by NTS — the National Alliance of Russian Solidarists. Today also an important factor in émigré affairs, NTS was one of the non-Nazi émigré organizations in Germany. Since its foundation in Belgrade in 1930, it was distinguished for its Mussolini-like philosophy of "solidarism" and intense Russian nationalism, and because — unlike most old-émigré organizations — it was exceptionally skilled organizationally and propagandawise. Thus, side by side with straight Nazi propaganda — with some of which many, if not all, NTS members heartily agreed — the lectures at Wustrau included a strong emphasis on the preservation and furtherance of Russian national objectives. In an atmosphere otherwise permeated with *Untermensch* sentiments and policies, the influence of this nationalist group upon the at first largely dazed Soviet collaborators was of the greatest importance and had considerable effect upon the crystallization of wartime Soviet opposition. Indeed, the fact that coöperation continued between the old-émigré NTS and the wartime Soviet opposition movement, even though many recent defectors subsequently became ideologically and organizationally critical of the solidarists, may probably be attributed largely to the force of this initial NTS impact.

Extreme nationalist sentiment among the old émigrés — and some Soviet nationals — was, however, by no means solely Russian. Within wartime Germany there were Byelorussians, Ukrainians, Caucasians, Turkestani — indeed, all the various Soviet minorities. Many of them were organized into innumerable groups and subgroups, each with its separate history, leaders, cleavages, program, and aspirations. Endlessly diverse, these nationalist organizations shared one basic plank — the break-up of the USSR and the independence of their own nationality. Also, as might be expected, they usually shared the support, material as well as political, of Rosenberg and his *Ostministerium*.

The fortunes of these various groups were nearly as complex as their composition, and far too complex to be dealt with adequately here. One of the facts that should be mentioned in the broadest and most general terms, however, was that those nationalities most remote from and least important to Germany fared best. Thus it was the Ukrainians, alone of the non-Russian nationalities, who most of the time had no German-recognized National Committee. True, they had their brief day of glory when a Ukrainian State was proclaimed triumphantly in Lvov, in July 1941, by followers of Bandera, the leader of OUN. OUN, like NTS, again prominent in present-day émigré affairs, is the anti-Communist, anti-Russian, and, it may be added, also anti-democratic Organization of Ukrainian Nationalists, a group with roots not in the USSR but in the Ukraine's smaller western part, Galicia, which was under Poland until 1939. But the Ukrainians were too numerous, the nationalism of the Galicians too extreme, and their homeland's exploitation too important to Germany to permit such independence for long. Indeed, the OUN's "State" was dissolved in less than a month, after which the Ukraine was the least favored of the potentially separatist areas.[9] In contrast, the also largely old-émigré North Caucasian, Armenian, and Azerbaijan-Tartar National Committees, and especially the United Turkestan National Committee, enjoyed some measure of independence. Their weaker and more isolated border regions were far less crucial to Hitler's future plans.

In the past century, nationalism has frequently been hopelessly complex and emotionalized. This explosive situation was applicable during World War II, and is today, to anti-Stalinists from the Soviet area. Among these exiles the issue has been even more divisive than the familiar political cleavages of émigré existence. This is so although the outside observer lacks sufficient data to determine to what degree these inflamed exile emotions are representative of moods within the USSR.

On the national question, as on their attitudes on Hitler, the old émigrés may be divided into three different groups. The same tends to be true of the Soviet defectors. In a sharply polarized situation, one pole (itself of course not uniform) is that of the Russian nationalists like the solidarist organization, NTS, and the still active prime minister of the 1917 Provisional Government, Alexander Kerensky. It is significant that among the Russian nationalist group are to be found an unknown percentage of Soviet defectors who are of non-Russian origin. These are either Russianized culturally, or they strongly favor a post-Stalin federation among the component nationalities of what is now the USSR. Exemplified by the New York monarchist daily *Rossiia*, the extremists in the Russian nationalist group seem committed unalterably to the official Tsarist doctrine of "Russia one and indivisible."

The other pole is that of the non-Russian separatists. This group is pressing for post-Stalin separation from Russia proper, and independent statehood for the other nationalities of the USSR. They insist equally strongly on recognition of such plans without delay by exile groups and foreign governments. A continuingly important feature of the separatist group is that the extremists among it cherish a hatred for the Russians as a *race* of oppressors and imperialists as great as, if not greater than, their hatred for the Soviet regime. Just as the monarchist newspaper *Rossiia* is typical of the extremists in the Russian nationalist group, so the extremists in the separatist group are symbolized by the already-mentioned Ukrainian organization, OUN, and its leader, Bandera. During World War II this Russophobia not only fitted perfectly with the Rosenberg Conception; its fanatic racism also bore an obvious affinity with Hitler's and Himmler's *Untermensch* theory, and was not without significance in the over-all development of German *Ostpolitik*.

Between the two poles of the émigré nationality strife is the self-determination group. This group favors the settlement of the national issue, after the overthrow of the Stalin regime, by the population affected — and not by either exiles or foreign governments. In addition to the convinced, the self-determination position tends to attract those who are less immersed in the national issue. It has therefore lacked, during World War II and after, both the fanaticism and the organizational drive of the two other currents. Although it perforce provides the one meeting ground on which the two other groups might possibly compromise, the chaos and passions unleashed first by the 1917 Revolution and again by World War II provide little ground for optimism — or for any certainty as to what, if any, formula might succeed short of protracted post-Soviet anarchy and bloodshed

The old émigré element of the Other Germany played a crucial role in the history of the Vlasov Movement. Alongside the anti-*Ostpolitik* grouping of Germans, it daily influenced, protected, guided (and misguided) the Soviet-bred neophytes in the jungle of Nazi politics. But the old émigrés also brought with them the ever-devisive germs of nationality antagonisms. They also added the demoralized émigré passions of bitter decades of exile to the Inertness, the bewilderment, the demoralization of the Soviet defector.

Neither the anti-*Ostpolitik* nor the old-émigré components of the Other Germany could have had their great influence on the Vlasov Movement but for another phenomenon within the Nazi system. This was the existence, within the great German sea of totalitarianism, of islands on which individuals and their activities could survive with relative safety. This phenomenon is of the greatest significance. It involves the immensely complex question of just how total Nazi totalitarianism — and modern totalitarianism in general — has been.

At this point, two basic differences between German and Soviet totalitarianism should be noted. One of these is the duration: twelve years of National Socialism in power, thirty-five of Soviet Communism. The other basic difference between the two systems is that whereas over the years the social revolution in the USSR was drastic and radical, changing property, employment, and practically every other human relation, the same certainly is not true of Hitler Germany. This difference is of the greatest importance for this study. German groupings on *Ostpolitik* were decisively affected by the partial preservation of such once-sovereign institutions as the *Wehrmacht*. Perhaps even more important, tactically as well as psychologically, was the retention by a number of non-Nazi officials of private incomes and estates, or the opportunity of earning a livelihood outside the realm of immediate and intimate Nazi control.[10]

These islands of economic and occupational pluralism in the sea of German fascism make up one of the lacunae in contemporary studies of totalitarianism. These islands — so strikingly smaller in Soviet life — must be made a vivid reality in the mind of the reader before he can understand fully the position of the non-Nazi officialdom and its relation to the wartime *Ostpolitik*. In a profoundly paradoxical manner, this is a combination of the dread and terror essential to every totalitarianism with islands on which individuals could pursue their activities with an astonishing degree of independence. This is a subtle combination indeed, and to date the tendency has been to reject — or at least to neglect — the second of its basic components.

Hence most remarkable, and most important for our study, was the existence of the Other Germany group — and of like-minded old émigrés as well — whose opinions and actions differed so strikingly from official policy. The preservation of these islands within German totalitarianism influenced the course of wartime Soviet opposition decisively.

On the Vlasov Movement the impact of Germany was to a very

large extent the impact of the Other Germany. Rarely indeed did a decision by a Soviet national during World War II to collaborate with the Hitler regime take the form of direct contact or direct coöperation with Nazi officials or organizations. On the contrary, the most effective and persuasive German advocates of Soviet-defector collaboration came from the ranks of those German officials and old émigrés who dissented from the official *Ostpolitik*. What in fact was unquestionably collaboration with the Hitler regime had thus been effected largely through German officials and old émigrés whose words and actions bespoke disapprobation of that regime.

Wartime Soviet opposition appears in a different light, and has to be judged differently, as a result of this situation. There is an enormous difference in how the first step toward collaboration was decided upon. Entering upon a course of collaboration under the influence of Nazi doctrines and officials is one path. But the whole picture is altered when the step is guided by the Other Germany, a current apart from the ugly core of German fascism and far more sympathetic toward the aspirations of these Soviet citizens. The Other Germany thus played a dual role in the evolution of the Vlasov Movement. It not only aided and furthered the anti-*Ostpolitik* aspirations of the Vlasov Movement itself. In effect, although not in intent, the Other Germany also was outstanding in smoothing the Vlasovites' first step to collaborating with Nazism.

The search for a suitable Soviet figure to head a German-backed anti-Stalin movement of Soviet nationals gained momentum in 1942: the increasing German reverses on the Eastern Front hastened the growth and strengthened the position of the Utilitarian and Other Germany dissents from Hitler's *Ostpolitik.* There were those who, like Strikfeldt, favored an independent-minded leader; others sought only a German stooge or quisling. Thus even the *Ostministerium* showed interest; in a "Top Secret" memorandum to Rosenberg, dated October 25, 1942, Dr. Bräutigam, deputy chief of the Ministry's Central Political Department, wrote: "As the best means, the establishment of a sort of counter-regime to Stalin with a captured Red general was indicated; or if the word government should be avoided, then just a rebellious general somewhat after the model of de Gaulle, who should become the point of crystallization for all the Red soldiers who are dissatisfied with Stalin." [1]

It was not long before a candidate was found who was both acceptable and willing. He was Andrei A. Vlasov, Lieutenant General of the Red Army, now to become the leader of the German-sponsored Russian Liberation Movement. Soon this movement became synonymous with the name of its leader. In popular parlance its name became the Vlasov Movement.

The fullest single biography of Vlasov is contained in a pamphlet published in Germany in 1944. Its complete text, in English, is reproduced in Appendix I.

**Chapter III**

**General Vlasov**

Its author, V. Osokin, was a former Red Army lieutenant who in Germany became a junior aide to Vlasov. The biography was published by the Soviet opposition movement itself. It may therefore be assumed that the biographical data either originated with Vlasov or were approved by him. This is not to imply that the "official" biography may not contain certain exaggerations or glorifications in Vlasov's favor; it probably does. Nevertheless, it is the only more or less first-hand source of information regarding numerous aspects of Vlasov's life.

## 1. The Life of Vlasov

"Andrei Andreevich Vlasov," states this "official" wartime biography, "was born on September 1, 1900, in the family of a peasant of the village Lomakino in the Nizhni Novgorod province. His grandfather was a serf." In reference to Vlasov's peasant origin, it is significant that some question exists regarding the subsequent status of his father. This is brought out in an as yet unpublished essay by Gustav Hilger. A German diplomat with long service in the USSR, he was during World War II Schulenburg's deputy in the Foreign Office "Committee on Russian Affairs." Active in the Other Germany grouping, Hilger first met Vlasov soon after his capture and maintained close contact with him through much of the war. Stating that his information came directly from Vlasov, he writes that "by diligence and stamina, Vlasov's father had succeeded in exceeding the average level of the Russian peasantry by achieving a certain grade of prosperity which — though even a very modest one — sufficed under Soviet rules for blaming and treating him as a 'kulak.' " [2] Evidently, Vlasov's father did at some phase of the Soviet period fit into the kulak category, although he was never by any means a wealthy peasant. Indeed, "Andrei was able to enter school, and later a theological seminary only because his oldest brother Ivan provided for him. . . but he still had to pursue his studies on a scanty subsistence, living a hand-to-mouth existence in a corner which he rented from the family of a hack driver on the outskirts of Nizhni Novgorod."

But the account of Vlasov's education presents a still more significant aspect. "The February Revolution and the October *coup d'état* found Vlasov a student in the fourth year of the theological seminary. . . In 1918, Vlasov entered the first-year course of the Agricultural School of the Nizhni Novgorod University. But the times were not right for studying. . . The young Soviet Republic was living through difficult days. . . The last economic resources were being used, the last human resources were being mobilized. In the spring of 1919, Andrei Vlasov was drafted into the 27th Infantry Volga Regiment. . . In a few weeks he was sent from the regiment to the first officers' school of the Red Army. . . In four months Vlasov was sent to the Southern front as a lieutenant." Thus Vlasov, unlike many of his fellow Red Army generals, had never been a Tsarist soldier, nor did he, after October 1917, promptly enlist in the Red Army or a pro-Bolshevik guerilla unit. On the contrary, young Vlasov continued his university studies until he was drafted. This suggests that Vlasov was not at that time a convinced or active Bolshevik sympathizer.

The "official" biography raises no doubts regarding Vlasov's loyal Civil War service as it relates his routine though successful progress as a junior officer in the Red Army. Rather it seeks to explain the now potentially ticklish problem of his loyalty to the Soviet cause. "During the Civil War, Andrei A. Vlasov had devoted all his energy and strength to the struggle against the White movement. In that period he deeply believed that the Bolsheviks were bringing happiness, freedom and bread to the Russian people. . . It is true that rumors were reaching him of the Kronstadt rebellion, of the unrest among peasants . . . of the terror of the Cheka, but . . . it seemed to him that the country was waging a cruel war, that all means had to be used to achieve victory . . . and that afterwards everything would be settled more to everyone's liking." This was written in the atmosphere of Hitler Germany, under Nazi and old-émigré pressure. But it was aimed primarily at Soviet nationals under German control who themselves were not wholly ready to repudiate this early Soviet period.

Following a further typical account of the rise of a young career army officer, the "official" biography contains a sentence of the greatest interest. "In 1930 Vlasov also joined the Communist Party of the Soviet Union." This poses the significant question: why did Vlasov join the party now, after a dozen years of nonparty service in the Red Army?

One possible answer to this query is supplied by the Wladimirow compilation, published in Berlin in 1944 and devoted to the major latter-stage organization of the Vlasov Movement. According to this source, "Vlasov remained outside the party, although this hindered him considerably in his military career. For these reasons he left military service in 1930 and moved to Leningrad, where he taught . . . in the Officers' Retraining School of the Red Army. From the year 1930 on, the five-year plan began to come into reality. It appeared as if the time of a revival for Russia had really started. . . This constructive enthusiasm excited many; it also excited Vlasov. At the end of 1930 he submitted application for membership in the Communist Party." [3] This variant is not repeated elsewhere, nor is its questionable statement that Vlasov actually left Red Army service rather than merely changing army assignments.

A more cynical answer is suggested by a wartime biographical essay in the Vlasovite press: "Under the conditions of the Stalin dictatorship, a commander of the Red Army could not fully apply his talents without a party card." [4] As a factual statement, this appears to be valid. But as a factor in Vlasov's move to join the party it lends itself to varying interpretations. One possible inference is that Vlasov acted out of sheer opportunism and hypocrisy, spurred on by personal ambition. Another is that Vlasov's long failure to join the party indicates his strong opposition to the Soviet regime, and that he only joined in order to infiltrate the Red Army command more successfully. Both of these interpretations, and that advanced in the Wladimirow compilation as well, seem too fanciful. On the basis of our general knowledge of the USSR, and of Vlasov's subsequent history, something else seems far more likely. Vlasov sought party membership when he could no longer advance without it, but this step was not considered, by him or his fellow officers, as anything suspect or out of the ordinary. The lateness of this step, however, taken together with his earlier history, does appear to indicate that Vlasov's commitment to the Soviet regime was never maximal.

It is not until 1938 that the account of Vlasov's career again demands close attention. At that time he "was appointed Chief of Staff to the military advisor in China, General Cherepanov. . . The Chief of Staff . . . had the task of lecturing to the commanding group of the Chinese Army on the foundations of operational tactics. Andrei A. Vlasov carried out this task and some time afterwards was assigned the extremely responsible position of military advisor to General Yen Hsi-shan. . . After the recall of General Cherepanov to Moscow, Andrei A. Vlasov performed the duties of chief military advisor to Chiang Kai-shek." Implicit in this account is the fact that Vlasov, unlike many of his military colleagues, was not arrested in the great Soviet purges of the late 1930's. Moreover, his post as a Soviet military advisor to Chiang Kai-shek is one of those referred to whenever Vlasov's promising military career is stressed. Finally, it was this tour of duty that took Vlasov outside the USSR and gave him an opportunity to see the non-Soviet world, even though his field of vision was not the West but war-torn China.

After his return to the Soviet Union, "in December 1939, Vlasov was named Commander of the 99th Infantry Division." This was a division that "contained representatives of forty-four nationalities. It was difficult to fuse these elements, but under the guidance of Vlasov the division soon improved its fighting qualities sharply. . . In the fall of 1940 . . . the division was awarded simultaneously . . . the banner for the best infantry regiment, the banner for the best artillery regiment, and the banner for the best division as a whole. Vlasov himself was decorated with an inscribed gold watch by Timoshenko, and with the Order of Lenin by the government."

The most important aspect of this second high point in Vlasov's Red Army career is that it probably did in fact direct official attention toward him. This is further suggested in a postwar study of Vlasov: "How great an importance was attached to the results [of Vlasov's 99th Division] can be seen from the *Krasnaia Zvezda*, official organ of the People's Commissariat of Defense: from September to November 1940, Vlasov and his division are mentioned in well-nigh ten issues."[5] Not possessing the *Krasnaia Zvezda* for this period, I cannot judge how prominently Vlasov's name was displayed. Moreover, a further qualification must be made, even if the praise was as lavish as stated. The Soviet press makes a practice of singling out a certain local achievement to further the propaganda objectives of the moment. Nevertheless, in this post Vlasov did indeed acquire a limited degree of prestige and prominence.

With the recital of the grim events following the German surprise attack on the USSR, Vlasov's "official" biography becomes more dramatic. As the prevailing chaos and disorder are increasingly emphasized, so is Vlasov's own performance painted in ever more glamorous colors. Thus, the 4th Tank Corps, of which Vlasov was named commander, is described as "in a very poor condition. There was a shortage of fuel, there were no spare parts," there was "incompetent leadership" from above. Yet "Vlasov with the remnants of his Corps, under the blows of the mailed fist of German armored-tank units, fought his way out of encirclement to Berdichev." Later, "in conditions of total disorder and demoralization, Andrei A. Vlasov defended Kiev" until, having received the order to withdraw, "for 550 kilometers, all the way to Kursk, they battled through encirclement."

The tendency, not only of his "official" biographer but of nearly all sympathetic chroniclers of the Soviet opposition movement, to glorify the final stages of Vlasov's Red Army career is nowhere so pronounced as in discussions of the role played by Vlasov in the fateful defense of Moscow in 1941. "In November 1941," the "official" biography recounts, "Vlasov was called back to Moscow. There was panic in the capital; factories and organizations were being evacuated, old men and students were hurriedly herded together to dig trenches and antitank ditches. Under such conditions Vlasov was faced with the difficult task of forming the 20th Army and defending Moscow. With his army Vlasov was able to stop the enemy and push him back from the approaches of Moscow to Rzhev. For this operation he was decorated by the Soviet government with the Order of the Red Banner and promoted to the rank of Lieutenant General."

This adulation was carried to its greatest extreme in an interview with the German woman whom Vlasov married at the close of World War II. The interview was published recently in a Swiss journal. "That Andrei Andreevich was a traitor," Mrs. Heidi Vlasov said, "Stalin already knew for a long time. But he needed my husband in the moment of Russia's great need more than almost anyone else. Only to him did [Stalin] entrust the big action for the saving of Moscow, despite his now obvious rejection of Bolshevism. . . It was known that only he could free [Moscow]. The wonder occurred which no one had believed possible." [6] Even the more moderate phraseology of the "official" biography leaves the impression that Vlasov had played an almost unrivaled role in the heroic defense of Moscow. Before accepting or rejecting this verdict, let us look at the available facts.

The Battle of Moscow, in which Vlasov played a part, took place between November 16, 1941, when the third and last great German sweep to capture the city began, and the completion of the Soviet counteroffensive some three months later. On December 13th of that year, *Pravda* published on its front page the announcement of *Sovinformburo* that on December 6th the Soviet counteroffensive had begun. On the same page it both named and pictured the Red Army commanders in charge of this operation. Of the nine photographs on this page, one is twice as large as the other eight, that of General G. K. Zhukov, who had recently replaced Marshal Timoshenko as commander of the Western Front. Surrounding Zhukov's picture are the other eight. It is here, in the lower left-hand corner, that we find "Major General A. A. Vlasov." Five of these subordinate commanders were Lieutenant Generals, three, including Vlasov, Major Generals. And while it is true that Vlasov was raised to the Soviet two-star rank of Lieutenant General following the action, the Lieutenant Generals were also promoted to Colonel Generals, thus remaining a rank above Vlasov.

Walter Kerr, an American war correspondent, interviewed several of these Generals, including Vlasov, in mid-December 1941. In his book, *The Russian Army*, he states that during the German offensive in November "the most dangerous drive was the one made by the central column, for Vlasov was pushed as far as Krasnaya Polyana, just twenty-five miles from Moscow." Kerr also compares Vlasov to his sector colleague, Lieutenant General K. K. Rokossovskii, now a Marshal of the Soviet Union and in command of Poland's army, whose component "constituted the bulk of the northwestern group" and "had a far tougher assignment than Vlasov." [7] This evaluation may be colored by the fact that Kerr, writing in the middle of World War II, was either unwilling to praise Vlasov, who had already become a German collaborator, or was influenced in this direction by subsequent Soviet statements on the defense of Moscow. Nevertheless, Kerr's comments, the issues of *Pravda* covering the period, and the later standing of Vlasov's fellow commanders, taken together, definitely suggest one thing: the importance of Vlasov's role has probably, and quite naturally, been magnified by his followers.

Nor is this contradicted in the reports of two other Western writers who met Vlasov at the time. C. L. Sulzberger of the *New York Times*,[8] and Eve Curie, in her widely read *Journey Among Warriors*,[9] stress — together with Vlasov's expression of loyalty to Stalin — one feature about Vlasov: the high post he held in view of his age (Curie) and rank (Sulzberger). While Kerr also commented that "most generals were in their early forties, for the simple reason that the older officers had been killed off or eliminated in the great purges of 1937 and 1938," [10] neither Curie nor Sulzberger otherwise singles Vlasov out.

Unquestionably Vlasov was among the dozen or fewer Red Army generals who led what became Germany's first major defeat in World War II. This defeat was probably far more a turning point than the later one that is usually stressed, the Battle of Stalingrad. Vlasov's competence in this operation may well have presaged a still greater wartime future in the Red Army. He was indeed *one* of the *young* generals rising rapidly. But in the defense of Moscow, Vlasov was an equal among equals rather than the outstanding figure; his role was considerable but not unique.

After the Battle of Moscow, to continue with the "official" biography, "in March 1942, Vlasov was named deputy commander of the Volkhov

Front. General Meretskov was commanding the front. A shock army had been created for the liberation of encircled and starving Leningrad, but this army was itself soon surrounded and cut off from the rest of the front. Assuming command of the army . . . [Vlasov] was able to breach the German ring and form a narrow corridor. . . But he lacked the forces to widen the breach . . . General Meretskov did not come to the rescue . . . Vlasov saw that the hungry army — Red Army men were receiving 50 grams of bread a day — encircled in forests and swamps, was doomed to perish. . . Andrei A. Vlasov together with the remnants of his army was captured." The precise date of his capture is not recorded. However, the German diplomat Hilger has made the statement that he first met Vlasov near the latter's Winniza prison camp on August 7, 1942; [11] Captain Strikfeldt's recollection, as stated to me, was that the general became a prisoner in either June or July. It therefore may be assumed that the capture occurred during the summer of 1942.

Hilger's and Strikfeldt's testimony permits another justifiable conclusion: that it was not long before Vlasov was not merely questioned, but encouraged, even courted, by the German advocates of a Soviet opposition movement. Nor was it long before they discovered that in Vlasov they had found the captured Red general they were looking for. On September 10, 1942, Vlasov, from the Winniza camp for prominent prisoners of war,[12] made his first extant statement of opposition to Stalin.[13] Later in the fall he was transferred to Berlin to the Victoriastrasse center. Operated by the Soviet section of the OKW propaganda department, Victoriastrasse had become the nucleus of wartime Soviet defection. It is at this point that Vlasov's "official" biography brings the story of his career to its climax and conclusion. "In December 1942, Andrei Andreevich Vlasov placed himself at the head of the Russian Committee, organized by him, and thereby became the head of the spontaneously conceived Russian Liberation Committee."

## 2. The First Step

What is known of *why* Vlasov took the first step toward Nazi collaboration? Vlasov has issued several statements in Germany on the "why" of his collaboration. His first, of September 10th, 1942, was a leaflet from the Winniza internment camp. Opening with an appeal to officers and "comrades of the Soviet intelligentsia," it lays the blame for "the immeasurable suffering of our people in this war" squarely upon the "Stalin clique," listing among its particular crimes the ruination of the land through the kolkhoz system, the destruction of millions of honest people, the murder of the best cadres of the Red Army, and the involvement of the country in an unnecessary and senseless war for foreign interests. After an apology for Hitler Germany — "A lying propaganda wants to scare you with fascism, with executions and cruelties in German captivity. . . Millions of prisoners can testify to the contrary" — it appeals to its audience to "strive with all strength and means to overthrow the universally hated Stalin regime." [14] In tone the leaflet sounds very much like straight Nazi propaganda. It probably was such, since it was issued by the Propaganda Department of OKW over Vlasov's signature.[15] It offers little in the way of an explanation of Vlasov's first step.

More interesting is the "Open Letter," second of Vlasov's two known signed statements on the subject. Entitled "Why I Entered Into the Fight Against Bolshevism. An Open Letter by Lieutenant General Vlasov," this document is both longer and far more extensive in its political statements. There are serious doubts, however, as to how faithfully it mirrors Vlasov's own thinking on the subject of Soviet collaboration with Nazi Germany. At the time of its preparation, Vlasov was in close contact with Zykov, his legendary ex-Soviet aide, and Strikfeldt. By himself, Vlasov, like so many thoroughly disoriented Soviet prisoners of war, might again have lent himself to far greater concessions to Nazi propaganda, as he had done in his initial appeal. But he was prevented from repeating this now by Zykov's cool, perhaps cynical, realism regarding what would appeal to Soviet nationals, and Strikfeldt's no less cool and steadfast warnings against collaborating with the official *Ostpolitik*. Nevertheless, despite these major qualifications, the "Open Letter" is worthy of examination.

As if to emphasize that Vlasov's opposition to the Stalin regime was in no wise founded on purely personal grounds, the "Open Letter" begins: "I must start out with the statement that the Soviet system had in no way mistreated me." This persuasive approach — one in which Zykov's brilliant mind may have had a share — may explain why in the following paragraph (as in all subsequent wartime "official" accounts) no mention is made of the fact that Vlasov's father had at one point evidently been classified by the Soviet regime as a kulak. "I was born the son of a peasant. . . In the ranks of the Red Army I joined to win the Russian peasant his land, the Russian worker an easier life, and the whole Russian people a brighter future." Throughout, the "Letter" emphasizes that Vlasov was not only born, but remained, a "son of the people." Yet even though no mention is made of his father's status, an eyewitness [16] states that this was much on Vlasov's mind during the lengthy talks they had. This indicates that his father's treatment as a kulak may have sown in Vlasov's mind seeds of bitterness toward the Soviet regime.

After reiterating his early faith in the Revolution, the "Open Letter" goes on to reveal Vlasov's growing disillusionment. "I came to recognize that nothing of what the Russian people fought for in the Civil War had been realized through the victory of the Bolsheviks. I saw the heavy life of the Russian workers, I lived through the peasant being forced into the kolkhoz, [I saw] how millions of Russians were liquidated, how they were arrested without sentence or investigation." Now comes an especially bitter denunciation of the treatment accorded his own profession. "The institution of commissar demoralized the Red Army. Lack of responsibility, being spied upon, and steady supervision made the officer a plaything in the hands of civilian or uninformed party officials. . . When I returned to the Soviet Union [from China], I learned that in the interim the higher command of the Red Army had been liquidated and wiped out by Stalin without any reason. Many thousands of the best officers, including the marshals, were arrested and shot or locked up in concentration camps to disappear forever." Vlasov does not spell out just when this disillusionment came — probably because, as with so many foreign adherents to Soviet Communism, it was gradual and indirect, and required a shock such as the initial Soviet reverses in 1941 to crystallize the process.

Vlasov then goes on to make a striking justification of his continuing loyalty, which might be of considerable significance for present-day Western speculation on potential Soviet opposition. "The Army was weakened and the terrorized people looked with dread into the future. For they anticipated the war for which Stalin was obviously preparing. . . Since I foresaw the vast sacrifices which the Russian people would have to make in such a war, I did all that was within my strength to make the Red Army powerful for such a struggle." After citing his prize-winning 99th Infantry Division as an instance of his peacetime policy, Vlasov repeats the same attitude when he reaches his role in World War II. "As a soldier and as son of my homeland I of course fulfilled my duty honestly." Yet, as he saw the "innumerable hardships" suffered by every citizen, "more than once did I have to chase away the question which constantly forced itself upon me: Stop, am I really defending the homeland, am I sending people to their death really for its sake? Is it not possibly only for Bolshevism, hiding behind the sacred name of the homeland, that the blood of the Russian people is shed?"

In an outburst of emotion, Vlasov's "Open Letter" appears to link the general's final decision to break with the Soviet regime with his experiences in the "Volkhov encirclement" immediately preceding his capture by the *Wehrmacht*. "Probably nowhere was Stalin's contempt for the lives of Russian men shown as clearly as in the use of the 2nd Assault Army. The guidance of the army was concentrated in the hands of the Supreme Command [in Moscow]. Of its actual situation no one knew anything. And no one was interested in it. One order was contradicted by the next. The army was doomed to destruction. The troops and officers . . . were bloated from starvation and could hardly move in the swamps where the orders of the Supreme Command had led them. . . At this time the question arose in full force: Should the blood of the Russian people be shed any longer? . . . There in the forests and the swamp I reached the decision that it was my duty to call upon the Russian people to destroy the Bolshevik system." What to him seemed like abandonment by the Soviet government evidently aroused bitter resentment in Vlasov.

The following portion of the "Open Letter" suggests another, though highly speculative, factor in Vlasov's opposition to Stalin. Presumably while still encircled in the forests and swamps, Vlasov "realized clearly that the Russian people were drawn into this war by Bolshevism for the interests of foreign powers, the Anglo-American capitalists. England has always been the enemy of the Russian people. But in service for the Anglo-Americans Stalin saw the chance to realize his plans for world domination, and for the sake of these plans, Stalin tied the fate of the Russian people to the future of England. He pushed the Russian people into the war. . . Neither Stalin nor Bolshevism fights for Russia." Though this is reminiscent of undiluted German propaganda, one postwar study states that Vlasov did indeed feel strongly antagonistic toward England. This study advances the theory that the agitation of the Soviet Communist Party among its members, particularly in the Red Army, implied a geopolitical preference for continental ties with Germany and an animus toward the English-speaking powers, especially Great Britain. It further suggests that Vlasov's own Anglophobia was reinforced during his tour of duty with Chiang Kai-shek.[17] Some eyewitness testimony contends, however, that this is farfetched and that Vlasov was not in fact anti-British.

A last specific motive may have been Vlasov's at first great, if naïve, faith in a genuine alliance of equals between Hitler Germany and the Soviet opposition to Stalin. Regarding Vlasov's attitude toward Germany, the "Open Letter" is unequivocal. "The interests of the Russian people are linked to those of the German people. . . In alliance and in coöperation with Germany it must create a new happy homeland in the circle of equal and free peoples of Europe. . . With these thoughts, with this decision, I was taken prisoner. . . As a prisoner and behind barbed wire I became in no way disloyal to my decision; on the contrary, my conviction hardened further. . . In this struggle for our better future I enter openly and honestly upon the road of alliance with Germany."

In this statement of his reasons for collaboration with Germany, the language of the "Open Letter" is significant. Though it sounds highly pro-Nazi to Western ears, it was in fact far from it in contemporary terminology. It is "coöperation" and "alliance" that Vlasov states he entered into, not "collaboration." And here, as elsewhere, Vlasov referred not to Hitler Germany, its leader, or its government (as German propaganda unfailingly did), but to the "German people." The difference between ally and collaborator, between German government and people, was in reality slight. But Vlasov's selection of words evidently reflects the direction that he came to insist upon. That Vlasov made a determined effort to create an independent opposition movement is borne out by a German Foreign Office memorandum of that period. "[Vlasov] is not . . . a mere seeker after political glory and accordingly will never become a purchasable hireling and will never be willing to lead hirelings." [18] In Vlasov's case, specific motives for the first step thus not only include his father's persecution either as an average peasant or as a kulak and resentment against Moscow's "abandonment" of Vlasov's troops in the Volkhov encirclement. His first step was also premised on Vlasov's stubborn hope for a genuine partnership for equals with Germany.

As in the case of most others, Vlasov's first step was definitely more tortuous and gradual than the early date of his postcapture proclamation would indicate. Not only was this first appeal motivated strongly by a nonpolitical, humanitarian urge to lessen German excesses against Soviet prisoners. It was also followed by numerous occasions when he contemplated not going through with the first step at all. Above all, Vlasov — very much like Tito — failed to make a break with the Soviet government or evidently even to contemplate one until the confluence of two circumstances. One of these was an unmistakable change in power positions (for Vlasov, his capture by the Germany army; for Tito, the public Cominform demand for removal of the Yugoslav leaders). The second, concomitant circumstance was the existence of an equally unmistakable alternative. In Tito's case this was a geographically viable state whose party, police, and army he controlled (and the expectation, operative before long, of powerful outside support); in Vlasov's case, it was a crusade against Stalin, again with powerful outside support, at a time when military reverses made total Soviet defeat appear distinctly feasible. How exceptionally rare is the confluence of these two circumstances in the Soviet world! Yet even given both, Vlasov no less than Tito hesitated to the last.

From the end of 1942, with the founding of the Russian National Committee, Vlasov was not merely the titular head of the movement to which his name has become attached. We do not possess sufficient detached, unbiased data to attempt a full-scale portrait of him as the wartime leader of Soviet opposition. Most eyewitness accounts are either much too worshipful or too scanty. One French book, *J'ai Choisi la Potence, Les Confidences du General Vlasov* (I Chose the Gallows, The Confidences of General Vlasov), published in Paris in 1947, which claims to record Vlasov's wartime thought and actions, is made suspect not only by its sensationalism but also by its failure to name either its author or its editor. We therefore do not know to what extent Vlasov's dominating role is due to his own qualities. Nor dare we hazard an opinion on the degree to which his preëminence might be traced to his Soviet-bred followers' craving, conscious or otherwise, for a leader-symbol to replace those of the USSR. Of the impressions that I gathered from oral and written testimony, however, one fact about Vlasov is certain. Brilliance or above-average intellectuality were evidently not among his characteristics. But Vlasov possessed the great qualities of leadership that the German sociologist, Max Weber, has popularized by the term "charisma." Vlasov's personality, appearance, language, and statements were such as to inspire an exceptional loyalty on the part of practically all of his followers. Wartime photographs show Vlasov as being extremely tall and sparse in build, with heavy horn-rimmed glasses usually accentuating the bony thinness of his face. The following characterization of Vlasov, by a Soviet defector, comes close to a satisfactory appraisal of Vlasov as a "charismatic" leader, although here, too, adulatory notes merge with straightforward description. "Vlasov himself was probably not distinguished by a particularly sharp mind. He often said the wrong thing or more than necessary. But he possessed something which the others did not: great personal charm and an inner power which set him off from the people surrounding him and made him the perfectly logical choice for the leadership of the whole movement. It was said that his influence on the mass of the soldiers was almost unlimited and that whenever he spoke invisible threads of mutual understanding stretched between him and every member of his audience. One could feel that he was a man of the people who had not lost his spiritual connection with the people. He fully shared the life of his comrades in arms." [19]

### 3. Vlasov's Associates

Though Vlasov was indeed the leader in both dominance and popularity, there were other figures of importance and influence within the anti-Stalin movement of Soviet nationals. Among them were three others who, like Vlasov, fit into one of the potential sources of Soviet opposition: the military. These were the ex-Soviet generals Malyshkin, Trukhin, and Blagoveshchenskii.

Major General W. F. Malyshkin was the leader second only to Vlasov in the Russian Liberation Movement. Malyshkin, it appears, was born in 1894, son of a coal-mine bookkeeper. Having graduated from a gymnasium in 1915, he was conscripted, and completed an officers' school by 1917. In 1918 Malyshkin enlisted as a volunteer in the Red Army, and by the end of the Civil War he held the post of commander of an infantry brigade. His peacetime service included a number of staff and field assignments. One of them, from 1933 to 1936, was as commander of the 99th Infantry Division — the same post that was subsequently to bring fame to Vlasov. In 1938 Malyshkin was arrested in the Tukhachevsky affair and confined in Moscow prisons, from which he was released after fourteen months. At the outbreak of the German-Soviet conflict, Malyshkin was named, in July 1941, Chief of Staff of the 19th Army. Four months later he was captured by the *Wehrmacht* in the double battle of Briansk and Viazma. [20] We first encounter Malyshkin as a figure in the opposition movement at Wullheide, near Berlin. Here the OKW had set up a center for training propagandists from among Soviet nationals under German control, to be used primarily in camps for Soviet prisoners of war. Malyshkin was made an instructor in the Wullheide propaganda school.

Also at Wullheide was Major General R. F. Blagoveshchenskii, until his capture in command of a coast-artillery unit of the Red Army.

Blagoveshchenskii is universally described as an aging but sharp-tongued and sardonic man. Unlike Malyshkin, he never put his heart into the opposition movement and spent much of his time deriding it and some of its top leaders. He appears to be the best known of the group of Soviet officers who, though persuaded to collaborate, nevertheless remained uneasy and unenthusiastic about it.

The final military figure to be mentioned here is Major General Fedor I. Trukhin. Trukhin was born in 1896 in Kostroma, the son of a retired officer of noble background. Having served as an officer in World War I, he was drafted into the Red Army in the summer of 1918 and fought in it throughout the Civil War. From that time on he followed the career of a Red Army officer. This career came to an end in 1941 when, as deputy Chief of Staff and Operations Officer for the Baltic Military District, he was wounded and captured soon after the outbreak of Soviet-German hostilities.[21]

Outstanding among Vlasov's associates was an unusually colorful and intriguing former member of a Communist Party alignment, Milentii A. Zykov. Zykov has attracted extraordinary attention and controversy in all subsequent discussions on the wartime opposition movement. He, more than any other leading figure in the movement, mystified his associates. The mystery was caused at least as much by his Soviet past as by his wartime behavior, which was haughty, sharp, and often tactless enough to win him a considerable number of ill-wishers.

Zykov fell into German hands in the summer of 1942. He held the Red Army rank of Captain, and was serving as Deputy Commissar of a Soviet division. But, almost unanimously, postwar accounts place Zykov's actual status in the USSR far higher. One writer, commenting on Zykov's last Soviet title of Battalion Commissar states "there is no doubt that this was not true. He was a creature of far greater scope." And an eyewitness says: "I am not sure that [Zykov's description of himself] was precise, but, in any event, in the entire ex-Soviet world which found itself on [the German] side, I did not meet a man of his caliber, of his capabilities." [22] Michael Kitaev, a close wartime associate of Zykov and a great admirer, states flatly that he was "unquestionably a man with the mind of a statesman, who stood a head above all of his colleagues."

It is from Kitaev's unpublished account that we can obtain the most data on Zykov's Soviet past — a subject on which Zykov was uncommunicative even to his closest wartime associates. Like all other writers on the topic, Kitaev suggests that Zykov was not his real name. He adds the following: Zykov, who in 1943 said he was forty but looked younger, was born in the family of a man of letters. He was raised in the midst of political arguments, since his father was a supporter of the Menshevik faction of the Social Democrats. Under the Soviet regime, Zykov edited a provincial newspaper in Uzbekistan, and subsequently served as assistant editor of *Izvestia*. This top organ of the Soviet Government was then still in the hands of Nikolai Bukharin, Lenin's favorite ideologist, who was condemned to death at the second of the Great Trials, as a right-wing oppositionist and "traitor." During this period, Zykov was arrested and exiled to Siberia. But like a strikingly large number of fellow victims, he was released shortly before the German attack on the USSR, reinstated in the Communist Party, and assigned to the Red Army as a political officer.

One of the most fantastic aspects of the Zykov story is the question of his ethnic origin. As Kitaev states, "Zykov was repeatedly accused of being of Jewish origin . . . although no one knew anything definite . . . Zykov himself frequently made ironic remarks regarding his supposedly Jewish origin. However, he did not once call himself directly a Russian and did not once categorically controvert the opinion that he was a Jew." [23] Another written source insists that he was not Jewish, a third that he was.[24] One of my outstanding German sources on the entire subject states that Zykov himself had told him that he was a Jew. But how could a Jew or one suspected of being Jewish survive, even if he were so anti-Stalin as to collaborate with Hitler Germany? This question did not remain unanswered. In mid-1944 Zykov vanished, with all traces pointing toward the SS.

Soon after German capture in 1942 — it appears definite that it was not surrender — Zykov was flown to Berlin for interrogation, passing through little of the grueling experience of prisoner-of-war camps. Before long he was at Victoriastrasse, the same center for the preparation of Soviet-directed propaganda to which Vlasov was taken. There Zykov became intensely busy writing, negotiating, arguing. When the Russian National Committee was set up in December 1942, with Vlasov at its head, Zykov was one of its members. Increasingly he became Vlasov's ghost writer.

Georgii N. Zhilenkov was, like Zykov, a Communist Party official. But unlike him, Zhilenkov defies categorization as a precapture oppositionist. He had not belonged to a party alignment. Nor was he a persecutee. Alone among the leaders of the Vlasov Movement, he was thoroughly at ease in collaboration with Hitler Germany. Zhilenkov had only recently been party secretary for one of the largest districts of Moscow. This made him the outstanding and highest ranking representative of Communist Party officialdom among all Soviet collaborators. With the start of the Soviet-German war, Zhilenkov had been named a member of the top Military Council of the newly activated 24th Assault Army — not as a military commander but as a high-level political commissar. But his post entitled him to take command of his unit in an emergency, and when the 24th Assault Army was encircled by the *Wehrmacht*, Zhilenkov in fact did so. This is the reason why the nonmilitary party official was eventually designated by the German authorities and by the opposition movement a Lieutenant General.

After being captured — again *not* surrendering — Zhilenkov served for several months as a *Hilfswilliger*, or volunteer helper, on the Eastern Front. Upon transfer to the Victoriastrasse propaganda center, he soon became outstandingly opportunistic in his dealings with the German officials. The Soviet exiles that I interviewed emphasized that Zhilenkov lived an extraordinarily luxurious life in Germany. They add that though he held responsible positions in the Soviet opposition movement, Zhilenkov showed little sense of responsibility, loyalty, or consideration for his colleagues or subordinates. This opinion was unanimous regardless of the outlook of the informant. All-powerfulness and a material well-being out of all proportion to both the average living standard and past Bolshevik spartanism have bred in the USSR a new type. This is the "Soviet *barin*," the Soviet parallel to the arrogant, spoiled, ruthless old Russian landowner. Zhilenkov was certainly a Soviet *barin*. As such, he was unique — this deserves emphasis — in the anti-Stalin movement.

Vlasov, Malyshkin, Trukhin, Blagoveshchenskii, Zykov, Zhilenkov — these were the leaders of the Vlasov Movement. What were the motives and the implications of their collaboration with Hitler Germany? And that of their followers? Part III of this study delves into this central problem. But first we must trace *how* wartime opposition to Stalin took form within its double context of Soviet origins and German habitat.

A fundamental assumption of Stalin's Soviet opponents in World War II was that their greatest effectiveness would be in the form of a military formation of Soviet nationals fighting beside Hitler Germany, but with a considerable degree of autonomy. It is this aspiration of Soviet opposition that became embodied in the Russian Army of Liberation (Russkaia Osvoboditelnaia Armiia, or ROA). It was mentioned from the outset by the pronouncements of the Russian National Committee, a Vlasov venture to be discussed in the following chapter. Today ROA still remains the most widely known and used synonym for the Vlasov Movement.

Chronologically, ROA was preceded by a series of lesser ventures which were local but nonetheless extremely interesting ones. Among these early units, which had not only ex-Soviet personnel but also ex-Soviet commanders, three may be cited in particular.

Probably the best known was RONA, or Russian National Army of Liberation. At its start, this was a local military detachment in Lokot, Byelorussia. First established in 1941 for self-defense against Soviet partisan units, RONA got its ambitious name, its expansion, and finally its status as an SS Division from its own ex-Soviet little Führer, Kaminsky. It was under his leadership that the "Kaminsky Brigade," a volunteer unit from the otherwise unenthusiastic RONA, played a bloody role in the German suppression of the August 1944 uprising in Warsaw. The pay-off came quickly and unexpectedly. With his

Warsaw contingent committing extremes of plunder and savagery, Kaminsky was secretly killed by his erstwhile SS sponsors.[1] Thereupon RONA was dissolved.

A second early experiment originated in a German prisoner-of-war camp, also in Byelorussia. Its leader was an ex-Soviet officer, Gil-Rodionov. His unit, officially designated *Druzhina I*, came to be known as the "Gil-Rodionov Druzhina." Soon it, too, came under SS tutelage. In 1943, however, his unit was also dissolved, when friction with German authorities developed. This friction had impelled Gil-Rodionov himself to defect to the Soviets — an exceptional action, despite the Germans' mistreatment of their anti-Stalin collaborators.

The third and last venture is RNNA, the Russian National People's Army, not to be confused with Kaminsky's RONA. (Neither "army" ever exceeded the size of a division.) RNNA, also known as *Verband Graukopf* after the gray hair of its first native commander, was activated late in 1941 not far from Smolensk, at Osintorf, a large industrial plant site near the Byelorussian village of Osinovka. Unlike the other two early units, RNNA was initially headed by old émigrés; it had German tutelage from the very outset, and the tutelage came not from the SS but the army. By mid-1942, friction developed between some German officials and the old-émigré leaders of RNNA, including Colonel K. G. Kromiadi, in 1943 named chief of General Vlasov's chancellery. They were then replaced by two other Vlasovite figures, Zhilenkov and Colonel Boyarsky, after whose name RNNA came to be known as the "Boyarsky Brigade." However, by the winter of 1943, RNNA, too, was disbanded.

Three major features characterize all of these forerunners, chronologically at least, of ROA. For one, they were all sponsored to fulfill narrowly utilitarian military needs on the Eastern Front: combatting Soviet partisan detachments or dropping propaganda and intelligence agents behind Soviet lines. Broader political motives were in no way discernible. Secondly, all three ventures were centered in Byelorussia and the Smolensk-Pskov area of Russia, and not in the Ukraine. Thus these units were not in direct contact with either the Ukrainian nationalist problem or the Ukraine's satrap Koch, one of the most fervent and faithful followers of Hitler's antagonistic policy toward Soviet defection. Lastly, each of the experiments ended in a similar fashion: friction, frustration, and finally, failure. In every instance, the surviving members of the units were scattered into the German-commanded *Osttruppen* formations.

*Osttruppen* was the designation applied to those Soviet nationals who fought within German units. They wore German uniforms, and served under German commanders, usually without even the semblance of independent organization. From the first days of the conflict thousands of ex-Soviet soldiers offered to serve in the ranks of the *Wehrmacht*. This willingness to fight their native regime is in part attributable to genuine anti-Stalin conviction, for without it Soviet citizens were no more likely to take the first step than most Americans were. But in greater measure the compelling reason must have been that only through such action could they hope for life itself.

No more terrible example of the results of the *Untermensch* theory of *Ostpolitik* exists than the treatment of the vast numbers of Soviet prisoners taken early in the war. That in these prisoners of war the Germans were faced with a tremendous problem is undeniable. Campaign conditions in 1941–1942 were such that the German army was in neither the mood nor the position to care adequately for the Soviet soldiers it captured, and this difficulty was compounded immeasurably by the enormous size of their human booty. We have already cited the official German statistics, according to which the major battles prior to November 1, 1941 resulted in a total of 2,053,000 prisoners, 665,000 having been captured in the single battle of Kiev,[2] and the Rosenberg letter which speaks of 3,600,000 Soviet prisoners of war.[3] Though we may readily grant these extenuating circumstances, the fact remains that these millions of men were subjected to conditions far more harsh than the imperatives of the situation could account for.

*Untermenschen* indeed these Soviet prisoners were considered. Using for sanction the fact that the USSR had not signed the Geneva Convention, Goering quickly pronounced: "In the care and feeding of Bolshevik prisoners we are, contrary to that of other prisoners, not bound by any international obligations."[4] And, fearful lest German guards should not be sufficiently severe, the general responsible for the supervision of the Soviet prisoners included in his official regulations the warning that "any indulgence of even friendly disposition [by German guards] is to be punished very severely ... Slackness is out of place even with a PW who is obedient and willing to work."[5] Precisely what this treatment accomplished was later attested to by German officialdom itself. In October 1942 there came from the *Ostministerium* the statement: "It is no longer a secret from friend or foe that hundreds of thousands [of Soviet prisoners of war] literally have died of hunger or cold in our camps."[6] A speech by Himmler in

October 1943 not only corroborates this statement, but also suggests the basic reason why the treatment of Soviet prisoners was later somewhat mitigated, and why indeed a group like the *Osttruppen* was permitted to come into being. "The attack [on the USSR] succeeded. The Russian army was chased together, wiped out, captured in large encirclements. Then we did not value the mass of [Soviet] people as we value them today as raw material, as labor force. What in the long run, when I think in terms of generations, is not regrettable, is yet regrettable because of the loss of manpower: that the prisoners died by the tens of thousands and hundreds of thousands from exhaustion, from hunger." [7]

Hitler's initial stand on the use of Soviet prisoners of war as *Osttruppen* was blunt and unequivocal. On July 16, 1941, he insisted: *"It must never be permitted that anyone but the Germans bear arms!* This is particularly important; even if in immediate terms it appears easier to draw on some other conquered nations for armed assistance, this is wrong! One day it shall hit out against us, inevitably and unavoidably. Only the Germans may bear arms, not the Slav, not the Czech, not the Cossack or the Ukrainian!" [8]

Yet before the end of the war, ex-Soviet citizens serving in the *Wehrmacht* totaled at least half a million. The figure may well have been closer to or as much as a million. In 1943 the General of *Osttruppen* cited 427,000 such ex-Soviet soldiers who would have to be replaced on the Eastern Front alone by German troops if the *Osttruppen* were disbanded. The same year, the Chief of Staff of the German Army cited *Osttruppen* units which — if computed at 100 men per company, 1,000 per battalion, and 3,000 per regiment — would total 373,200. This total does not include the more than 100,000 individual *Hilfswillige*. Again for 1943, Wallace Carroll gives the figure of 800,000 Soviet citizens in the German forces. And in an unpublished postwar essay, Köstring, last General of *Osttruppen*, states: "The total strength of the Volunteer Units may be assumed to be at least a million," while a former *Ostministerium* official estimates that "at the end of 1942, almost one million so-called '*Hilfswillige*' served in the German *Wehrmacht*." [9]

That Hitler's stand on the use of *Osttruppen* was modified only gradually and with great reluctance is indicated by a complaint from the *Ostministerium* in October 1942: "Only in the last few weeks under the pressure of danger from the partisans was the formation of native units allowed and that only for combat with the bandits." [10]

As might be surmised, the major source of this pressure was the military Utilitarians, and the major reason, the ever-increasing need for manpower. The reasoning behind this Utilitarian position is presented clearly and forcefully in a secret memorandum from General Hellmich, then General of *Osttruppen*, dated March 23, 1943. "Relation between space and the available forces necessarily led to self-help by the troops; thus were created the *Hilfswillige* and later on the *Osttruppen*. This improvisation, undesirable in itself, [was] brought about by lack of manpower . . . To renounce . . . the units would only have been possible if at the right time sufficient German forces had been available . . . Consequently, the population's readiness to help had to be exploited as far as possible in order to (*a*) fill the empty positions in German units, (*b*) pacify and secure the undefended areas (partisan combat, etc.), (*c*) reconnaissance and information activity before the front." To justify further the use of *Osttruppen*, Hellmich continues: "The use of indigenous units so far has had the following advantages. (1) The appearance at the front of indigenous units increases the incentive for the Russian soldier to 'go over to his countrymen.' (2) The German soldier receives an ally trained in battle who is well acquainted with the terrain and way of fighting of the enemy and speaks the latter's language. (3) The fact that their own husbands and sons are fighting on our side also obliges the civilian population to favor our cause. (4) The use of indigenous units saves German forces and German blood."[11]

The tone of this memorandum indicates that the military Utilitarians were willing to, and did, put up a rather stiff fight for the retention and expansion of the *Osttruppen*. In this they were joined by the forces of the Other Germany contingent. Hellmich also noted in his statement that the almost spontaneous use of ex-Soviet soldiers on the Eastern Front had "led to a state of affairs which needed some direction from above." In the establishment of this office for *Osttruppen*, the Other Germany group played an important and consequential role.

One of the Other Germany prime movers in this activity was Count von Stauffenberg, at that time a major in the OKH Organization Branch and chief of the section charged with the establishment of new army units. He supported the idea of creating an OKH office for *Osttruppen*. "A separate complex of questions will form itself around these volunteers. Even now daily inquiries are received in headquarters from units regarding the clothing and paying of individual volunteers.

The army must not allow the SS to take the volunteers away from itself. We must therefore set up a general staff for the handling of all questions connected with the volunteers. The volunteers must have, as a representative of their interests, a general here in OKH just like the engineers, the artillery, and the others. The question is now who to find."

The quotation is taken from the book *Ost und West* by Captain Michel, a wartime associate and an eyewitness of this step. Although Michel's narrative is colored by the author's virtual hero worship for Stauffenberg, it is known that Stauffenberg made good use of his post in OKH, the post most likely to translate such a recommendation into reality. From the OKH's USSR intelligence section, *Fremde Heere Ost* — throughout World War II the main center of the Other Germany group — came the over-all proposal and also the answer to Stauffenberg's query: Whom to find? The candidate for the position — one that required both knowledge of the USSR and a readiness to resist official Nazi polity — was Lieutenant General Heinz Hellmich, a former superior of Colonel Rönne's, also a July 20 martyr serving in *Fremde Heere Ost*. Both Hellmich and Lieutenant General Ernst Köstring, the colorful former military attache in Moscow who early in 1944 succeeded him as General of *Osttruppen*, belonged to the military Utilitarian category. But, particularly during the early development of the *Osttruppen*, their objectives were so similar to those of the Other Germany group that the actions of the two currents were, in many instances, nearly indistinguishable.

Though the two groups acted together, it is clear that they continued to think separately. Michel quotes Stauffenberg as saying: "This Russian volunteer movement is a great opportunity . . . for the Russian people, for the other peoples of the East, for a free Germany, for the West, for the whole world." [12] What a contrast this is to the Utilitarian Hellmich's memorandum already quoted, a part of which reads: "The situation therefore demands the utmost increase in the exploitation of the Russian population. They must not only give their strength in the form of work but must be ruthlessly exploited to the last and sacrifice their lives for us . . . If, in exceptional cases, these auxiliary peoples also fail, this fact can be used at the given time, in order to weaken exaggerated demands which may come from their ranks. For this reason it is even desirable. It gives us the right to set them limited political aims." [13] Allowing for Michel's probable glorification of his hero, allowing for the fact that Hellmich may well have used arguments he did not share in his attempt to convince the *Untermensch* foes of the *Osttruppen* — these two attitudes still remain irreconcilable.

It was not just the Utilitarians and Other Germany dissenters who took an interest in and had their effect upon the development of the *Osttruppen*; Rosenberg and his *Ostministerium* were actively concerned about these ex-Soviet soldiers fighting for Hitler. Though Rosenberg also frequently condemned the *Untermenschen* treatment of the Soviet war prisoners, he characteristically directed his attention primarily upon a matter having direct bearing on his conception of *Ostpolitik* — the national composition of the various *Osttruppen* units.

Throughout the war, the *Wehrmacht* continued to use Soviet nationals in very small units, even as individual recruits (officially called *Hilfswillige*, or HIWI for short). But in time most of them were organized into *Ostbataillone*, units that varied from somewhat smaller to somewhat larger than the traditional 1000-man battalion. The majority of these *Ostbataillone* were separated from each other, scattered throughout the great German army, and without any special identification. Most of them were lost in the huge mass of German formations into which they were integrated. Only on a few — *Ostbataillone* whose names carefully omit the word "Russia:" "Volga," "White Command," "Berezina," "Dnieper" — were even brief, opaque reports published during the war.[14]

There was, however, a considerable minority of which this was not true, and the way in which these were organized was in perfect accord with the Rosenberg Conception. A "top secret" memorandum, dated as early as December 30, 1941, states: "The Supreme Command is to set up: (1) A 'Turkestan Legion' consisting of members of the following nationalities: Turkmenians, Uzbeks, Kazakhs, Kirghizs, Karakalpaks, and Tadjiks; (2) A 'Caucasian-Mohammedan Legion' consisting of members of the following nationalities: Azerbaijanis, Daghestans, Ingushes, Lezghins, and Chechens; (3) A 'Georgian Legion'; (4) An 'Armenian Legion.'"[15]

The term "legion" was applied not to military formations but to training and collection centers for units of each nationality. A considerable number of these units were formed. One of the larger and better known was the 162nd Turk Infantry Division. According to its "Old Russia Hand" commander, the German General von Niedermayer, it "consists of German, Turkestan, and Azerbaijani soldiers. The latter will be formed into separate units, except for a few units that will be mixed for military reasons. The Division is now on a par in all respects with every German field division." [16]

Probably the most favored were the Cossack troops; their preferential treatment was largely due to the Germans' admiration for this warrior type of anti-Communism, which overshadowed whatever nationalist tendencies some Cossacks had. A Cossack Division, under the command of the German General von Pannwitz, was eventually expanded by the *Wehrmacht* to the size of a corps, and before the end of the war transformed into the XV. SS "Cossack" Cavalry Corps.[17] One of its ex-Soviet regimental commanders had the distinction of being the first *Osttruppen* volunteer to receive the high German decoration of the Iron Cross.[18] In 1945 the entire unit was praised by both Hitler and General Jodl.[19] It might be added that the preferred status accorded the Cossacks was so marked that many other Soviet nationals attempted, and managed, to identify themselves as Cossacks. As a further confusion in nomenclature, it was the tendency of the German population at large to regard all members of Soviet nationalities fighting on the German side as "Cossacks."

Byelorussians, Ukrainians, and Russian volunteers, fared by no means so well. These peoples were Slavic, and the Slav had long been the Nazi symbol of depravity, cowardice, and disloyalty second only to the Jew. German designs for controlling a vanquished Eastern Europe were concentrated on these areas, and a not unreasonable fear existed that to arm their nationals would invite future difficulties. As a result, only a very few Ukrainian, Russian, and Byelorussian national units were established. The *Osttruppen* did contain numerous soldiers from these territories, but they were more likely to be found within the larger number of *Ostbataillone* which had no distinct national individuality. In the case of Ukrainian *Osttruppen* a peculiar difficulty in estimating their number results from the fact that after the war the Western Allies often tended to describe *Osttruppen* as "Ukrainian," whatever their national origin, as the wartime Germans had done with the "Cossack" label.

The decision to form the *Osttruppen* into various separate national units with emphasis on the non-Slavic nationalities, was clearly a victory for the Rosenberg Conception, while it was a defeat for the Other Germany point of view. Those holding the latter position had contended that it was of foremost importance to unite rather than to particularize the representatives of the various Soviet nationalities, that only through such unity could forces be adequately pooled and the "Soviet patriotism" in the USSR successfully combatted. Most of them added that, while each nationality certainly should have the right of self-determination, the appropriate time for that would be after the successful overthrow of the Soviet regime, not in the midst of a bitter struggle. Obviously, this attitude was too opposed to both the official *Ostpolitik* and the Rosenberg Conception to have much of a chance. Little if any German attempt was made to unite the great bulk of the *Osttruppen* under any flag or symbol.

Yet the fortunes of war were to raise this issue again. As the huge German war machine on the Eastern Front rumbled to a halt and reversed, many perceived the need of furnishing the *Osttruppen* with more of an ideological incentive. To cite once more the memorandum of General of *Osttruppen* Hellmich: "The [German] troops were able to supply the *Osttruppen* with food, clothing, and arms, but they could not provide them with a lasting purpose. In the beginning, in order to ask their bloody sacrifice, there was hardly any need for a stronger incentive than to be on the side of the victor. The critical winter months of 1942–43 have shown that the anti-Bolshevik spirit of the Eastern troops suffices to keep these units together, but it has no longer any power for the recruiting of new ones. The thesis 'We know whom we are fighting but we do not know what we are fighting for' is no longer sufficient . . . A political purpose is necessary for carrying through the total war." [20]

In this situation, the Other Germany group once more pressed for German recognition of an independent anti-Stalin force of Soviet nationals. It urged definite guarantees to respect present and future independence of the movement and its native land, stating that this was needed in order to provide the *Osttruppen* with the desired morale. Hitler, however, and some of his military entourage as well, were unalterably opposed to this view. Rather than risk disaffection among the ex-Soviet soldiers, it was Hitler's intention to disband, or at least seriously cripple, the ever-growing *Osttruppen*. This is clearly shown in the minutes of his June 16, 1943 conference, reproduced in Appendix II. Between these two profoundly incompatible alternatives, the military Utilitarians proposed a compromise solution. Caring little for the nationalist aspirations of various Soviet anti-Stalin groups, they were still determined to preserve the usefulness of the *Osttruppen* for the German war effort. They therefore recommended the shift of most of the *Osttruppen* away from the Eastern front, where their loyalties and fears of Soviet retaliation were most involved, to other parts of Nazi-dominated Europe. In the summer of 1943 began the gradual transfer of 70 to 80 per cent of the *Osttruppen* away from the fight against their own enemy to a fight against foes purely of Germany's choosing.[21] This expedient, though it prevented the dissolution of these units, deprived them of much of their rationale. By dispersing them far and wide, the move drastically reduced whatever hopes and illusions they may have retained of becoming more and more an independent opposition movement.

What this dispersion throughout Europe meant is illustrated in a wartime memorandum by Caucasian leaders in Germany.[22] Stating that the total number of Caucasians bearing arms for Hitler's Germany was 102,300, the memorandum shows the location of the units situated elsewhere than the Eastern Front:

| | |
|---|---|
| 812th Armenian Battalion | Holland |
| 807th Azerbaijanian Battalion | Near St. Raphael |
| 804th Azerbaijanian Battalion | Temporarily in France |
| 822nd Georgian Battalion | Zandwort |
| 795th Georgian Battalion | Cherbourg |
| 823rd Georgian Battalion | Island of Guernsey |
| 797th Georgian Battalion | Near La-Haye-du Poys (Graneville) |
| 798th Georgian Battalion | Near St. Nazaire |
| 799th Georgian Battalion | Near Perygeux |
| Georgian Battalion No. II/4, I/9 | In the Albi-Castre area |
| 800th, 835th and 836th North Caucasian Battalion | Normandy |
| 803rd North Caucasian Battalion | Holland |

Never had the duties demanded of the *Osttruppen* been of a particularly glorious or honored character. Some units were actually engaged in front-line combat. But far more often they were assigned to rear-area police duties, and, especially, to antipartisan activity. The shift initiated by the Utilitarians meant that throughout the second half of the war most of these anti-Stalin troops were largely engaged in combatting resistance movements in Poland, the Balkans, Slovakia, Italy, and France. These resistance movements were as often anti-Communist as Communist.

Participation by the *Osttruppen* during the Allied landings in France was extensive. German-controlled old-émigré papers reiterated: "In difficult war conditions, they fulfill their soldierly tasks in Normandy";[23] "In northern France . . . our *Ostbataillone* fought superbly. Some of them stubbornly defended their bases, surrounded by units of the invading army."[24] A contrasting picture was drawn, however, in the *New York Times* report that, during the Allied invasion of Southern France, "Russian, Caucasian, Georgian, and Ukrainian troops showed a propensity to shoot their German officers and desert. Therefore they have been disarmed and sent to the rear areas as labor battalions."[25] Between these versions lies Rosenberg's, which, while denying any mass disaffection, suggests rather subtly that all was not well with the ex-Soviet troops. "The officers and men [in the *Osttruppen*] were constantly saying that they had left one side but the other would not admit them . . . They were very brave at times, but one should not overlook the fact that they had to face the Americans and English with inferior weapons . . . They themselves had captured their weapons from partisans. They did not have any artillery . . . I just learned . . . that the desertion rate lies between 2 and 6 percent. This number appears to be fully satisfactory."[26] In fact, the prevailing German neglect and contempt of the *Osttruppen* in the West often led to the decimation of their units. That they fought on is a reflection not only of their now-crystallized anti-Stalin convictions but also their Soviet-bred physical and emotional stamina and above all the hopelessness of their situation.

There is still another reason for the absence of more disaffection among the *Osttruppen* during these later years, which were for them so discouraging. During this time they were bombarded on all sides with a particular type of German propaganda. It was propaganda reiterating a theme on which, for once, the Other Germany, the Utilitarian, the Rosenberg, and even the official views of *Ostpolitik* all agreed. This theme none but the Other Germany group believed, but it was used by the rest to further their own ends: the promise that there was in formation an independent, united, anti-Stalin force of Soviet nationals, and that soon all Soviet opposition could join in its crusade. The force they spoke of was the Russian Army of Liberation, a name abbreviated in Russian to ROA.

When German and Vlasovite propaganda spoke of ROA, it was no more than a combination of hopes and promises. ROA was to be created by placing the hundreds of thousands of Soviet nationals in the

*Osttruppen* under the unified command of a native ex-Soviet general. This was the dream, the blueprint. Until this date the survivors' references to ROA, to the "Vlasov Army," are in terms of this blueprint, rather than of what actually happened.

It was at the fateful Hitler Conference of June 8, 1943 that the aspirations of ROA, like those of the Russian National Committee, were relegated forever to the dust heap. Here was revealed just how deep and unremitting was Hitler's opposition to arming non-German troops, or in any way relying upon them. Throughout, he made it clear that he was willing both to use ROA for propaganda directed behind Soviet lines and to maintain most if not all of the *Osttruppen* already in existence. But to place the *Osttruppen* under a unified, ex-Soviet command was to Hitler totally out of the question. "I can only say this: we will never build up a Russian army, that's a phantom of the first order."

That is what the ROA, the "Vlasov Army," was in fact — a phantom. To speak of ROA as anything else, and particularly as an actual formation under Vlasov's command, is wholly erroneous. Yet the practice persists, not only among outsiders but even among surviving Soviet defectors themselves.

The reasons for this continuing confusion are not difficult to fathom. Though Hitler categorically forbade the ROA to become a reality, he readily agreed to "let the appeal of the 'Army of Liberation' continue to go across." Moreover, while primarily directed across Soviet lines, this was not the sole use made by the Germans of this propaganda appeal. General Köstring, German general for the *Osttruppen*, explicitly stated in a postwar memorandum that "the designation ROA arose with the purpose of giving the *Osttruppen* the feeling of community." [27] It takes little imagination to see how eagerly and stubbornly Soviet nationals in *Osttruppen* throughout Europe would cling to any suggestion that they were not mere isolated particles in the alien, often unfriendly, German world, but instead formed a part of a united, and therefore much stronger, native force. Nor, similarly, is it any wonder that these same Soviet nationals who in World War II were under German control now persist in referring to ROA as if it really had been what they and others had dreamed at the time it was or soon would be.

Moreover, propaganda can be highly effective in obscuring the true picture — especially when this propaganda enjoys the monopoly of a totalitarian regime. Every wartime reference to Vlasov spoke of him as commander of ROA. Most *Osttruppen* units were continually referred to in the press as ROA units. Such propaganda distortions were repeated again and again without any other information becoming available. The result of all this is vast and continuing confusion about ROA. And it was the Vlasov Movement and its own propaganda activities that did most to fasten the image of a genuine ROA in the minds of Soviet nationals.

A revealing illustration is the shift of *Osttruppen* from the Eastern Front to other parts of Hitler-dominated Europe, which began in mid-1943. This was the Utilitarian compromise solution to the tense three-cornered battle over the disposition of these units. The scattering of the *Ostruppen* throughout Europe, away from their former concentration near their homeland, was clearly a body blow to the Vlasov Movement. No Soviet opposition movement could ever have as much weight under these new conditions as it might have had while several hundred thousand Soviet nationals in German-controlled units were stationed on the Eastern Front. And yet in public statements the Vlasov Movement not only sought to explain away to its followers, but continually reiterated that ROA was an existing and growing force.

Thus Vlasov himself went on record on this subject in a letter to "the soldiers and officers of the Russian Army of Liberation," which occupied the front page of the *Dobrovolets* of November 17, 1943. "By order of the High Command of the German army, a part of the detachments of the Russian Army of Liberation are being shifted from the east for the struggle in the west. Our people in the detachments of ROA will preserve their idea of the Russian Liberation Movement wherever they are located. The idea of an equal, mutually advantageous friendship of two great peoples is growing and getting stronger, despite all trials." Subsequent issues of the same paper pressed the idea that "to fight Englishmen and Americans for us means, above all, to fight Bolsheviks," [28] and that in the West, ROA was "defending Europe." [29]

A somewhat different explanation of the east-west transfer, and one probably more truly expressive of the hopes of the Vlasov Movement, was offered by Vlasov's deputy, General Malyshkin. In the *Dobrovolets* of February 27, 1944, Malyshkin is quoted as having declared that the shift was strictly temporary; that a major reason for it was to enable the ROA troops to rest and regroup; and that Vlasov was constantly concerned with the ROA's return east.

A final vivid instance of how the Vlasov Movement identified itself and the name ROA with the scattered *Osttruppen* units is provided in a speech given by another key opposition figure, Zhilenkov, reported in the March 8, 1944 issue of *Dobrovolets*. "I have returned from an extensive trip west, where I visited our troop units and detachments . . . our troops shifted to the west have completely preserved their officer and soldier personnel . . . from the organizational point of view, from the point of view of military training, our troops [in the west] have taken a considerable step forward."

Surely the total impression given by these various Vlasov Movement statements is that "our" troops were indeed formed into a genuine Russian Army of Liberation — not the phantom army that it was in actuality. This propaganda-induced confusion was compounded when the German authorities subsequently authorized the use of a uniform set of ROA insignia, shoulder patches, and rank epaulets for *Osttruppen*.[30] It is hardly surprising, then, that wartime foreign newspapers, and also some writers since World War II, have reflected the confusion in references to the Vlasov Movement.

At times the Vlasov Movement did seek to suggest publicly its dissent from German policy on the ROA. Several statements by General Vlasov stressed the training purposes of the east-west shift, and that the eventual role of the ROA was, of course, against the USSR on the Eastern Front. Malyshkin's statement also emphasized the temporary nature of the shift and Vlasov's constant concern with getting the ROA returned to the Eastern Front. From Zhilenkov comes the fullest report on how the leaders of the Soviet opposition to Stalin truly felt about the ROA. In this instance, Zhilenkov's views are expressed not in print but during informal remarks, in January 1944, to the 439th *Ostbataillon*. There is extant a summary sent by the German commander to his superior: "It was stated in the remarks to the soldiers that the soldiers are not here in the west to fight against Englishmen and Americans, but mainly for reorganization of the units, until Germany has activated its new formations. The *Osttruppen* are now to be used not in battalion size but unified in the ROA . . . The ROA is here not for the liberation and establishment of the new Europe, but solely and exclusively for the liberation of Russia from Bolshevism."[31]

But these hints and veiled pleas against *Ostpolitik* did not stand out in the midst of Vlasov Movement double talk on its relation to the phantom ROA. A notable example of this double talk is a pamphlet issued for "ROA propagandists," entitled *Answers by the Editors of the Newspaper "Dobrovolets" to 50 Questions.* The pamphlet is made up of a series of strikingly direct questions on the complex of problems that must have worried every Soviet national under German control: maltreatment of *Ostarbeiter* and other Soviet nationals in Germany, Hitler's plan for a post-Stalin Russia, the political and other rights of the opposition movement. Throughout this booklet, the ROA is spoken of as an entity, as a functioning organism, even though the questions and answers most pertinent to the subject tell a radically different story.

"*Question 1:* How can an army exist without a government?

"*Answer:* We are against the creation of a puppet government. There are already plenty of such governments without army and state in the streets and cheap hotels of London. As for ROA, it exists, and this fact is well known to those who meet it on the field of battle in the East and in the West.

"*Question 7:* Why is there a majority of German officers in Russian battalions?

"*Answer:* The volunteer units are working together with units of the German army. Therefore the presence of German officers in ROA is absolutely essential, especially at the present time. The units of ROA are grateful for the fact that the German army finds it at all possible to assign trained officers to ROA.

"*Question 9:* Are the Russian Committee and General Vlasov recognized by the German government?

"*Answer:* The Russian Committee, headed by Lieutenant General Vlasov, is the spiritual center of leadership of the Russian Liberation Movement. Contrary to the English and the Bolsheviks, the German government rejects the creation of would-be governments. . . The civil government begins to carry out its functions after the decision has been reached with arms in hand. In wartime the decisions must be left to those who are willing to sacrifice their life. The high command of the German armed forces therefore recognized ROA as the embodiment of the desire of the Russian people to rid itself of Bolshevism.

"*Question 10:* Will General Vlasov be given direct command of ROA?

"*Answer:* ROA is fighting against the common enemy together with the German armed forces, and, like all the anti-Bolshevik troops of other countries, is under a central [German] command. The role of General Vlasov at the present time is that of collaboration with the German high command. The day will come when these understandable questions may be given a more clear and detailed answer.

"*Question 27:* Why is there no independent headquarters for the Russian Army of Liberation?

"*Answer:* As is known, there exists in ROA the various appropriate headquarters. We see no reason to inform our enemy about this.

"*Question 28:* What is the size of ROA? From what source will come its replenishments?

"*Answer:* The size of ROA is a military secret. . . That ROA is not a mirage, but does exist in reality and is moreover not a propaganda organization is known, we believe, on both sides of the front. However, it may be said that together with its reserves ROA represents a mighty force, which in alliance with the German army will guarantee victory over Bolshevism.

"*Question 29:* Will ROA in the future act separately or together with the German army?

"*Answer:* At present the volunteer units are acting together with German formations. What forms this will take in the future, especially when we will again begin a victorious advance on the Soviet Union, will be revealed by future events." [32]

The pamphlet reveals the true situation. The ROA is not a unified force. Its scattered units are commanded largely by German officers. Vlasov does not have command over it. The Russian National Committee is not recognized by the German government. The Vlasov Movement is merely the "spiritual center" of what is called the ROA. But despite all these admissions, the *Dobrovolets* pamphlet as well as all Vlasov Movement pronouncements kept on designating the ROA as a living, functioning unit that was the embodiment of the Soviet opposition movement.

Actually, the vaunted Russian Army of Liberation was merely a meaningless collective term for scattered *Osttruppen* units.

"In December 1942, Andrei Andreevich Vlasov placed himself at the head of the Russian Committee, organized by him, and thereby became the head of the spontaneously conceived Russian Liberation Movement." Behind this seemingly straightforward statement by the general's "official" biographer, there lies a far from simple story. If the ROA was a phantom army, in Hitler's own words, the whole Vlasov Movement remained in a phantom stage.

Originally it had been the central Other Germany group that first decided to promote Vlasov as leader of a German-sponsored anti-Stalin movement. This group was *Fremde Heere Ost*, the Army (OKH) section primarily concerned with combat intelligence about the Red Army. Recognizing the need for caution, these *Fremde Heere Ost* officers thought it best to promote the project on the grounds of its value to military propaganda on the Eastern Front. More specifically, they cited leaflet-dropping behind Soviet lines. This justification for sponsoring Vlasov led to Strikfeldt's temporary-duty assignment from *Fremde Heere Ost* to WPrIV (*Wehrmacht* Propaganda Section IV), a section of the Armed Forces (OKW) Propaganda Department dealing with military propaganda for Soviet personnel on both sides of the Eastern Front. Here the attitude toward Soviet opposition to Stalin was far more Utilitarian than Other Germany in outlook. But by retaining throughout a "temporary-duty" status, Strikfeldt gained both protection and an unusually high degree of independence in his actions as chief of one of the branches of WPrIV.

Thus it was that Strikfeldt, toward the end of 1942, came to Victoriastrasse, the WPrIV propaganda center where Vlasov, Zykov, and Malyshkin would converge. And it was here, under the guise of writing leaflets used for Soviet areas, that birth was to be given to the Russian National Committee, the long-awaited political organization of the entire Soviet opposition movement.

The original plan called for the establishment of a Russian National Committee, with General Vlasov at its head, at Smolensk. The advantage of this site was that it was the largest Russian city occupied to date. Moreover, the headquarters of Field Marshal von Kluge's Army Group Central were located there, and von Kluge, though somewhat wavering, was nevertheless a Utilitarian dissenter from the official *Ostpolitik*. The formation of the Committee was to be proclaimed in a special radio broadcast from Smolensk. It was for this occasion that one of the major documents of the opposition movement was prepared — "The Smolensk Manifesto," the first of the two programmatic manifestoes issued by the Vlasov Movement.

The Smolensk Manifesto is built around its thirteen programmatic points:

1. Abolition of forced labor and guarantee to the worker of a real right to labor leading to material welfare;

2. Abolition of collective farms and planned transfer of land into private peasant property;

3. Reëstablishment of trade, handicrafts, and artisan trades, and the creation of opportunity for private initiative to participate in the economic life of the country;

4. Opportunity for the intelligentsia to create freely for the welfare of its people;

5. Guarantee of social justice and the protection of working people from exploitation;

6. Introduction for working people of a real right to education, to leisure, to a secure old age;

7. Termination of the reign of terror and violence; introduction of actual freedom of religion, conscience, speech, assembly, and press; guarantee of the inviolability of person and personal residence;

8. Guarantee of freedom for subject nationalities;

9. The liberation of the political prisoners of Bolshevism, and the

return from prisons and camps to the Motherland of all those who suffered detention in the struggle against Bolshevism;

10. Reconstruction of the cities and villages destroyed during the war, at the expense of the state;

11. Rebuilding of the factories belonging to the state, which were destroyed during the war;

12. Refusal to make payment on the enslaving agreements concluded by Stalin with the Anglo-American capitalists;

13. Provision of a minimum living wage to disabled veterans and their families.[1]

The complete text of the Smolensk Manifesto added a note quite contrary to these thirteen points, which, with the exception of Point 12, are impressively liberal and non-Nazi. This was the statement that "Germany, led by Adolf Hitler, pursues the aim of creating a New Order in Europe without Bolsheviks or capitalists."[2] The second significant statement of the Smolensk Manifesto's main message is: "The Russian Committee appeals to all soldiers and officers of the Red Army to join the Russian Army of Liberation, fighting shoulder to shoulder with the Germans."

The issuance of the Manifesto was the first step called for by the plan for the Russian National Committee. But all did not go according to plan. Though innumerable conferences occurred between the various military and civilian German agencies concerned, high-level approval for the action had not yet been obtained. Thereupon Captain Strikfeldt and Captain von Grote, the Utilitarian but at times Other Germany-minded chief of a second branch of WPrIV, undertook a phantasmagoric adventure. The purpose of it was to present German authorities with a *fait accompli*, a Russian National Committee already in existence. Through the spreading net of Utilitarian as well as Other Germany dissenters within German officialdom, including the Propaganda Ministry — there were even a few in the SS — Strikfeldt and von Grote were able to make progress. Thus it came about that, despite the absence of official authorization, the Russian National Committee was established in December 1942.

It was, however, a sorely limited triumph. Strong Nazi protests were lodged against the activities centering around Vlasov. The immediate result was that no German-controlled publications announced either the establishment of the Committee or the issuance of the Smolensk Manifesto. The inaugural radio program was canceled. The Committee's seat never became Smolensk, as originally proposed. Indeed, the only way its existence became known at all to Soviet nationals under German control was by another of the flukes engineered by the enterprising WPrIV branch chiefs and their German sympathizers. A consignment of leaflets announcing the Russian National Committee which was destined for the Soviet side of the Eastern Front was, "by mistake," dropped on the German side.

Again there followed a stage of countless conferences within the German government which now resulted in a modification of the official attitude toward the Vlasov Movement. This was first visible in March 1943. Then, in lieu of the more grandiose and official Smolensk Manifesto contemplated originally, Vlasov's own personal "Open Letter" was published in *Zaria*.

At this time also Vlasov was allowed to make the first of his two tours through occupied Soviet areas. According to an American account, "German intelligence officers reported that the Manifesto aroused enthusiasm throughout the conquered territory. Vlasov himself spoke to mass meetings of Soviet volunteers and civilians. Everywhere, said German officers who heard him, his personality caught the imagination of his hearers." [3] We may assume that the German officers reporting on Vlasov's tour were guilty of some exaggeration because of their own pro-Vlasov attitude. But it is not hard to imagine that genuine eagerness may have greeted the appearance of a nationalist-minded Soviet general like Vlasov, after long months of brutal and politically negative *Ostpolitik*. This is especially true in view of the quite independent, unobsequious statements that Vlasov evidently made during his tour. For example, in one interview given and published at the time, Vlasov said: "I agree completely with Adolf Hitler when he says that he does not wish to transfer National Socialism to other states. To each his own. Another's suit does not fit the Russian. . . We will take over from the Germans that which suits us, but far from everything because we do not want to make Germans out of Russians and vice versa." [4]

During this favorable period, there also took place a major gathering: the "First Anti-Bolshevik Conference of Former Officers and Soldiers of the Red Army, now Prisoners of War, who have adhered to the Russian Liberation Movement." One wartime source described it as the constituent assembly of the Vlasov Movement. It was unlike the mass meetings Vlasov addressed, and was never repeated. This was in April 1943, at Brest Litovsk, and over two hundred Soviet nationals are said to have attended.[5] With Zykov opening the Conference, one of its high points was the adoption of a resolution strongly supporting General Vlasov, his "Open Letter," and the Russian Liberation Movement.[6] The other was a speech by General Malyshkin, who together with Vlasov and Zykov was one of the original three members of the Russian National Committee, on "The Tasks of the Russian Liberation Movement."[7] Malyshkin's speech sets forth the position of the Vlasov Movement with greater frankness and detail than any other extant published statement. It is summarized in the notes to this chapter.[8]

Speeches notwithstanding, the position of the Russian National Committee was far from good. One source of its troubles was Rosenberg, whose conception of *Ostpolitik* categorically excluded a Russian national committee of any size or strength. Thus, as Goebbels commented in a diary entry dated April 29, 1943, "The Russian General Vlasov, who is fighting on our side in the Separatist Army, has been pretty much shelved by the Ministry for the East."[9]

Gradually, however, Rosenberg's opposition appears to have lessened. An American writer has suggested that this less negative attitude toward Vlasov was brought about by the latter's concessions on the ever-ticklish national question. "Several months were lost while Vlasov tried to appease Rosenberg. In some of the statements which he made to German officials for this purpose, Vlasov not only conceded self-determination to the minorities but indicated — according to German sources — that in the future peace settlement he would be willing to give up the Ukraine and the Caucasus. At last Rosenberg was reassured."[10]

Although it may be doubted whether Rosenberg was ever really "reassured," the American writer's statement aroused considerable discussion in the exile world for a different reason. Typical of the reaction of surviving Soviet defectors close to Vlasov was the emphatic denial by Colonel K. G. Kromiadi, who became Vlasov's chief of chancellery in 1943.[11] In support of Kromiadi's position, one can cite subsequent Vlasovite opposition to German-backed separatist movements, and its continued emphasis on self-determination as the solution to the nationalist problem. Yet the balance of power within Hitler's Germany and the compulsions inherent in the logic of compromise lend some credence to the disputed statement. Moreover, it is confirmed by a subsequently published letter from Rosenberg to Hitler, dated October 12, 1944. In this letter Rosenberg speaks of an earlier letter of May 28, 1943 which, he states, had as an enclosure "a declaration by General Vlasov, expressing a renunciation of the Ukraine and the Caucasus." [12] Certainly, by the time of the conference that Hitler held on June 8, 1943 on the subject of Soviet opposition, Rosenberg had at least agreed to the OKW plan for a propaganda campaign built around Vlasov's name, for Field Marshal Keitel placed particular emphasis on the fact that the leaflets involved had been "coördinated word for word with Reich Minister Rosenberg. He approved and authorized them."

It is a mistake, therefore, to think that the main or most effective opposition to Vlasov's venture came from Rosenberg and his *Ostministerium*. It was after Rosenberg himself had begun reluctantly and belatedly agreeing to it that a far more decisive obstacle came to the fore. This was Hitler himself. At the conference on June 8, 1943 he put an end to the early hopes of the Soviet opposition movement. The complete minutes of this crucial conference are reproduced, in translation, in Appendix II. Hitler decreed that Vlasov was to keep out of the occupied Soviet areas. Though propaganda to the Soviet side of the front might keep on using Vlasov's name, neither he nor his Russian National Committee were to be granted further scope. Irate at a report regarding the *Hilfswillige* — that formerly they had been willing to work "for bread and maintenance," but "now Vlasov has whipped up in them the idea of independence" — Hitler said: "I don't need General Vlasov at all in the occupied areas . . . That must be stopped . . . He will function only across, to the other side." Solely on the condition "that not the slightest practical consequence will ensue" did Hitler agree to any further activity of the Vlasov Movement. And what those activities would be was clearly summed up in Keitel's restatement of the Führer's decision: "Then it may be said that we look upon the Russian Committee, the originator of the propaganda leaflets signed by Vlasov, as purely a propaganda weapon."

If politically and militarily the Vlasov Movement was reduced to a phantom existence, there was one area in which, logically and ironically, it was permitted to flourish and was even encouraged. As spelled out by Hitler and Keitel, the Vlasov Movement became engaged, practically full time, in German-directed propaganda activities. The scarcely functioning Russian National Committee and the non-existent ROA served as outlets, as external trappings, for this propaganda.

The center of the Vlasov Movement's propaganda work was a German military post or camp near Berlin that had formerly been used to house captured enemy generals. Dabendorf, the name of this center, is one of the key terms in the entire history of Soviet opposition in World War II. To the extent that the Vlasov Movement, the chief manifestation of Soviet opposition, did achieve cohesion and popularity, this occurred at Dabendorf or through activities initiated or controlled by Dabendorf. Other propaganda and training centers were set up. One of them in France was reportedly even larger than Dabendorf. Dabendorf itself had a preliminary staging camp, Lückenwald. But none of the comparable undertakings ever approached Dabendorf in the extent or significance of their role in wartime Soviet opposition.

Dabendorf was made into a Soviet collaboration center at the turn of 1942–1943, soon after the establishment of the Russian National Committee. The latter and Dabendorf had in fact the same origin: the Propaganda Department of the German Armed Forces (OKW). Specifically, this meant the Victoriastrasse center of the section dealing with the USSR, WPrIV. More specifically still, after Captain Strikfeldt was attached to Victoriastrasse, a unit of WPrIV was established under his command as part of what already existed under Captain von Grote. The latter continued to supervise the output of German material for the Soviet side of the Eastern Front, and published material in general. Strikfeldt's new unit was given the status of a battalion, and was to draw together selected Soviet prisoners of war who at the time could not obtain the kind of civilian status desired for key opposition figures.

It was Strikfeldt's unit in WPrIV that early in 1943 was transferred wholesale from Victoriastrasse to Dabendorf. Strikfeldt himself, a stanch Other Germany activist within German officialdom, was thus in charge of Dabendorf, and he made considerable use of its simultaneous subordination to as many as four different German headquarters. But in this uniquely favorable arrangement at least two complications appear. One is that Strikfeldt's Utilitarian and less unreservedly pro-Vlasov colleague, von Grote, also had some control over Dabendorf affairs. He and his section were given considerable censorship powers over the publications issued from Dabendorf. Another complication limiting Strikfeldt's freedom of command was that among the increasing personnel at Dabendorf there were a number of only partially disguised agents of various German organizations ranging from other branches of OKW to the Gestapo and to SD, intelligence branch of Himmler's SS.

But within these considerable limitations on his own command of Dabendorf, Strikfeldt, according to all oral testimony available to me, turned the internal operation of the center over to recognized leaders of the Vlasov Movement. Vlasov himself remained in Berlin. But Zykov and Zhilenkov shared responsibility for one of Dabendorf's chief activities, the publication of newspapers. The other major activity located at Dabendorf — the School for ROA Propagandists — was headed by another top leader of the Vlasov Movement. This was Major General Trukhin, who became Vlasov's chief wartime associate on military matters. (Initially, the publishing as well as the school activities were headed by General Blagoveshchenskii, but he was soon forced into the background.)

Since the propaganda school was the larger, numerically and spatially, it was Trukhin who among the Soviet collaborators was considered the native commander of Dabendorf. Not only did Strikfeldt, without any formal German authorization, transfer internal control of Dabendorf to Trukhin. In turn Trukhin, again without formal German authorization, placed himself under the command of Vlasov, although Vlasov had no formal control whatever over Dabendorf affairs. In this paradoxical manner, and through the presence at Dabendorf of key figures like Zykov, this propaganda center became closely identified with the Vlasov Movement.

The two newspapers first issued at Dabendorf were *Zaria*, which early in 1943 replaced the German-published *Klich* as the principal publication for Soviet prisoners of war, and *Dobrovolets*, directed at Soviet volunteers in German military units. *Zaria* and *Dobrovolets* were in fact published largely by the same staff. Like the Vlasov Movement itself, its publications had no formal hierarchy, and thus in the postwar period many claimants appear to the key posts. But there is little doubt that it was Zykov, brilliant, brash, at times rude and often domineering, who lorded it over *Zaria* and *Dobrovolets*.

In ascribing the outstanding role in the publication of the Vlasov newspapers to Zykov, two qualifications must be made. One is that Zykov's influence was limited throughout by considerable German interference. This took the form not only of censorship, but also of repeated insistence on the inclusion of some material and the omission of other. But a far more total and final limitation occurred when Zykov himself disappeared forever. This came in the summer of 1944. One evening Zykov, together with his secretary, was called from his house in the village of Ransdorf to answer a telephone call in the restaurant across the street. Neither Zykov nor his secretary ever returned.

Zykov's disappearance, like his Soviet past and his ethnic origin, are among the aspects of the Vlasov Movement most frequently speculated on. Of two theories entertained at the time, one was that during a trip to Serbia in the summer of 1943 Zykov may have discussed with representatives of Draja Mikhailovich the possibility of continuing anti-Soviet resistance after Germany's defeat — to German ears a rankly "defeatist" thought. Others thought that Zykov was found to be a Soviet agent.

The explanation actually most tenable is that supplied by a wartime German officer, writing on the matter recently in a Soviet exile journal.[13] According to him, in the summer of 1944 certain SS officials turned to General Zhilenkov, whose relations to the SS were reputedly of the best, in connection with a major propaganda project, Operation Scorpion, for the southern sector of the Eastern Front. The project was to be staffed by Zhilenkov and a number of other Vlasovites active at Dabendorf. Key among these was to be Zykov, who would edit a large front-line newspaper for Soviet troops. It was at this point that Zykov vanished. "One Gestapo employee told me," the German informant states, "that this was done by that SS group which did not believe the Russians [the Soviet opposition movement]. In Zykov they saw a Bolshevik and a Jew and, knowing his capabilities, feared that his presence at the front would bring much harm." From this and other testimony the fact is now practically established that Zykov was indeed eliminated by the SS faction which distrusted the Soviet opposition movement.

Zykov's disappearance is probably a fitting symbol of the entire publishing venture of the Vlasov Movement. The circulation of *Zaria* and *Dobrovolets* evidently reached into the hundreds of thousands. Therefore the papers played a dual key role: drawing together all likely opposition elements, and improving the German treatment of Soviet nationals by publicizing and stressing the most favorable among German policies. But much of its content was either sharply altered by German censorship or forced upon the editors by outright German pressure. Therefore this aspect of the Dabendorf propaganda activities of the Vlasov Movement was at times as frustrating, as unrepresentative of its own nationalist, non-Nazi aspirations, as the two myths that this published propaganda furthered — the Russian National Committee and ROA.

The second major activity at Dabendorf, also, by its very name, played a part in perpetuating the myth of the actually nonexistent ROA. This was the School for ROA Propagandists. Established early in

1943, it graduated, according to former instructors of the school, a total of several thousand "ROA propagandists."

Naturally, since its purpose was to train propagandists, or information officers, the emphasis of the school was primarily political. But it had its military aspect as well; military training was included in the curriculum. Although it was only a minor part of the course of study, this became highly significant in the future of the Vlasov Movement. It was under the disguise of military exercises and drill that General Trukhin was able to build up what became the Vlasov Movement's closest approximation to a military headquarters and general staff of its own. This was accomplished by padding the staff of the Dabendorf school with numerous high-ranking Red Army commanders and military specialists. When, in its second stage, the Vlasov Movement was to develop a military organization less nebulous than ROA, the senior military instructors at Dabendorf could readily be transformed into a general staff and a cadre for headquarters and military units. In the meantime, these ex-Soviet colonels and majors had little to do but drill and parade, to the not infrequent annoyance of the intellectuals at Dabendorf.

Turning to the political side of the School, an extensive statement on the political indoctrination carried on is contained in a pamphlet published at Dabendorf. Dated 1943, it is part of a series put out by the School, paralleling its own course of instruction.[14]

The introduction to this pamphlet gives a good formal summary of the activities — lectures, trips, assignments, schedules — of the Dabendorf School. Of greater interest is its statement of the purposes of this School for Propagandists:

1. Familiarization with Germany, its historical past and its achievements under the National-Socialist Party.

2. Proof of the complete bankruptcy of the Bolshevik system and its unacceptability for the Russian people, as well as its advantage for world Jewry.

3. Familiarization with the ideas and positions of the Russian Liberation Movement. Detailed study of materials connected with the indicated questions had in turn as its purpose the preparation of qualified propagandists for work in units of the Russian Army of Liberation and among its camps for prisoners of war.

This pamphlet's detailed summary of the material purportedly taught as political indoctrination (reproduced in translation in Appendix III) makes sorry reading. It abounds with hymns of praise to National

Socialism, violent and lengthy tirades against every aspect of life under the Soviet regime, ugly characterization of Jews as "a people-parasite . . . inventors and carriers of destructive ideas . . . war mongers." All this reads like a veritable echo of Goebbels, of Julius Streicher, of the *Völkischer Beobachter*, of Hitler himself. Only in its final, and briefest, section on the Russian Liberation Movement does it appear to deviate in any way from the most extreme and primitive kind of Nazi propaganda.

How can this official contemporary description of the Dabendorf School (and similar material published in *Zaria* and *Dobrovolets*) be reconciled with the Vlasov Movement's distinctly non-Nazi aspirations?

The most immediate explanation, of course, is that German interference, German pressure, German propaganda were constant, never abating in intensity. A major share of what finally found its way into published form reflected the views, not of the Vlasov Movement, but of the least Other Germany-minded Nazi officials surrounding it. Even if its immediate German environment had been less restrictive, the Vlasov Movement would have been forced to publish large doses of vile Nazi stuff merely in order not to arouse outside suspicion.

Much of the Vlasov Movement's published material does sound practically indistinguishable from Nazi utterances, but a careful comparison of it with the contemporary output of official Nazi propaganda reveals a difference. Although liberally sprinkled with bows to the party line, it is, on the whole, noticeably restrained in its parroting of Nazi dogma. Seen from a Nazi point of view, even the vulgar anti-Semitism of the Dabendorf pamphlet is remarkably moderate and "unorthodox."

It was, moreover, not in its censorable printed material but in its oral instructions that the Dabendorf School showed the extent of its deviation from Nazi doctrine. By definition, no published wartime sources exist to substantiate this statement. But postwar testimony unanimously tells of the relative freedom, and impudence, with which the instructors at the Dabendorf School preached what was utter heresy in Hitler's Germany. Such heretic notions began with the absolute need for a far more independent Soviet opposition movement, and ended with frank discussions on just what kind of post-Stalin regime the USSR should have. In little of this Dabendorf oral instruction, lectures and more informal discussions, did the Nazi regime or its leaders apparently fare very well. To repeat: no wartime substantiation of this is likely to have been published under German control. But the suggestion has been strongly advanced since the war, not only by eyewitnesses, but also by the unpublished study of A. E. Jolis, an officer in OSS, the U. S. Office of Strategic Services. Jolis had access to classified Allied documents, and made his study of the subject in France immediately following its liberation in 1944.[15] Like the centers of the Vlasovites' Other Germany patrons, Dabendorf in effect became one of those unique islands of relative privacy within the totalitarian sea of Hitler's Germany.

If Zykov dominated the Dabendorf publications, the political activities of the school were dominated by the "solidarist" NTS. This old-émigré organization, characterized as "right wing" but on the whole non-Nazi, held this ascendant position even though no old émigrés were employed as instructors. In part, this can be explained by the fact that General Trukhin had passed through the NTS-dominated Wustrau center, and at some early stage of the war had joined the NTS. He was now a member of its Central Bureau and, although not activist, did not oppose its influence at Dabendorf. A number of ex-Soviet intellectuals, recently captured and considerably disoriented by their first months in Hitler Germany, were also drawn to the sole organization in wartime Germany. The NTS had not only a strong Russian nationalist position, but an elaborate ideological scheme as well. Equally naturally, when the Dabendorf School was set up early in 1943, it was from this group of intellectuals that its original instructors were chosen. This combination of circumstances accounts for the influence wielded by the NTS in Dabendorf's political affairs. To the extent that the Vlasov Movement ever did evolve a crystallized ideological position, its two wings were represented by those in charge of the two major political activities at Dabendorf. The most important and lucid spokesman for the "left" wing was Zykov; the position of its "right" wing closely resembled that taken by the NTS. We shall return in Part III to the subject of the Vlasov Movement's ideology.

The influence of the various activities at Dabendorf extended far beyond its physical boundaries. Its newspapers, *Zaria* and *Dobrovolets*, published hundreds of thousands of copies. Its several thousand "propagandist" graduates went out to prison camps and *Osttruppen* units as Vlasov Movement proselytizers. Four branch offices were maintained in Paris, Verona, Copenhagen, and Riga. Reaching a majority of Soviet nationals under German control, the Vlasov Movement, itself puny in size and importance, in this fashion garnered much publicity and support.

Dabendorf may be ascribed two basic roles in the history of wartime Soviet opposition to Stalin.

One was internal: Dabendorf soon became the spiritual as well as the physical center of the ideological and organizational activities and developments of the Vlasov Movement. It was here, in this least uncongenial spot under German control, that the Soviet opposition movement developed what cohesion it was able to attain. Although the results were pathetically slight, this Dabendorf atmosphere created an *esprit de corps* within the Vlasov Movement which still plays an important role among surviving Soviet defectors.

The second, the external, role was played by Dabendorf's newspapers, Dabendorf's school, the whole Dabendorf center. Everything was furthering propaganda for and under the control of German authorities. As it was only in propaganda that the Russian National Committee and the Russian Army of Liberation achieved a semblance of reality, Dabendrof becomes a fitting symbol of the entire Soviet opposition movement in its phantom stage.

# The Vlasov Movement:
# Himmler Stage

The Vlasov Movement might have remained in its phantom stage until the end had it not been for one very remarkable phenomenon. Heinrich Himmler, Nazi Germany's ever more powerful police chief, changed his stand on *Ostpolitik*. In its first phantom stage the Vlasov Movement had been kept above water by the Other Germany and Utilitarian military around the Armed Forces (OKW) Propaganda Department and the Army (OKH) *Fremde Heere Ost*. But in its final stage this Soviet venture owed most of its progress to Himmler.

How ironical, how paradoxical this turn of events truly was. Himmler had done so much early in the war, through the notorious *Untermensch* pamphlet, to popularize the ugliest aspects of the official *Ostpolitik*. And it was Himmler who, as late as the autumn of 1943, delivered what remains one of the most extensive and brutal monuments to the *Untermensch* position. In an address to a conference of SS generals, held in Posen on October 4, 1943, Himmler said: "What happens to a Russian, to a Czech, does not interest me in the slightest. . . Whether nations live in prosperity or starve to death interests me only in so far as we need them as slaves for our culture; otherwise it is of no interest to me. Whether 10,000 Russian females fall down from exhaustion while digging an antitank ditch interests me only in so far as the tank ditch for Germany is finished."[1] This same speech also contains several sharp outbursts against Vlasov himself. What particularly infuriated Himmler against Vlasov was plainly detailed ten days later when Himmler spoke at Bad Schachen to a gathering of high Nazi representatives in the *Wehrmacht*. There he declared: "I may bring up here quite frankly the name of General Vlasov. Very great hopes were placed on this General Vlasov. The hope was not as well founded as some assumed. . . Mr. Vlasov then — and this surprised me immensely — proceeded to make propaganda within Germany itself, and gave lectures to us Germans, sometimes in a form which I must call outright grotesque. . . Mr. Vlasov, with the arrogance typical of the Russian, of the Slav . . . stated: 'Germany has never been able to defeat Russia; Russia can be defeated only by Russians.' . . . This sentence alone shows him as the swine he is." [2]

Together with this unmistakable evidence of Himmler's contempt for Soviet nationals, Vlasov's real efforts toward independence, and Himmler's loyalty to the *Untermensch* approach, these 1943 speeches indicate just how the SS chieftain would be willing to use the Vlasov Movement: "I would have had nothing against it if General Vlasov, like any other Slavic creature in Russian general's uniform, had been employed by us in order to do propaganda with him against the Russians. I would have had nothing to object against that. Wonderful." [3] But what persuaded Himmler of the need for such a move, and how did the new relation come about?

All of the answers are related to the position that Himmler held in Hitler Germany. Until the final days of the Third Reich, when his futile negotiations with Count Bernadotte led Hitler to excommunicate him, Heinrich Himmler's rise under the Hitler regime continued unabated. He was chief of the SS, the Nazi party's elite guard, before its coming to power. Soon after 1933 he was strengthened by being named chief of the German Police, including the ever-expanding secret police, the *Gestapo*, and also by the gradual decline of the more plebian Nazi force, the SA. During the war he became first Minister of the Interior, and subsequently (after July 20, 1944) Commander of Reserve Troops, thus holding a military post. But even this impressive list does not tell the whole story. For Himmler managed to make his own *Waffen-SS* into an ever-larger combat force, which gave him an increasing voice in military affairs. And the whole wartime evolution of Germany, the internal political strains together with the vast policing problems throughout *Festung Europa*, made it likely that Himmler, as the gendarme of Hitler Germany, would come more and more to the fore.

In his Bad Schachen speech of October 1943, Himmler remarked that there were some six to seven million foreigners in Germany at the time.[4] A year later, on October 12, 1944, Rosenberg put the number of Soviet nationals in Germany at five million.[5] It can well be imagined that Himmler, as chief police officer for all German-held Europe, would be interested in these aliens, particularly in the morale of those within Germany proper. This provides one explanation of why Himmler should revise his view of the Vlasov Movement. He could speculate that if this independent-minded and so far repressed venture could be given more German support, it might well help him in pacifying by far the largest single group of foreigners in Germany — the Soviet nationals.

Some writers state that Himmler's change of attitude toward the Vlasov Movement followed the abortive *Putsch* of July 20, 1944, since this event called attention to the Soviet nationals under German control, and specifically to the *Osttruppen*, as a potential danger.[6] Himmler had in fact approved some changes in SS policy as early as the spring of 1944; moreover, his first decisive meeting with Vlasov was originally scheduled for July 21, 1944, the day after the anti-Hitler *Putsch*. Although this does not preclude the possibility that the impact of the *Putsch* accelerated Himmler's interest in the Vlasov Movement, it suggests that the July 20 events were probably no more than a contributing element.

Another contributory factor is the well-known animosity within the hierarchy, and the striving of the SS for predominance throughout the government. In view of Himmler's acknowledged enmity toward Rosenberg, as well as the probable *Waffen-SS* rivalry with the *Wehrmacht*, this power struggle furnished additional motivation for Himmler's sponsorship of the Vlasov Movement. Specifically, if he could thus project himself into the entire problem, and place the potential nucleus of a vast *Osttruppen* armed force under his own jurisdiction, Himmler would certainly gain considerable general advantage over both Rosenberg and the *Wehrmacht*. This is related to one further explanation — the growing hunger for troops, any kind of troops, that was felt by the competing *Wehrmacht* and SS.

There is a final factor in explaining Himmler's change toward the Vlasov Movement which at the same time is an answer to the further question of precisely how the change came about. Just as the *Wehrmacht*'s earlier tutelage of Vlasov had been piloted by a small group of activists — notably Strikfeldt and his associates in *Fremde Heere Ost* — so Himmler's backing of the Vlasov Movement in this second stage was in large measure similarly engineered within the SS. Here the central figure is SS Standartenführer (Colonel) Gunter D'Alquen.[7] Influential in the SS and personally close to Himmler, he was founder and editor of the SS organ *Das Schwarze Korps*. During World War II, he had become the publicity and propaganda chief for the growing military formations of the SS. D'Alquen's leading role is confirmed by a wartime report of the Propaganda Ministry office of Dr. Taubert, its expert on Soviet-directed propaganda: "Credit for the carrying through of the Vlasov line belongs to Standartenführer Gunter D'Alquen, who proposed it to the Reichführer [Himmler] through whom it was then submitted to the Führer." [8]

The issue that most immediately aided D'Alquen's pro-Vlasov effort was Himmler's order to him in the spring of 1944 to start a major SS propaganda campaign against Soviet troops on the Eastern Front. D'Alquen soon began to build much of this propaganda "Operation Scorpion" around Vlasov Movement personnel, notably Zhilenkov. (It will be recalled that Zykov, too, had been slated for a key role in this operation.) Every effort was now made to channel to Himmler all reports that would subtly suggest the value to Germany and the popularity among Soviet nationals of General Vlasov and his presently restricted venture. Eventually, after special urging by D'Alquen, Himmler agreed to receive Vlasov, and the date was set for July 21, 1944. But just as Vlasov was ready to entrain for Himmler's headquarters in East Prussia, came the word of the anti-Hitler *Putsch*, and the consequent cancellation of the meeting. Then followed an even more frustrating period of delays and machinations, a period spent by Vlasov mostly at an SS rest home, where he first met the German woman (manager of the home) whom he was to marry at the very end of the war, Heidi Bielenberg. But finally, despite postponement, internal friction, and external opposition, the Himmler-Vlasov talks actually did take place.

D'Alquen occupied a unique position in Himmler's change toward the Vlasov Movement. A Nazi intellectual who combined a propagandist's skill with personal influence and aggressiveness, D'Alquen arrived at a definite conclusion as World War II went on. This conclusion was affected by his frequent contacts with SS combat units on the Eastern Front, and above all by the large-scale "Operation Scorpion" there which he conceived and then executed. D'Alquen's conclusion, in short, was that the official *Ostpolitik* was wholly inadequate and that a major change was called for. Gradually, but unmistakably, D'Alquen reached the parallel conclusion that in the Vlasov Movement his homeland had been provided with a unique tool with which to execute this reversal of previous German policy.

Within the SS, D'Alquen emerges as a one-man crusade for the Utilitarian grouping. But D'Alquen was not the only one inside the Himmler camp who in 1944 began to develop an interest in the whole problem, and particularly in the Vlasov Movement. A second trend is embodied by Dr. Fritz Rudolf Arlt, who in 1944 became responsible for the SS military units made up of Soviet nationals. Arlt's function encompassed both the military supervision exercised in the Wehrmacht by the General for *Osttruppen* and the political and welfare tutelage of Rosenberg's *Ostministerium* over the non-Russian nationals of the USSR. If D'Alquen embraced the Utilitarian position, Arlt favored the Rosenberg Conception. He therefore supported non-Russian nationals as against Russians such as Vlasov. Although both Rosenberg and Arlt had gradually acceded to Vlasov's leadership of Russian defectors, they continued to resist the extension of his scope to other Soviet nationals under German control.

A third group in the Himmler camp that at this point took an interest in the Vlasov Movement is represented by SS Colonel Kröger. Kröger at the end of 1944 became head of Arlt's section for Russian formations within the SS. A distinguishing feature of this third group was its late and least considerable shift away from the *Untermensch* approach, and at the same time the intense pro-Russian sentiment as opposed to the other national groupings of the USSR. Another special characteristic of this group was that most of it, including Kröger, were officers of the SD, the independent secret police of the SS headed by Kaltenbrunner. Lastly, Kröger and again almost all others were younger Germans of Baltic origin.

An interesting contrast exists between these younger Baltic Germans and Vlasov's earlier champions in the Other Germany group, who were primarily Germans reared in Russia. Though exceptions may be cited in each case, the Germans born in Russia of middle-class, usually merchant, families possessed not only a knowledge of the Russian language and habits but also a reflection of the values of the prerevolution Russian intelligentsia. Those who were Baltic born, although familiar with the language and customs of Russia, were on the whole typified by an irredentist type of German nationalism and far more likely to become believing members of the Nazi party. If the Vlasov Movement's principal backers in the first stage were non-Nazi officials in the *Wehrmacht* and Foreign Office, the Russian-speaking figures among those who furthered the Movement's progress in its later developments were on the whole zealous party members in the SS.

If D'Alquen, Arlt, and Kröger can be divided into three distinct currents, what it is that they — and above all their common superior, Himmler — wanted from the Vlasov Movement, and in turn were willing to give to it? The answer to this puzzling question emerges from the event that climaxed and also sealed the new *rappochement* — the September 16, 1944 conference between Himmler and Vlasov. Valuable eyewitness testimony on this conference and its background has only recently been presented by D'Alquen, Arlt, and Strikfeldt. This testimony is recorded in the account on the Vlasov Movement by Jurgen Thorwald, a German journalist-chronicler of World War II.[9]

The Himmler-Vlasov meeting took place in the morning of September 16, 1944, in the SS chief's field headquarters at Rastenburg, East Prussia. Present besides the two principals were D'Alquen and SS Colonel Ehlich, as representative of the SD, and SS General Berger, head of the SS Central Office and at the same time a top deputy of Rosenberg in the *Ostministerium* in form if no longer in fact.

It is noteworthy that Vlasov had neither an interpreter nor an advisor of his own — Strikfeldt was stopped from entering the conference room without prior warning either to him or to Vlasov. Moreover, neither the Foreign Office nor the *Ostministerium* was represented.

The major decisions taken at this conference centered around the organization of a new committee and an armed force to unite Soviet nationals under German control for political and military action against Bolshevism.

After approving the idea of the committee and promising it his support, Himmler raised the question of its national composition. Vlasov strongly reiterated the Smolensk Manifesto's stand which he had originally spelled out a year and a half earlier in a *Zaria* statement of March 28, 1943: "[In the New Russia] every people will obtain national freedom, including the right of self-determination. The realization of this right to national freedom and independence is possible, however, only after destroying Stalin and his clique. Without this the happiness of any people in the country is inconceivable." Himmler assented to this, and hence also to the proposed name of the committee: *Komitet Osvobozhdeniia Narodov Rossii* (KONR); in English, Committee for the Liberation of the Peoples of Russia. Although it was agreed that the KONR would function initially as a political committee rather than as a government in exile, Himmler also promised that as soon as German forces reconquered major Soviet areas the KONR would be given the status of a provisional government.

Extensive, too, were Himmler's promises regarding the formation of a KONR army. Vlasov would be permitted to activate, to begin with, five divisions from among Soviet *Ostarbeiter* and prisoners of war. Though *Osttruppen* units could not be transferred immediately to the new army, this would eventually be done in gradual stages.

Himmler's generosity was not, however, without its qualifications. Concessions and restrictions characterized, for instance, the outcome of the discussions regarding German treatment of Soviet nationals. Himmler expressed a willingness, in principle, to urge upon Hitler a change in the much-hated *Ost* patch of the *Ostarbeiter*. But he limited his commitment by stating that he did not think it wise to make the recommendation until the KONR army had proved itself successful in the front lines. At Vlasov's request, Himmler did agree to halt the circulation of the defamatory *Untermensch* pamphlet and to have it confiscated by the Gestapo. This occurred, however, only after he had assured Vlasov that each society has its *Untermenschen*, and the pamphlet had merely sought to emphasize that, whereas in Germany they are in jail, in the USSR they are in power.

Despite these and other stipulations, the potential consequences of this conference were very far-reaching. Himmler had in effect endorsed the unification, both political-organizational and military, of the Soviet nationals under German control. Thus, in the final stage of World War II, in the days of crushing German defeats, it appeared that the cherished hopes and dreams of the Soviet defectors were at long last to be realized. But all was not as yet to be smooth sailing.

One of the great questions regarding this whole development is just how much Hitler knew and approved of Himmler's new policy toward the Vlasov Movement. There is a postwar Rosenberg lament that Himmler began influencing Hitler in Vlasov's favor toward the end of 1944,[10] and a wartime letter from Rosenberg which stated that Hitler had approved of the first meeting between Himmler and Vlasov.[11] It is now established that Himmler obtained Hitler's approval for his new orientation at least twice — before the initial conference date in July and again before the September 16 meeting. But in each case Hitler's blessing was qualified. It was limited to propaganda and left open the questions of Vlasov's political and military role.[12] It is also known from every available document, however, that Hitler was growing short-tempered with the military, and ever more suspicious of both their loyalty and their competence. Hitler's reliance on Rosenberg, the other primary claimant to control of the Soviet nationals, had steadily declined, not least because of the anti-Rosenberg intrigues of Hitler confidants such as Bormann, Goebbels, and Himmler himself. While it is inconceivable that Hitler should ever have abandoned his original *Ostpolitik*, it is still quite plausible that he did not object to Himmler, his loyal and efficient gendarme, moving in on the prerogatives of both the military and Rosenberg's increasingly ineffectual *Ostministerium*.

If not faced with active and adamant opposition from Hitler himself, the Vlasov Movement had by 1944 developed a number of powerful enemies within Hitler Germany. Inside Himmler's own domain there had been active opposition. Earlier in June 1944, the Gestapo had jailed most of the top leaders of the "solidarist" NTS,[13] and had sought also to arrest the leaders of the Vlasov Movement. Though this plan had been blocked (with the exception of the disappearance of Zykov), the Gestapo's animosity toward the Soviet opposition movement did not lessen. Well-placed tory old émigrés and *Ostministerium* personnel were also vehemently anti-Vlasov. And despite Himmler's ever greater ascendancy over the whole German scene, this opposition not only continued but increased following the Himmler-Vlasov conference.

It was the always explosive national issue, and Himmler's apparent approval of a united, multinational Committee for the Liberation of the *Peoples of Russia* led by the *Russian* General Vlasov, that consolidated the opposition. On October 12, 1944, Rosenberg wrote a lengthy, worried protest to Hitler on this subject.[14] First he made several references to his own past position and to Hitler's negative reaction to it. "I suggested once again the formation of National Committees, and enclosed a declaration by General Vlasov containing a renunciation of the Ukraine and the Caucasus. To this suggestion I remained without answer, which I was forced to accept as a rejection." But now, Rosenberg asserted, this new action "had reopened the Eastern problem in all its vastness. . . With your approval a discussion has now taken place between the Reichführer SS [Himmler] and General Vlasov, which went far beyond military coöperation and which made the aspirations of the Russian general clear."

At this point Rosenberg helps to explain what became a great disappointment for the Vlasov Movement, a disappointment visible in the proud and yet restrained announcement of October 1, 1944 in the Vlasovite *Zaria* regarding the Himmler-Vlasov meeting. "A subordinate office gave a press announcement at the national press conference to the effect that agreement had been reached on all measures on the use of extensive forces of the *peoples of Russia*. I raised objections against this form of announcement, because just this terminology contradicted all that I have thought necessary in the spirit of your ideas to defend all these years. A German official terminology about the peoples of Russia means the recognition of the entire old territory as Russian property and the inclusion of all non-Russians into this conception." The upshot of this was that the major press announcement was called off and in the end only a small and insignificantly displayed notice appeared. The actual announcement, according to Rosenberg, "took place on the basis of changes according to which General Vlasov was designated as leader of the *Russian* Army of Liberation and that his task consisted of assembling the forces of the *Russian* people for the struggle against Bolshevism." Rosenberg goes on to state that "General Vlasov, nevertheless, always without my participation, evidently received further assurances and subsequently talked with the leaders of different national groups. The natural consequence of this claim as military-political leader also of the non-Russian peoples, and their subordination to his command, has now led to the unanimous protest of all."

To date the general view has been that it was Rosenberg and his *Ostministerium* which did most to counteract and minimize the success of the second phase of the Vlasov Movement. The foregoing excerpts from Rosenberg's letter certainly confirm that he did all within his power to sway Hitler away from Himmler's promises to Vlasov. But the same letter also reveals just how pathetically slight Rosenberg's influence with Hitler was at the time. "I ask you, my Führer, to tell me whether you wish me still to continue my activities in this direction; for since it has not been possible for me to report to you orally, but the problems of the East are brought to you from different directions and discussed, I must therefore in view of this give consideration to the assumption that you, my Führer, no longer consider this activity of mine necessary." Indeed, indications of his weakness are numerous enough to warrant a definite conclusion: Rosenberg's anti-Vlasov stand would have carried little if any weight had it not received powerful support from other branches of the German government.

That such backing did exist is clearly shown in a memorandum by Dr. Taubert of the Propaganda Ministry, dated September 22, 1944. "Vlasov is trying to unite all the National Committees of the Eastern peoples into one large committee. . . Opinions are divided on the question of whether this is right. As far as we [the *Ostabteilung* of the Propaganda Ministry] are concerned, we as well as [SS General] Berger's representative Arlt and Reichminister [Rosenberg] believe that this should *not* be allowed, for in this manner a large united organization would be created for all Eastern nationalities. It is furthermore in the interest of Germany not to unite but to disunite these peoples." To this general reason for his disapproval Taubert adds a more specific one. Plans were under way to unite all the various Ukrainian groups, including those with whom, "while still occupying the Ukraine, we clashed in partisan struggles." This "unity with them, which it is hoped now to achieve" would "create the possibility of collaboration with the Ukrainian partisans behind the Soviet front." Thus Taubert also opposed the proposed KONR organization on the grounds that "under such a set-up common work with the Ukrainians will be made impossible." [15]

This is Utilitarianism in the best Goebbels style! Not only were the Soviet nationalities to be kept split up because Germany could thus manage them more easily, but peace was to be made with the formerly anti-German Ukrainian partisans for the very Utilitarian consideration that they had become a force behind Soviet lines. The entire Taubert memorandum indicates that it was this Utilitarian opposition to a predominance of the Vlasov Movement, rather than Rosenberg's persistent but ineffectual protests, that was in fact the chief counterforce against Himmler. As additional evidence, we know from an *Ostministerium* minute of November 28, 1944, that General Köstring, OKH General for *Osttruppen*, and one of the most influential (and most pro-"Great" Russian) military Utilitarians, on this issue sided not with the Vlasov Movement but with its opponents.[16]

We are now back to a basic theme of this work: throughout, the prevailing German approach to Soviet opposition to Stalin was at best Utilitarian. And the significance therefore of the national issue was twofold. For one thing, it rallied and united against the Vlasov Movement whatever elements may have been suspicious of such a united, independent-minded undertaking of Soviet nationals. But equally important is the second way in which the national issue of this period is significant. For here it is clearly revealed that both the basic opposition and the basic support stemmed from the same source — the narrowly defined self-interest of wartime Nazi Germany.

What we have here, in this militarily disastrous last year of the Third Reich, is the coming to the fore of leaders and impulses which might be described as Nazi "neo-Utilitarian." While earlier D'Alquen was described as a Utilitarian and Arlt as representing the Rosenberg Conception, the term "neo-Utilitarian" can well be applied to the other SS elements that at this late stage developed an interest in the Vlasov Movement. This is true not only of the Kröger group but also of their SD superior Kaltenbrunner and two other top Himmler deputies, Schellenberg and Ohlendorf. All three at the end became sponsors of the Kröger combination of Russophilia and Nazism. Himmler, too, can well be described as a neo-Utilitarian. They all believed that the Vlasov Movement might be worth gambling on in this desperate stage. But even now these neo-Utilitarians were incapable of shedding their basic Nazi predilections and commitments. This is one of the basic differences between the earlier backers of the Vlasov Movement — the Other Germany officials like Strikfeldt and Hilger — and the by comparison far more powerful Himmler group that now replaced it more and more. At this time Captain Strikfeldt, the Vlasov Movement long-time German supporter, was replaced as chief of the appropriate branch of the OKW Propaganda Department by SS Colonel Kröger, Himmler's recently named delegate on Soviet opposition matters. Thus Kröger now headed not only the SS *Russische Leitstelle*, the office that was increasingly dominating decisions on Soviet defection, but also the OKW branch that had most immediate charge of Dabendorf, the organizational center of the Vlasov Movement.[17] At about the same time, SS Colonel D'Alquen replaced Strikfeldt's superior as chief of WPrIV, Colonel Martin.

That now the German use of the KONR was to be essentially neo-Utilitarian is suggested not only by this change in personnel. It is also clearly indicated by the already-quoted memorandum of Dr. Taubert. "Basically all propaganda must be conducted externally in the name of the National Committee at the same time that it is internally directed by us."[18] Altogether, there is little reason to suppose that Himmler's attitude toward the Vlasov Movement ever varied substantially from that expressed so revealingly in 1943 at Posen: "I would have had nothing against it if General Vlasov . . . had been employed by us in order to do propaganda with him against the Russians."[19]

This provides the final answer to the earlier query why exactly

Himmler reversed himself. He, and also his SS associates, did so primarily to use Vlasov for German propaganda purposes. Grasping at any means that might help lessen the probability of Germany's losing the entire conflict, Himmler thus became the patron of the Vlasov Movement in its latter stage. But the powerful patron's neo-Utilitarian motivation was inadequate at this late stage of World War II.

In the history of the Vlasov Movement, the city of Prague twice played an outstanding role. It did so once in 1944 and once in 1945. On the earlier occasion, Prague was the happy scene of the establishment of General Vlasov's KONR — the Committee for the Liberation of the Peoples of Russia. But if the Vlasov Movement had by then embarked upon its Himmler stage, and hoped for the neo-Utilitarian backing of the powerful SS chieftain, there remained one decisive obstacle.

This obstacle was the war situation. By that time, disastrous and unceasing defeats were being suffered constantly by Hitler Germany. If Himmler's concessions to the Vlasov Movement were caused to a large extent by these war reverses, the entire brief life of the KONR took place in an environment of unmitigated disaster. Only four days after its founding in Prague on November 14, 1944, General Patton's Third U. S. Army entered German territory. By the end of December 1944, the Red Army had flooded into the Balkans and was fighting inside Budapest. The Western Allies were driving ever deeper into Germany. And all along, increasingly heavy bombing raids were destroying the major cities of Germany as well as its communications.

This widespread defeat and destruction, the thorough disorganization and disruption of the entire German governmental apparatus, affected the KONR deeply. Now even those German officials who either from conviction or from bureaucratic habit were quite ready to furnish the KONR with the military, organizational, or propaganda aid needed for its new activities were often unable to do so. It would be erroneous to attribute all of the KONR's many frustrations to conscious and organized German opposition.

But the KONR was affected by the war situation in an even more fundamental way. When wartime Soviet opposition at last attained a semblance of German recognition and assistance, that Germany was unmistakably crumbling. The KONR was born in an atmosphere of defeat and black pessimism. Behind every action, every thought, every hope of its leaders was the haunting vision of failure, of doom, of death — a devitalizing, dispiriting atmosphere indeed.

Yet on the occasion of the founding of the KONR, the specter of defeat was pushed away. So many frustrations had marked the whole path of the Vlasov Movement that it was only natural that this formal, even ceremonial, recognition of long-cherished hopes should have been greeted as a notable achievement. And indeed this attitude still prevails. Despite its ominous future, despite the fact that neither the achievements nor the drama of the event were great in absolute terms, the Prague meeting of the KONR is remembered as the most historic event in the annals of wartime Soviet opposition.

The activities preceding the founding meeting of the KONR were of a kind all too familiar in the story of the Vlasov Movement. The Vlasov Movement's proposal that the founding take place in a non-German city was adopted. The meeting was scheduled not for Berlin, as first planned, but in the Slavic capital of Prague. But with plans well under way, Rosenberg addressed one more protest, an unusually sharp one, to Bormann, Ribbentrop, and Lammers, as well as to Himmler. The outcome of this was that Himmler gave orders to conduct the Prague meeting on a far smaller scale than had initially been proposed. Instead of the four undersecretaries slated to represent the German government, there was actually only one — SS General Lorenz, as a deputy of the German Foreign Minister and President of the Society of Interstate Associations.[1]

Vlasov and other key KONR figures arrived in Prague, and returned to Berlin, on the day of the meeting, November 14, 1944, in a special section of the Berlin-Prague night express. They were escorted to Prague's best hotel, the Alcron, in front of which a German honor guard was posted for the occasion. An exclusive luncheon was given for Vlasov and his closest associates by Karl-Hermann Frank, Reichsminister for the "Protectorate" of Bohemia and Moravia (not to be confused with

Hanns Frank, Gauleiter for occupied Poland). The KONR meeting itself began at 3:00 P.M. in Prague's most festive hall, the Spanish Hall of its ancient palace, Hradčany.[2] The meeting was first chaired by the oldest member of the KONR, Professor Rudnev. (The other published names of original KONR members appear in Appendix IV.) Vlasov was then elected chairman, and took over the conduct of the meeting.

After a welcome by Reichsminister Frank, Lorenz delivered a speech which conferred official endorsement upon both the KONR — "an ally of Germany" — and its Prague Manifesto. "In the manifesto issued today by you, the foundations for a joint struggle against Bolshevism are outlined with conclusive clarity. On the path to the realization of the aims cited in the manifesto, you may be assured of the support of the German government."[3] Following the reading of a congratulatory telegram from Himmler came the principal address of the day — that of General Vlasov.

Vlasov stressed that although opposition inside the USSR never abated, Soviet totalitarianism made a struggle practically impossible. It was only World War II that gave opposition an opportunity to organize itself outside the USSR. Thus, "for the sake of saving the motherland, we sought an honest alliance with Germany. We know that the help which is being furnished to us by the German people is today our sole real possibility to organize an armed struggle against Bolshevism." Vlasov next described his recent interviews with Himmler and Ribbentrop, apparently with the desire of stressing the "spirit of mutual understanding" and the "full support" of these Nazi chieftains. At the same time that he made his formal bow to Hitler, Vlasov once again struck his usual independent note in concluding: "On the basis of trust and common interests between the German and Russian peoples, with an unswerving will to victory, we build our collaboration on the basis of mutual respect. Today we can assure the Führer and the whole German people that in their difficult struggle against the worst enemy of all peoples — Bolshevism — the peoples of Russia are their best allies and will never lay down their arms but rather will go shoulder to shoulder with them to full victory."[4] After Vlasov's speech, and one by General Trukhin, came the climax, the adoption of the Prague Manifesto.

The Prague Manifesto is the only major ideological pronouncement of the Vlasov's Movement's second stage. It is also the most detailed and most famous programmatic statement issued by the Russian Liberation Movement. In the postwar period, and to this date, the Prague Manifesto is cited by a broad range of Soviet exile groupings, and unaffiliated émigrés, as the most acceptable credo for a future struggle against the Soviet regime. It thus enjoys a unique standing in the annals of postwar as well as wartime Soviet opposition to Stalin. Two circumstances stand out as the Prague Manifesto is analyzed. One is the changing status of Germany and the West. The other is the ideological picture within the Vlasov Movement, a subject to be discussed further in Part III.

Faced with imminent defeat, German officialdom by the fall of 1944 had far less absolute self-confidence. This meant an easing of the prohibitions and restrictions that had for so long hampered the Soviet opposition movement. Hence the Prague Manifesto comes closest to reflecting the beliefs of Soviet opposition in World War II. But the counterpart to German defeat was Allied victory. With this prospect ever closer, the Vlasov Movement began to think far more in terms of the Western world and the slogans that might appeal to this possible new ally of Soviet defection. This adjustment to a changing power situation was in large measure not conscious. Even the assertion of its existence might well be met with indignant denials by surviving key figures of the Vlasov Movement. Nevertheless, along with genuine non-Nazi convictions, the shift of the offensive from Germany to its opponents increasingly affected the ideological position of the Vlasov Movement.

Though united in its opposition to Stalin, the Vlasov Movement was otherwise an ever-fluctuating gathering of varying, and sometimes conflicting, currents. And these currents changed considerably between 1942 and 1945. The Vlasovite ideology itself was nonexistent except as an amorphous consensus between the "left" and "right" currents. Articulated ideological positions should be ascribed throughout only to the Vlasovite elite, and far less to the Movement's rank and file. In the latter case, sympathy with the middle grouping intermingled with ideological confusion and apathy. To divine any, or particularly a single, ideological pattern for such an amalgam is immensely difficult at best. It is only necessary to recall the situation that existed at Dabendorf, that least uncongenial spot in Hitler Germany, which was the spiritual and ideological center of the Vlasov Movement. It is a curious paradox that the two groups most responsible for this were the two extreme groups within the Movement, its "right" and "left" currents. The influence of Zykov, or the "left," is generally thought to have been considerable on Vlasov Movement thinking. The "right" wing has claimed that "the Vlasov manifesto . . . was inspired by NTS philosophy." [5]

There is much of interest in the Prague Manifesto, the full text of which is reproduced in Appendix IV. Notable in the Manifesto are the brevity and the stanchly independent tone of its sole reference to Hitler Germany. "The Committee for the Liberation of the Peoples of Russia welcomes Germany's help under conditions which shall not impair the honor and independence of our country. This help is at the moment the only tangible opportunity to organize an armed struggle against the Stalin clique." Interesting, too, is its unequivocal "self-determination" stand on the national issue. While insisting on "the unification of all national forces and their subordination to the common cause of destroying Bolshevism as the prerequisite for victory," in its first programmatic point it firmly endorses "equality of all peoples of Russia and their real right for national development, self-determination, and state independence." Its list of reasons why the Vlasov Movement's crusade will be victorious in the end seems incredibly unrealistic when one considers the date of its issuance. But it remains worthy of attention not only as a reflection of the Vlasov Movement's frame of mind but particularly if the crusade's terminus is seen not in German victory but after a continuing anti-Stalin struggle. Yet these and other points are all subordinate in interest to the ideological blueprint of the Prague Manifesto and of its theme: "A new free People's political system without Bolsheviks and exploiters."

One of the most significant aspects of the Prague Manifesto is its position on the Bolshevik Revolution and the Soviet regime. Despite its bitter indictment of "Bolsheviks" and the "Stalin clique," neither the Prague Manifesto nor the Vlasov Movement in general ever disavowed the Bolshevik revolution of 1917. According to the Vlasovite picture, the Czarist regime was "bankrupt," and in the February Revolution, the people themselves won for Russia the fullest political freedom it has ever enjoyed. It was not only "the overthrow of Stalin's tyranny" but also "the restitution of those rights . . . won in the people's revolution of 1917" for which the Vlasov Movement was fighting. "All reactionary projects involving a limitation of the people's rights" were categorically rejected. But though political liberty had been won in the February Revolution, the Provisional Government proved vacillating and undynamic, "unable to decide on bold and consequent reforms." Therefore the Prague Manifesto does not deny the necessity for the October Revolution with its social and economic innovations. Only after the Soviet government had entrenched itself did it become clear that the people had been betrayed into new tyranny.

"Genuine freedom of religion, conscience, speech, assembly and press" are guaranteed. So are the "inviolability of persons, their property, and homes," and "equality of all before the law." Laboring people are guaranteed "the right to free labor." The land is to be turned over gratuitously "to the peasants as their private property." "Trades, crafts, artisan enterprises" are to be established. "Private initiative" will be granted "the right and opportunity to participate in the economic life of the country." "Free education, medical care, vacation and old-age security" are to be guaranteed by the state "to all." Apparently it is only private property that is "earned by work" that is to be inviolable. The "free choice of land use" assured to the peasants endorses not only individual farming, but also coöperatives as well. Intellectuals are to be provided "with the opportunity to create freely" but only "for the well-being of their people."

An illiberal monarchy, such as Tsarism, is repudiated, but liberal capitalism fares no better, and not merely because, despite the encouragement offered to "private initiative," the great Vlasovite emphasis on state planning automatically excludes large-scale capitalist enterprise. The Prague Manifesto reveals a deep distrust of the Western capitalist democracies, the "plutocrats of England and the U.S.A., whose powers are based on the suppression and exploitation of other countries and peoples." The image of the capitalist as the wanton exploiter of destitute, defenseless wage earners was firmly fixed in the minds of the Soviet-bred members of the Vlasov Movement.

There is no place in the Prague Manifesto for truly international concepts — the "powers of internationalism" are too indelibly identified with "the Stalin clique." Although it is "convinced that the united efforts of the peoples of Russia will receive support from all the freedom-loving nations of the world," it is in nationalism, the peoples of Russia united, that the Vlasov Movement really puts its faith. And finally, the great majority of Soviet defectors stressed emphatically that neither Marxism nor any form of socialism, with its "inevitable" similarity to Stalinism, could lead to a happy and free post-Stalin USSR.

The same issue of *Volia Naroda* that published the Prague Manifesto published other data of considerable interest to this study — the names of thirty-seven signatories who were members of the KONR, and of twelve more who were candidates. Any analysis of KONR membership is at once complicated by the *Volia Naroda* statement immediately following the listing: "The names of some members and candidates of the Committee for the Liberation of the Peoples of Russia are not published in view of their presence in the territory of the USSR or for reasons of personal safety." And although it is known that the membership was subsequently enlarged,[6] no complete membership list is available. This is not least because the top officers of the KONR as well as about half of its final total of some eighty members are no longer alive (or are in Soviet hands).

Of the thirty-seven identified full members of the KONR, the following categorization may be made: thirteen former members of the Red Army, including Generals Vlasov, Malyshkin, Zhilenkov, Trukhin, and Zakutnyi; nine Soviet professors and docents; seven old-émigré leaders; and eight others, including one peasant and two workers.

A second type of breakdown is of interest, particularly in the light of the furor and friction that previously arose regarding the national issue. On the basis of very incomplete analysis — based partially on the names themselves, partially on the testimony of surviving members — thirteen, or just above one-third of the original identified membership, were non-Russian by nationality. The later additions to the Committee were largely non-Russian. As a result, the proportion of non-Russian members rose to half by the time the KONR reached its maximum of eighty members.

Yet the KONR was not able to recruit outstanding representatives of the existing non-Russian National Committees. The one exception from the outset was Shamba Balinov, identified in the *Volia Naroda* of December 13, 1944 as chairman of the Kalmuk National Committee. Moreover, since Cossacks in part sought to be treated as a nationality, the adherence to the KONR of their Lieutenant General E. Balabin may be mentioned. Finally, a subsequent addition was a former wartime general secretary of Kaium Khan's United Turkestan National Committee. But on the whole the major figures of these separatist groups, unwilling to subordinate themselves to Vlasov in a united movement, remained adamantly separate. Vlasov himself [7] and the Prague Manifesto emphatically backed the "self-determination" rather than the Russian nationalist position. But the gap between the Russian-led KONR and its separatist opponents on the national problem was too great to be bridged under the prevailing conditions, key among them being continuing German cleavage and intrigue on this issue. As a result, despite numerous negotiations, the Vlasov Movement was unable to gain the support of the separatist National Committees, notably that of the Ukrainian National Committee and its Ukrainian National Army, both formally established under Lieutenant General Pavlo Shandruk only on March

17, 1945, as a last-minute counterpart — and counterbalance — to Vlasov and his KONR.[8] Being at the same time unwilling to leave the field to these national committees, the KONR by 1945 set up five national councils of its own.

As interesting as the national element in the KONR is its old-émigré component. Many tory old émigrés retained their hostility toward this, as toward other manifestations of wartime Soviet opposition, to the end. Thus General Biskupskii, who acted as Hitler's plenipotentiary for Russian émigré affairs in Germany, even while a guest of the KONR at its Prague meeting, reiterated his opinion that Vlasov was an unrepentant Communist and his venture not to be trusted. Yuri S. Zherebkov, however, who filled a similar position in France, became an original member of the KONR. Though Zherebkov is said to have been a German agent within the KONR, his Paris organ, *Parizhskii Vestnik*, was more pro-Vlasov than any other Russian-language newspaper under German control except the Dabendorf publications. In addition to the six old émigrés identified as members by *Volia Naroda*, at least three others held key positions in the KONR apparatus. These were D. A. Levitsky, chief of the KONR secretariat, A. S. Kazantsev, managing editor of *Volia Naroda*, and K. G. Kromiadi, chief of Vlasov's personal chancellery. Thus, while the overwhelming majority of KONR members and of Vlasov Movement leaders in general were of recent Soviet vintage, a number of old émigrés were active and important in the KONR. In general, the KONR stressed its hospitality to all who subscribed to its ideological position, and decried a formal division between "old" and "new" émigrés.[9] But, contrary to the situation since World War II, it was the recent Soviet defectors who at all times headed and dominated the wartime opposition movement.

The Committee for the Liberation of the Peoples of Russia met five times after the Prague gathering, once a month from December 1944 through April 1945. There is, however, general agreement that KONR matters were not transacted by the KONR itself. This committee of fifty, and later eighty, members was mainly a representative body which — not unlike Soviet procedure — would merely approve decisions made elsewhere. Formally, the governing body was a smaller group within the larger committee, the KONR Presidium. Another widely held opinion is that the membership was far from outstanding either intellectually or organizationally. In the make-up of the KONR the stress was on social and national cross section rather than on intellectual capacity or leadership. The truly decisive voices were those of the four ex-Soviet generals who headed the KONR apparatus, and, above all, Vlasov himself.

Not long after the Prague meeting, Vlasov issued the statement: "The Committee had hardly any time for what is usually called the preparatory period. The central organs of the Committee were created the day after the founding meeting, and immediately started practical work." [10] In the same statement, Vlasov named the four organs — administrative, military, civilian, and propaganda — that became the framework of the KONR apparatus, headed by Generals Malyshkin, Trukhin, Zakutnyi, and Zhilenkov, respectively, and described in the notes to this chapter.[11]

After the Prague meeting, the KONR apparatus returned to Dabendorf and to Dahlem, the fashionable Berlin sector where Vlasov had resided throughout most of the war and where the KONR had been granted three additional villas from which to carry on its activities. But the immense Allied bombings forced it, early in February 1945, to move from these centers to the Czech resort of Karlsbad, where headquarters were established in the principal hotel, the Richmond. The Dabendorf School was moved to nearby Joachimsthal. As if this one move were not sufficient to dramatize the nightmarishly uncertain and ephemeral existence of the venture, steady German retreats forced the KONR into a second move two months later, in the middle of April. This time the move was to what the Allies had feared would become the great, last-stand Nazi redoubt, the Bavarian and Austrian Alps. This new, and last, KONR center was in the Upper Bavarian town of Füssen.

If the KONR's actual physical existence was uncertain and ephemeral during this grueling last half-year of the Thousand Year Reich, its political existence was no less so. Though finally permitted to build up a comparatively formidable organizational structure, the KONR was still hampered and frustrated at practically every turn by the continuing rigidity of German officialdom. And the waiting had been so long, the collapse was now so imminent, that the total impact of the years of frustration, shattered illusions, and unrewarded compromises became particularly burdensome. A poignant and revealing eyewitness account comes from Dr. N., whose identity, as well as his prominence both in the KONR and previously in the USSR, is known to me. As a leading member of the KONR, Dr. N. speaks of the repeated shocks and disappointments that came with the Vlasov Movement's latter-stage dependence on Himmler. It was after the actual establishment of the KONR that "the greatest disappointment awaited us. It turned out that all our decisions had to be coördinated with the appropriate [German] commissar. Nobody had the right to write even the smallest paper without his commissar. . . Many times during this period both I and other members of the KONR doubted the correctness of our decision to join the KONR. However . . . all bridges had been burned, the departure of individuals from the KONR would not improve the situation. Therefore only one thing remained, to grit one's teeth and to try to accomplish at least the minimum which we might be able to." [12]

The brief life of the KONR not only began in Prague. Seven months later, it returned to Prague for its climax — the climax preceding the tragic end. In 1944, the prologue to Prague was Vlasov's *rapprochement* with Himmler and the SS. In 1945, the KONR return to Prague was preceded by the formation and the combat actions of the military arm of the Vlasov Movement — the KONR Army.

In many ways the experience of the KONR Army is strikingly similar to that of its political center, the Committee for the Liberation of the Peoples of Russia. As with the KONR, this seeming realization of the Vlasovite dream for an independent army began with high hope — and with formal ceremony.

In its January 31, 1945 issue, the front page of *Volia Naroda* was devoted to a major announcement:

ORDER No. 1

To: All Armed Forces of the Committee for the Liberation of the Peoples of Russia

Headquarters                    January 28, 1945

1. This date the Führer of Greater Germany transferred to me and I assumed command of the Armed Forces of the Committee for the Liberation of the Peoples of Russia.

2. The list of subordinate units is contained in a special appendix.

3. As Chief of Staff I appoint Major General F. I. Trukhin, whom I order

to form the Headquarters of the Armed Forces of the Committee for the Liberation of the Peoples of Russia according to approved tables of organization.

> Commander in Chief of the Armed
> Forces of the Committee for the
> Liberation of the Peoples of Russia
>
> Lieutenant General
> A. VLASOV

Two weeks after Vlasov's assumption of command of his new military force, a formal transfer took place. The units brought together to form the KONR Army were turned over to Vlasov by General Köstring, still OKH General for *Osttruppen*, or Volunteer Units, as these formations were now called.[1] Yet nothing describes the formation of the KONR Army so well as "too little and too late." It was now hardly more than three months before Hitler's Germany would surrender — and in these remaining three months the KONR Army would see much travail and frustration.

One of the sources of frustration was Himmler, who had promised Vlasov an initial formation of five KONR divisions. As Germany's fortunes declined catastrophically, he now withdrew more and more from his troublesome sponsorship of the Vlasov Movement. Finally it was decided that the OKH General for *Osttruppen*, Köstring, would be charged with the activation of the promised KONR divisions. With the Other Germany center in OKH *Fremde Heere Ost* decimated after July 20, the task fell to Köstring's former *Osttruppen* deputy, Colonel Herre. But the number of authorized divisions was whittled down from five to two, with more to follow if these proved themselves in combat. These were given the following German army designations:

1. First KONR Division — *600th Panzer-Grenadier Division;*
2. Second KONR Division — *650th Panzer-Grenadier Division.*

Vast difficulties still stood in the way of the actual activation of the long-delayed KONR Army. Most of these difficulties were not so much political as stemming from the immense strain under which Hitler's Germany was then seeking to keep itself from collapse. Weapons for the KONR Army were extremely scarce. Germany's economic and manpower chieftains protested vigorously against surrendering *Ostarbeiter* for the manning of KONR units. The *Wehrmacht* was equally reluctant to transfer *Osttruppen* units to the KONR Army. Vast administrative chaos began to predominate throughout what once was the vaunted German apparatus. Thus the KONR Army experienced never-ending difficulties in equipping even its meager formations. The extent of the chaos is revealed by an exclamation made by Hitler himself at a military conference on March 23, 1945: "We just don't know what is floating around. I have just heard for the first time, to my amazement, that a Ukrainian SS-Division has suddenly appeared. I don't know a thing about this." [2] Lastly, an ever-present obstacle to the expansion of the KONR Army was Hitler's continuing disdain for and suspicion of Soviet opposition and its military formations. At a staff conference on January 27, 1945 Hitler once again ranted against issuing German uniforms to any foreigners, particularly singling out the Soviet defectors. "One has no sense of honor around here. Every wretch is put in German uniform. I was always against it." [3] Even when a KONR Army was authorized, little practical progress was made.

It is remarkable that the KONR Army came into being at all. One primary explanation for this was the enormous influx from all over German-held Europe — particularly from areas being occupied by the Red Army — of refugees from among Soviet *Ostarbeiter, Osttruppen,* and prisoners of war. Thus one of the peculiar features of the KONR Army is its constant swelling in size, caused largely by this steady stream of refugees. It is reported that on one day, November 20, 1944, 60,000 voluntary enlistments reportedly had been received for the KONR Army.[4]

The other major reason for the growth of the KONR Army despite the many German obstacles is the already-mentioned skeleton general staff created at Dabendorf during the months preceding the formation of the KONR and its Army. When the signal finally came to go ahead, in the midst of chaos and flux, the KONR Army set up a strikingly elaborate headquarters and a number of units in addition to the two KONR divisions. At this time, too, on the recommendation of Vlasov and the KONR at its February session,[5] and with the approval of Köstring, the German army promoted five KONR ex-Red Army colonels to the one-star German rank of major general: Sergei K. Buniachenko, commander of the First Division; G. A. Zverev, commander of the Second Division; Victor I. Maltsev, head of the KONR Air Brigade located at Eger and Marienbad, near Karlsbad; Mikhail A. Meandrov, chief of the KONR Officers School; and B. I. Boyarsky, the deputy to Trukhin.

With a clandestinely organized general staff as its nucleus, the First

Division evolved. Its center was the Münsingen Staging Area in Württemberg, an old, undersize Army camp forty miles from both the Swiss border and Stuttgart. The early strength of the division came to 13,000, according to the ex-Soviet colonel who was chief of Trukhin's Operations Section. At Münsingen, the First Division had little if any German supervision. Following Vlasov's acceptance of the KONR units in February 1945, all remaining German insignia were removed from the uniforms. German headquarters were unwilling at this crucial moment to transfer *Ostbataillone* from front-line duty to the KONR Army. As a result, the base of the First Division was elements of two SS Divisions: Kaminsky's — including, according to one German account, those in the Warsaw uprising's suppression, though Vlasovites deny this — and Siegling's 30th Volunteer SS Division, comprising Byelorussian units badly mangled earlier in the Allied invasion of France.

The activation of the First Division began in November 1944 and was completed by the next January; it was only then that work on the Second Division really started. Therefore it was never as fully activated as the First. But a number of *Ostbataillone* formerly in Norway were assigned to it, as well as Soviet prisoners of war of recent vintage. By the end it was almost fully trained, and equipped at least with small arms. It was based in the Heuberg Staging Area in Baden, some 40 miles from Münsingen, and, like the latter, from Stuttgart. Also located there were the KONR Army's headquarters, its officer units, a Reserve Brigade, and a Construction Battalion. The total of these various units came to 25,000.

During the incredibly brief and chaotic period when the KONR Army was formed, numerous schemes were proposed for expanding it further. General von Pannwitz's Cossack Corps was formally assigned to the KONR Army, but the transfer was never actually consummated. The same was true of the old-émigré Russian Defense Corps formed in Serbia. At the last moment, the old-émigré pro-KONR generals Kreuter and Turkul were authorized by Vlasov to form a KONR division in Austria, but little if anything came of it. And throughout, German authorities either delayed or refused outright to transfer Soviet national units or *Ostbataillone* to the KONR Army. Yet despite chaos and obstruction, the KONR Army finally rose to about 50,000.[6] A considerable potential, this. But it was a puny number when compared with the Vlasovite blueprints of an All-Russian Army uniting all Soviet nationals under German control, with the hundreds of thousands of *Osttruppen* — and with the inflated numbers often ascribed to "Vlasov's Army."

One last feature to be noted about the organization of the KONR Army is that months and years of past usage led to its designation, even in print in the official *Volia Naroda*, by the old name of the phantom ROA. The KONR Army drew little of its personnel from the *Osttruppen* units that had been described by the fictitious collective term of ROA. But the Vlasov Movement's propaganda had succeeded in making ROA a vital symbol of the entire Soviet opposition movement. Thus the old term continued to be used, even in 1945, rather than the new name of KONR Army. The practice thoroughly obscured the great difference between the vast, scattered phantom army of *Osttruppen* and the small, united KONR Army commanded by Vlasov himself.

Between the tortuous formation of the KONR Army and the Vlasovites' return to Prague lies a fantastic episode — the brief history of the KONR Army as an active combat force.

The episode in question was preceded by a small volunteer unit's going into action on the Eastern Front early in February 1945.[7] The second instance of KONR Army combat was the outstanding one — and far more complex. At least two eyewitness versions exist, that of the Vlasovites[8] and that of the German officers closest to the First Division.[9]

According to both versions, what was in effect to be the grand finale of the entire wartime Soviet opposition movement began on March 2, 1945. On that date, General Buniachenko, Commander of the First KONR Division at Münsingen, received orders from the German command to proceed with his unit to the Eastern Front, where it was to occupy front-line positions between Stettin and Berlin. Instead of prompt compliance with these orders, Buniachenko informed the German command that the First KONR Division was under the sole command of the Commander in Chief of the KONR Army, General Vlasov, and that he could not act until ordered to do so by Vlasov himself. Thus, Vlasov was called hurriedly at Karlsbad, the Czech headquarters of KONR itself, and on March 5 he gave the order for the First KONR Division to proceed to the Eastern Front. The move of the division was completed by the end of March, when it was located north of Cottbus, about 70 miles southeast of Berlin and near the Czech border, with the front running at the time on the Oder and Nissen Rivers. During its move, the division had been joined by several thousand volunteers from among Soviet *Ostarbeiter* and *Ost-truppen.*

The decisive next step took place when General Buniachenko was ordered on April 8 to go into action at a peculiarly difficult spot on the Eastern Front, a Red Army salient near Frankfurt on the Oder River which the German army had not been able to capture during weeks of fighting, and to which access had now been made more difficult than ever by spring floods and continued Soviet entrenching. Buniachenko had not questioned the preliminary order to occupy a certain area just behind the front line of his German front commander. But now he refused to make the move until ordered to do so by General Vlasov. Once again Vlasov was swiftly summoned, and once again he agreed to a compromise with the German command. Thus, on April 11, the First KONR Division entered into combat. After the costly failure of the division's first assault, Buniachenko abruptly ordered withdrawal from its front-line position. It appears certain, from both the available versions, that Vlasov did not participate in this fateful decision. He failed to arrive at the near-front location of the First Division by April 15, the deadline set by its commander, and on that day General Buniachenko ordered the division to proceed southward.

It may be surmised, in the light of our entire study, that both the Vlasovite and the German versions were at least partially true. German coöperation, even if far from absent, evidently did fail to come up to high-strung Vlasovite expectations. On the other hand, Buniachenko's uppermost concern to extricate his unit from the foreseeable collapse of the Eastern Front also appears completely plausible. On these facts, the Vlasovite and the German versions agree. The difference between them lies in the interpretation. According to the Vlasovite version, the KONR had been promised that none of its military units would be used separately and that Vlasov would have immediate charge of combat operations by the KONR Army. As to the First Division's frontal actions, the Vlasovite version emphasizes the suicidal nature of the combat mission assigned to it, and also the criminal failure of German commanders to supply the artillery and air cover promised. Thus the emphasis is on the uniform ill-will and breach of faith on the part of German authorities.

The other version, that of the surviving German officers most closely connected with the First Division, emphasizes something rather different. Asserting that beginning with Himmler's agreement — in his latest capacity as Commander in Chief of the Weichsel Army Group

— to use the First Division in his sector, Colonel Herre and the other German associates of the KONR Army managed to overcome most if not all of the many obstacles placed in the way of both the activation and the combat use of the First Division. They add that most German field commanders involved approached the First Division with understanding, once its peculiar background had been explained to them. Lastly, the German version does not support the Vlasovite statement that promises had been broken when the First Division was moved to the front without the rest of the KONR Army. Instead, the German version heavily emphasizes the fact that Buniachenko's decision was motivated by his only secondary interest in the Eastern Front; his far greater concern was to preserve all of the First Division's strength for merger with the rest of the KONR Army before the final onrush of Soviet and Allied forces.

Now began a swift withdrawal, with the advancing Red Army following close on the heels of the mutinous division. On April 23, when the division was located east of Dresden, it was offered complete reinstatement in German service if it would agree to stand and fight there under the commander of the Army Group Center, Field Marshal Schörner. This offer General Buniachenko rejected, and, after a tense forced march, dodging both German and advancing Soviet forces, Czechoslovakia was reached on April 28. With Colonel Sakharov's unit added as its Fourth Regiment, the First Division by now had reportedly grown to a force of 20,000.

With its arrival in Czech territory, the First KONR Division entered upon the most dramatic single episode of the entire history of wartime Soviet opposition. On that day, division headquarters were visited not only by Vlasov but by the German commander, Marshal Schörner himself. Once again Buniachenko refused to reënter German service. By May 2, the First Division had moved on to a village some 50 kilometers southwest of Prague. Here Vlasov, still with the First Division, received an emissary who informed him that KONR Army Headquarters, together with the Second Division and other KONR units, were now in Austria, moving toward Czechoslovakia. The emissary also stated that the principal German concern was no longer to regain the services of the First Division, but merely to assure its neutrality toward German units.

At this time, with both Soviet and American forces pressing toward Prague, the Czechoslovak National Council had begun preparing for an uprising against the German occupants. By May 5, the revolt was under way, and the air waves of Central Europe were flooded with desperate appeals from the Council: "Calling the Allied armies. We need urgent help. Send your planes and tanks. The Germans are advancing on Prague. For the Lord's sake, send help." [10]

We know now that the Red Army did not enter Prague until after German surrender on May 9, and that the more rapidly advancing U. S. forces were kept from seizing Prague by an Allied decision to leave it — like Berlin — to Soviet capture. At the time, however, Czech resistance leaders were not aware of this. They were particularly anxious that the Western forces, rather than the Red Army, should be the first to enter Prague. But these were held back by a political decision, while the Red Army tarried, perhaps for reasons similar to its delay before Warsaw in August 1944, when the revolt in the Polish capital was led by anti-Communists, not pro-Communists. Therefore, seeing itself hard pressed by German forces, particularly by the SS concentration around Prague, the Czech resistance center repeated its urgent pleas for rescue to General Buniachenko.

And now the climax of our story is reached, with Buniachenko's decision on May 5 to throw the First KONR Division, the "Vlasov Army," into the Prague resistance against German units. By the evening of May 6, the First Division stood near Prague, and on the following morning it engaged in combat against SS troops within the ancient Slav capital. Here the Vlasov troops were given a jubilant reception by the populace, who were evidently never quite sure just who their saviors were — an understandable confusion resulting from the spectacle of Russian-speaking soldiers in German-type uniforms savagely opposing the SS forces. By the end of that day, May 7, after extremely bitter and widespread fighting, the scales were tipped in favor of the Czech uprising by the First KONR Division.

This, then, was the dramatic finale of the military arm of the wartime Soviet opposition movement. Founded as an act of collaboration with Hitler Germany, denied all but an insignificant, eleventh-hour part in combat, in its last moment it turned upon its erstwhile patrons — and played a leading role in the liberation of a major European center.

But if this episode may shine in glory in the annals of the Vlasov Movement, it was an all too brief glory. For on the same day, May 7, the commanders of the First KONR Division learned to their dismay not only that Red Army rather than U. S. forces were to occupy Prague, but also the more immediately disrupting news that the Czechoslovak National Council, the resistance center that had sought the aid of the Vlasov forces, was being rapidly replaced by representatives of Eduard Beneš's Czech government in exile. These new authorities wanted the First Division either to await the arrival of the Red Army and surrender to it or to make a speedy departure from the city it had just helped to liberate. And so at dawn of the next day, May 8, the First KONR Division began its final withdrawal, returning from Prague to the area of the near-by Czech town of Beraun, from which it had begun its liberating action. For a fitting summary of this episode, we have the account of an American foreign correspondent: "Prague really was liberated by foreign troops, after all. Not by the Allies, who did not arrive until the shooting was all over, but by 22,000 Russian outlaws wearing German uniforms. . . When I reached Prague on Tuesday, May eighth, General Vlasov and his men had melted away as mysteriously as they had come." [11]

Extreme charges — of treachery and of sheerest opportunism — have been lodged against the Vlasov Movement for this action. How can we explain this striking last-act Vlasovite defection from Hitler Germany?

As to the general charge of treachery, this entire study suggests that so shabby and insolent had been the German treatment of wartime Soviet opposition that concepts such as allegiance and loyalty appear inapplicable. Regarding the specific allegation that the defection of the First KONR Division was part of a long-prepared plan to betray Hitler's Germany, neither the written nor the oral testimony available to me reveals the slightest evidence that the KONR or General Vlasov had prepared this act in advance, either as treason to its former "ally" or for any other reason.

Opportunism, as a factor, cannot be dismissed so easily. Oral testimony to me by both German and Vlasovite officials involved in the events indicates that both Vlasov and Buniachenko were unquestionably concerned about the attitude the West would take toward the Soviet opposition movement, and were therefore undoubtedly motivated in part by the thought that liberating Prague from the SS might make a favorable impression on the Western allies.

At the same time, however, two considerations suggest that the Vlasovites' desire to ingratiate themselves with the West was not the most decisive factor. One of these — which we shall soon discuss at greater length — was their firm conviction that the West's outlook and intentions were essentially anti-Soviet. However erroneous this conviction may have been at the time, the fact that they were so convinced in this attitude greatly reduced any feeling that they might have had of the necessity of appeasing the Western powers.

The other consideration is that events developed far too spontaneously to allow for such premeditation. So much in flux and limbo was the entire war situation, so difficult had communications become between various KONR formations, that actions which might otherwise have been ruled out by cooler heads were given free rein. From all accounts, General Buniachenko was a quick-tempered, impulsive, and far from sophisticated military man. Not only the German authorities but Vlasov himself had difficulty in bridling his irascible temperament. And we know specifically that Vlasov was not with the First KONR Division the greater part of the time; in both key instances, at the Eastern Front and regarding Prague, the final decision was taken by Buniachenko without him. For throughout the month or two before VE Day, Vlasov had become so deeply despondent and fatalistic, with ever more frequent heavy drinking, that in the last critical weeks his leadership was well-nigh absent — as was he himself much of the time. Nor was General Trukhin, as KONR Army Chief of Staff Buniachenko's immediate superior, in Prague, as has been claimed by the German novelist, Edwin Erich Dwinger, in his highly fictionalized *General Wlassow*.[12] Moreover, it appears that to the end Vlasovite chieftains were deeply divided on whether to place the KONR Army at the mercy of the advancing Western Allies or to unite with anti-Soviet formations, either in the Balkans (Draja Mikhailovich, von Pannwitz's Cossack Corps, the old-émigré Russian Defense Corps) or around Prague (as Buniachenko then did on his own). All this suggests that actions which previously would have been given greater and more high-level consideration were now decided upon with a swiftness explainable only by the prevailing chaos.

Chaos was not the only result of the catastrophic decline of German power. The resentments within the Vlasov Movement against the long years of wanton maltreatment and abuse by German authorities now for the first time could be unleashed. As long as no other course than collaboration seemed open, the Vlasovites, like most men in similar circumstances, managed effectively to repress their resentments. But now, although German treatment had actually improved in objective terms, the changed situation made anti-Hitler actions not only more possible but more likely than ever before.

Rebecca West, in her masterly work on pro-Nazi treason in World War II, seems to mirror this explanation: "The Nazis were prone, in all sorts of circumstances, to make a peculiar error. When one of their enemies became their friend, they went on treating him as an enemy. However ready he might be to serve their interests, however much they might need his help, they continued to savage him. The great historic example of this curious trick is their treatment of the Russian soldiers and civilians who, by tens of thousands, gladly surrendered to them as they invaded Russian territory in 1941 and 1942. These people who might have been their most valuable aids then and forever after, they packed into cattle trucks and sent off to camps where they were starved and tortured. Later they were fetched out and invited to fight along-side the Germans, but by that time their enthusiasm was not what it had been, and the treatment they received in training and at the front failed to revive it." [13]

One factor emphasized by a German author [14] must not be over-looked. The liberation of Prague from German control would have taken place within a few days under any circumstances. The part played by the First KONR Division was only to speed the inevitable. But the Vlasov Movement itself, born and raised under German pat-ronage, did end with an anti-German act. Prague in 1944 saw the launching of the KONR. In 1945, Prague witnessed its last act.

With such a background as we have described, who could doubt that the Soviet opposition movement was doomed, from its very beginning, to tragedy?

The first dimension of the tragedy of wartime Soviet opposition derives from its Soviet context. Intellectually brutalized, morally crushed, and in large measure stripped of the capacity for spontaneous, independent action by his native regime, the Soviet national was peculiarly ill equipped to perceive clearly either the nature of the Hitler regime or the consequences of collaboration with it.

Neither Hitler nor his National Socialist regime had the desire, or the intellectual or moral capacity, to make even minimal political and nonpolitical concessions to Soviet opposition. Hitler Germany regarded the wartime opposition movement merely as a tool for its own war effort. Yet one of the basic factors in the collaboration with Hitler Germany of the Soviet opposition movement — or at least of its vanguard — was its fanatic hatred of the Soviet regime. Few convictions in recent history have been more compelling, more driving than the Soviet defectors' determination to use at all costs this first opportunity in decades to launch a major native crusade against Stalin. It is a second dimension of the tragedy of Soviet opposition movement that at that given moment in history it should have encountered Hitler Germany as the sole ally that appeared capable of furthering its aims. No ally could more

Chapter IX

The End of a Tragedy

☆

quickly and thoroughly corrupt and frustrate the aspirations of Soviet opposition than Hitler Germany could — and did.

In the half million or more Soviet nationals who served in the *Osttruppen* under German command and in German uniforms, the wartime opposition movement clearly had its most important trump card and its mightiest potential. This was true so long as the *Osttruppen* were fairly united in location and organization. But soon the divergences and conflicts within German officialdom regarding *Ostpolitik* added a third dimension to the tragedy of wartime Soviet opposition. The *Osttruppen* were scattered from the Eastern Front to all parts of Hitler-held Europe and were splintered into numerous national components, with mutual, and particularly anti-Russian, suspicions and passions. With this, the chief potential of Soviet opposition's bargaining power with the Nazi leaders withered away.

Once the *Osttruppen* had been particularized and scattered, the next step was almost inevitable. Scornful of the defectors' anti-Stalin aspirations, the Hitler government reduced the Soviet nationals in *Osttruppen* units to the status of mercenaries whose lowly task was to police Nazi Europe. Instead of fighting their own bitter enemy, they found themselves facing the foes of Nazi Germany, the often non-Communist resistance movements of Western Europe, Italy, the Balkans. At the same time, the small and harassed hard core of Soviet opposition — the Vlasov Movement — was equally compromised. Its fate was to serve as a propaganda weapon, and little more than that, of Hitler Germany. The fourth and last dimension is therefore not only a tragedy for wartime Soviet opposition but also its shame. Though the Soviet system had abjectly primitivized its citizens, it had not fitted them for a pro-Nazi role. Yet by a fateful combination of circumstances they were denied all but the lowliest of tasks. Ever tragically, these were tasks as unworthy as they were distant (objectively) from the independent anti-Stalin crusade to which (subjectively) most of the wartime opposition movement so ardently aspired.

The end of the Vlasovite tragedy had tragic poignancy of its own. The Vlasov Movement was not only tragically unaware of how its wartime actions would be interpreted by Western eyes; it was grossly mistaken regarding the West's attitude toward the USSR. And these two misapprehensions brought stark disaster to the leaders of wartime Soviet opposition and to many of their followers.

One of the basic premises of the Vlasovite leaders, almost from the outset, was that, should Germany lose, an early military conflict between the USSR and the West was inevitable. The corollary of this assumption — which sounded much more naïve in 1945 than it does today — was that the governments of the Western powers were well aware of this, and were no more wholehearted in their alliance than Stalin was. Hence, to the very end, the Soviet defectors clung to the belief that the West would welcome the Vlasov Movement and its army as a precious ally against the Soviet regime. Prompted by this belief, the Vlasov Movement, both during the war and just prior to the German collapse, sent representatives to make contact with high Western officials and arrange with them for the transfer of Soviet opposition forces from German to Allied jurisdiction. None of the negotiators met with any success. Most of them were interned as ordinary war prisoners or enemy agents without ever getting beyond Allied front lines.[1] Two higher-level Vlasovite contacts, with the headquarters of General Patton's Third U. S. Army and of General Patch's Seventh Army, were in each instance broken off in compliance with broad Allied policy. And yet, despite all failures and rebuffs, the hope persisted.

If it seems incredible that the Vlasov Movement should have held to this conviction in the face of all the evidence, one fact should be remembered. This assumption which guided the Soviet defectors was embedded deep in all their past environment. In the USSR the preaching of the inevitability of conflict with the capitalist powers is constant, and far more pervasive than is imagined by the outside world. In Hitler Germany as well, Goebbels did yeoman service in fostering the illusion. Not only was German victory predicted till the last, but, more importantly, all Nazi propaganda continuously reiterated that, should the Third Reich fail to destroy Bolshevism, Stalin would inevitably overrun Europe and thus promptly set off a third world war. Only a person who has lived through the unceasing, ever-present propaganda behind any Iron Curtain should feel wholly free to assert that he could not fall victim to one of its predominant themes.

Nor is it difficult to imagine that the Vlasov Movement must have been deeply reluctant to relinquish its hopes. Driven on by a fanatic zeal to unleash and continue their native crusade against the Stalin regime, their aspirations frustrated at almost every turn by Hitler and his *Ostpolitik*, these men had little if anything to cling to but this hope, this delusion.

Possibly in the attempt, conscious or unconscious, to shift the responsibility for this grave blunder to other shoulders, a considerable number of surviving Vlasovites have made serious charges against the

NTS, the old-émigré "solidarist" organization which played a considerable part in the Vlasov Movement. It is contended that these old émigrés, with a wide knowledge of European languages, customs, and political affairs, and with fellow members in Western countries, should have been more successful in establishing contact between the Vlasov Movement and the Western governments, and more astute in appraising the Western state of mind. The fact that they failed miserably is considered by many as highly suspicious, by some as evidence that the NTS is run by Soviet agents. These charges, however, appear unreasonable. In the first place, Western opinion was such that no amount of cosmopolitan skill on the part of NTS members in Western capitals could have had much effect upon it. And secondly, even if the NTS had judged the Allied attitude more accurately, the illusions regarding Western support of Soviet opposition efforts were so widespread and persistent throughout the Vlasov Movement that it would be far from correct to try to explain them by the actions or policies of any one group.

Just how unwilling the Vlasov Movement was to extinguish the hope that was all it had left to sustain it is vividly suggested by one eyewitness: "At that time, during the period of organizing our forces, help from the Western allies was counted upon as if [the Vlasovites] already had it in their hands. And they believed in it the more, the closer the decisive days drew. There were no grounds for believing this. Probably it was for this reason that people looked for them, created them in their imagination, and then, having created them, believed in them as in reality." [2]

However incapable the Vlasov Movement may have been of understanding the attitude and intentions of the Western powers, the West at the time was equally unable to comprehend the basic position of these Soviet nationals so inexorably opposed to their native regime.

The majority of the five to six million Soviet nationals under wartime German control may never have adhered to the Vlasov Movement, at least not actively. Only a major part of the 500,000 to one million in German-commanded *Osttruppen*, and the perhaps overlapping 50,000 total of the last-minute KONR Army, can be placed with certainty in the Vlasovite camp. Even here some separatist sentiment worked against the Vlasov Movement. Now, with the end of the war, the majority of Soviet citizens drifted back to the USSR.

One fateful consequence of the West's forced repatriation policy was that a large number of displaced persons of Soviet origin proceeded from 1945 on to forge their DP documents. Soviet citizens by the thousand thus turned themselves into any of the nationalities recognized at the time by UNRRA (United Nations Relief and Rehabilitation Administration, 1945–1947) and the IRO (International Refugee Organization, 1947–1951). As a result, statistics on displaced persons receiving UNRRA assistance include only 21,435 Soviet citizens for December 1945 out of a total of 736,014, and the low figure of 6,771 out of 642,749 displaced persons in June 1947. In the case of UNRRA's successor, the IRO, similar statistics mention a total of merely 44,109 (DP status on June 30, 1950, 6,306; resettled between 1947 and 1951, 35,972; repatriated to the USSR during the same period, 1,831).

An obvious loophole for Soviet DP's seeking to disguise their former citizenship was the Ukrainian category, which according to UNRRA and IRO referred to that part of the Ukraine that had been a part of Poland before World War II. Further substantiation for this conjecture appears in the jump in numbers of DP's registered by UNRRA as Ukrainians. In December 1945, the tabulation was 9,190. By June 1947 the figure grew more than tenfold, to 106,549. The IRO total for Ukrainian DP's is 120,227 (DP status on June 30, 1950, 12,649; resettled between 1947 and 1951, 107,578). A similar case is that of the Western, ex-Polish Byelorussians, 4,587 of whom were resettled by the IRO by mid-1951. It should be noted that no Ukrainian or Byelorussian DP's are listed as having been repatriated. The same is true of yet another loophole for Soviet DP's — the League of Nations "Nansen Status," applied to post-1917 émigrés from the Bolshevik Revolution. The IRO cites a total of 26,720 Nansen Status DP's (DP status on June 30, 1950, 7,980; resettled between 1947 and 1951, 18,740). Lastly there is the large Baltic DP category, for which the IRO gives a total of 173,381 (DP status on June 30, 1950, 14,969; resettled from 1947 to 1951, 155,292; repatriated to the USSR, 3,120).

How many of the DP's outside the USSR category were actually Soviet citizens before World War II it is impossible to estimate. Clearly a substantial fraction of these non-Soviet categories of DP's were in fact genuine Balts, Western (Galician) Ukrainians and Byelorussians, and Russian old émigrés from such concentrations as Belgrade, Sophia, Prague, and Berlin. On the other hand, in the pathetic postwar effort to dodge return by force to the USSR, a certain number of Soviet DP's through forged documents were registered as DP's in categories other than those mentioned as the most likely loopholes. Although such a contention is perforce based only on conjecture plus eyewitness impressions, it may be hazarded that the number of DP's of Soviet origin comes far closer to the total of Balts, Western Ukrainians, (Western) Byelorussians, and Nansen Status émigrés cited by the IRO (329,502) than it did to the USSR figure of 44,109 — only one-seventh as many. The same is probably true regarding the IRO statistics on DP's who have come to the United States between mid-1947 and mid-1951. Here the USSR figure is 11,014, while the Baltic-Ukrainian-Byelorussian-Nansen Status total is eleven times as large: 122,665 out of 282,785.[3]

What conjectures may be ventured as to the number of Soviet citizens who actually did become "nonreturners" following World War II? Allowance must be made not only for Soviet DP's registering under other national categories, but also for the likelihood that some "nonreturners" evaded altogether the DP censuses on which any conjecture depends. Above all, it must be kept ever in mind that the statistics and categories employed suffer from countless gaps, discrepancies, and overlapping.

In seeking a "nonreturner" total, it might be best to start with the wartime period. A U. S. Government compilation based on German and Allied data included as of January 1, 1945 about 2,500,000 "Russians" (1,900,000 Ostarbeiter, 600,000 prisoners of war, 11,000 political prisoners). They were part of a total of 6,691,000 described as "Approximate Number of Foreigners Put to Work for the German War Effort in the Old Reich." This is the most up-to-date, and the most complete, estimate available. Unfortunately, it fails to provide the total of Soviet nationals under German control. Rather, the figure given refers to the labor force ("Foreigners Put to Work") and evidently not to all German-held territory ("in the old Reich"). Hence, the compilation allows neither for nonworking prisoners and family members, nor for Soviet nationals outside Germany proper who during the war's last year had changed to Soviet or Western jurisdiction. This makes it necessary to turn to the least unreliable German figure available. It is a general reference to German-area Eastern Peoples (Ostvölker), the quasi-official wartime synonym for Soviet nationals. This reference, contained in a "Secret" letter by Alfred Rosenberg dated as late as October 12, 1944, cited the figure of five million. That this figure may not be too far off is indicated by the most inclusive analysis made to date of official UNRRA-IRO, Soviet, and Western data. This analysis was compiled by a leading specialist in population and refugee statistics, Eugene M. Kulischer. For our purposes, Kulischer offers two principal figures. He states that as of September 30, 1945 Soviet authorities had repatriated 3,200,000 to the USSR, and that some two years later, by June 30, 1947, the total of Soviet nationals repatriated by Western authorities and UNRRA was 2,126,445. The resulting sum is 5,326,445. While this sum excludes whatever figure we shall arrive at for "nonreturners," it on the other hand includes Balts and at least some Western Ukrainians and Byelorussians. Hence Kulischer appears to support Rosenberg's figure of five million for the number of Soviet nationals under wartime German control.

Regarding the period immediately following German surrender, U. S. officials stated at the time that in the fall of 1945 there were some two million Soviet citizens ("Russians") in the three Western zones of Germany. Similar figures for other parts of Western Europe (especially France, Italy, and the U. S., British, and French zones of Austria) are not available, but another half million may reasonably be allowed. Let it furthermore be assumed that the resulting total is not appreciably different from that of any earlier period during Germany's collapse. This is not done solely for convenience' sake; as was posited in the totaling above of the probably somewhat overlapping Kulischer figures, it is likely that large-scale repatriation to the USSR was delayed by the higher priority assigned during much of 1945 to combat and initial occupation tasks. The preceding leads to a figure of 2,500,000 Soviet citizens who in the fall of 1945 were in those parts of Europe not occupied by Soviet troops — or half of Rosenberg's wartime total of five million.

What, then, is the proportion of this estimated total who subsequently became "nonreturners"? Not infrequently in the past few years, the émigrés and their sympathizers have spoken in general terms of 1,000,000 or more "nonreturners." More recently, the figure of half a million was cited in the same month by two American statements: a survey for the Harvard Russian Research Center and a *Life* editorial. Our own first clue will be a conclusion reached earlier in the present discussion. This conclusion held that the "nonreturner" group (excluding inhabitants of territories annexed by the USSR since 1939) would in reality come closer to the IRO's DP total computed in 1950 for Balts, Western Byelorussians, Western Ukrainians, and Nansen Status émigrés — 329,502 — than to its USSR figure of 44,109. Corroborating this conclusion is another clue, Kulischer's 1947 repatriation estimate of 2,126,445 (repatriation diminishing sharply after that year). Following these considerations, the "nonreturner" total may be set at 250,000. It is of interest to note that in Moscow a pamphlet-form government statement was issued publicly in 1949, which spoke of 400,000 Soviet citizens who had not returned to the USSR after World War II, as against five and a half million who had. Official Soviet statistics receive limited credence abroad. But its 400,000 and 5,500,000 figures are not incompatible with our 250,000 and 5,000,000, as the Soviet statement included Balts, Western Byelorussians, and Western Ukrainians.[4]

The answer to our original inquiry as to the number of "non-returners" can thus be no more than a twofold conjecture: of the pre-1939 Soviet citizens outside their government's domain in 1945, approximately 10 percent did not return to the USSR, or 250,000 out of 2,500,-000. It is then conceivable that the new emigration, some seven years old, is in 1952 equal in size with the old emigration, five times its age.[5] As a working hypothesis on a recurring question, conjectures such as the above are clearly desirable. Yet need it be emphasized that this and similar conjectures are of very questionable value for generalizations of any kind? This is true not only because the figures employed are fragmentary in the extreme. Still more importantly, the world is never likely to know what portion of the great majority that *did* return to the USSR had done so under duress, Soviet or Western.

Although the Korean truce talks have recently made the issue of crucial importance, the whole subject of forced repatriation of prisoners is little thought about in the outside world as it applied to Soviet citizens at the close of World War II. But the subject is still daily remembered, and perhaps embellished, by the fear-ridden Soviet refugees of today. Nor can the survivors of wartime Soviet opposition forget that some of this repatriation took place with armed Western assistance. Their misreading of the West's general policies appears as innocent in retrospect as does the West's own misreading of the Soviet policies. But the defectors were also guided by their bedrock conviction that the worst that could happen to them in Allied hands was to be treated as political exiles.

In explaining the part played by the Western Allies in this forced repatriation, a variety of different factors must be taken into consideration. One of these — perhaps the most specifically decisive — was the Western concern for speedy and complete repatriation of its own war prisoners liberated by the Red Army in Eastern Europe. This concern was ever intensified by the USSR's reluctance to make the suggested plans and commitments, as well as by the Soviet's harshness and suspicion toward its own citizens who had been under German control,[6] and it was this concern that led to the symbol of forced repatriation, the repatriation agreement of the Yalta Conference. Article I of the repatriation compact called for segregation by the liberating power of Western and Soviet citizens into separate camps until they could be handed over to their own forces. Article II committed each party to inform the government concerned of the whereabouts of its citizens, and to give it access to and internal control of the repatriation camps containing its own citizens. Thirteen months after the Yalta Conference, in a press release of March 8, 1946, the U. S. Department of State made public the text of this compact. Entitled "Agreement Relating to the Prisoners of War and Civilians Liberated by Forces Operating under Soviet Command and Forces Operating Under United States of America Command," it had been signed on February 11, 1945 by Major General John R. Deane, wartime Chief of the U. S. Military Mission in Moscow, for the United States, and Major General A. A. Gryzlov for the USSR. The same 1946 press release contained an additional statement on U. S. repatriation policy. The statement specified that only pre-1939 nationals were affected, and that "The repatriation of Soviet citizens is not facilitated unless they so desire, with the exception of those who fall within the following categories: (1) Those who were captured in German uniforms; (2) Those who were members of the Soviet armed forces on or after June 22, 1941 and were not subsequently discharged therefrom; (3) Those who on the basis of reasonable evidence have been found to be collaborators with the enemy, having voluntarily rendered comfort to the enemy."

While the Western Allies adhered to the Yalta Conference repatriation agreement, we get a different picture regarding the USSR from *The Strange Alliance*, by General Deane. In what Deane describes as "my darkest days in Russia," in the winter of 1944–1945, the Soviets as a rule adhered to only two policies: procrastination and secrecy in their own plans, and continuous abuse of Western actions concerning repatriation of Soviet citizens. As Deane suggests, the reason may have been a typical maneuver to cover up the USSR's own failures and schemes. Perhaps it was also intended to keep the West, obviously anxious to please, on the defensive on a question of the greatest political import to the Soviet government.[7]

Casting a light on Soviet defection, General Deane also indicates that the Soviet government was not to be outdone in the task of myth-making on the complete wartime unity of the Soviet population. Thus, when the Soviet authorities were queried prior to the Allied invasion of France as to the desired disposition of Soviet nationals found serving in the German forces, "the Russian representatives at Eisenhower's headquarters replied that the question would not arise since there were no Russians so serving. About four months after the invasion we had accumulated twenty-eight thousand Russians in German uniform." [8]

In spite of its immediate and legitimate concern with the return of its own war prisoners, the West could hardly have agreed so readily to the policy of forced repatriation had it not been for the climate of opinion that prevailed at the time. Characteristic of this climate — perhaps difficult even to reconstruct today — was the intense desire to prove our unqualified friendship for the Soviet government, and, at the same time, the blithe confidence that Stalin was equally intent on international amity and intimate coöperation among the Great Powers. Imbued with this feeling of good will toward its great Soviet ally, it was almost inevitable that the West should view conditions within the USSR in only the most favorable light. Thus it seemed almost inconceivable that the axiomatic assumption that every war prisoner or forced laborer was eager to return to his homeland might not apply with equal force to Soviet nationals. And those Soviet citizens who were obviously reluctant to follow this expected pattern could be conceived of only as active Nazi agents.

Great also was the influence both of emotionalized Soviet "anti-Fascist" agitation and of the West's own genuine revulsion against most things not only Nazi but also German as being tainted with Fascism if not wholly Fascist. Neither the public opinion nor the governments of the Western world were in any mood to be charitable toward a phenomenon like the Vlasov Movement. In the eyes of a West that was so blissfully pro-Soviet and so passionately anti-German at that particular moment, members of such a group could not be considered anything but completely contemptible Nazi collaborators. It is part of the tragedy surrounding Soviet opposition that in such circumstances there was simply no place for what has been the proud Western principle of political asylum.

It should be noted here that the Western support of forced repatriation to the USSR immediately following World War II was a major cause of the continuing postwar dwindling of Soviet defection and desertion. A related cause was the Allied policy of returning Red Army deserters to Soviet authorities in Germany as part of a "gentleman's agreement." Thus Marguerite Higgins, at the time Berlin correspondent for the *New York Herald Tribune*, estimated in 1949 that in the four years since the war's end, 13,000 to 14,000 Soviet nationals were known to have defected.[9] This is vastly more than any free society would produce, but much smaller than the wartime defections. Although instances of U.S. return of deserters to Soviet authorities reportedly ceased with the Berlin blockade of 1948, even after that life for Soviet exiles in Western Germany — still their political center — remained insecure, ridden with fears of renewed Allied repatriations to the USSR. Only in 1951 did the U. S. authorities in Germany announce a major policy change aimed at furthering rather than discouraging future Soviet defection.[10]

It is clear that the West's immediate postwar policy boded ill for the future of the wartime Soviet opposition movement, and much attention has been drawn to this fact. Less frequently commented on, but, in my opinion, equally decisive, was the Vlasov Movement's own illusion regarding the West. It was because these two attitudes, so totally divergent and so incomprehensible to each other, met head on that Soviet opposition suffered so drastically calamitous a fate.

The end of the First KONR Division came on May 12, 1945, just four days after it had begun its withdrawal from Prague. This took place in the Czech town of Schlüsselburg, then under American control, where the division had compiled with the local U. S. Army request to lay down its arms. Soviet representatives — negotiators as well as propagandists — had been pleading with General Buniachenko to surrender the First Division to the Red Army. For a brief interim, Buniachenko stalled, evading the necessity of giving a definitely negative answer to the Soviet emissaries and all the while attempting to persuade the U.S. military authorities to intern his unit formally, or otherwise take charge of it. Vlasov, too, located in a castle nearby, sought unceasingly to obtain U. S. commitments. Then on May 12 came the word that Schlüsselburg was to be turned over that same day to the Red Army. The local American commander refused to admit the division as a unit into American-occupied areas. Only one possible loophole had been offered. This was the suggestion by a U. S. officer that the troops might trickle individually into American-held territory. Thereupon Buniachenko immediately formally dissolved the short-lived First KONR Division. Many soldiers fled southward to Bavaria, but most of the First Division were on the spot seized by Soviet units or turned over to them by the U. S. Army. At the same time, a similar fate befell the Second Division, which in April had moved first from Heuberg to Münsingen, and then to Linz, Austria. From there only one of its regiments, together with the KONR Army Headquarters, managed to evade capture by the Soviets and reach U. S. lines. Two other German-sponsored formations, made up of Soviet nationals, also fell into Soviet hands: General von Pannwitz's SS Cossack Corps in Austria and General von Niedermayer's 162nd Turk Division in Italy. In both of these instances, it was the British who first interned the units and then turned them over to the Soviets.[11]

The scattering of the First and Second KONR Divisions, it should be noted, was in striking contrast to the bitter-end combat on the Western Front of some Soviet-manned *Ostbattalione*. Their resistance was spurred on, ironically, by well-meaning Allied leaflets promising speedy return to the Soviet homeland.

It is the fate of the remnants of the Second KONR Division, those who came under U. S. control, that best and most tragically symbolizes the end of the Vlasov Movement. After a weary, wandering journey throughout the area where Czechoslovakia, Austria, and Bavaria meet, seeking unsuccessfully to establish contact with U. S. authorities and to do so while preserving the KONR Army's standing and unity as an anti-Soviet military force, these remnants were formally interned as prisoners of war by U. S. authorities in the western Bavarian town of Landau.

All this time, and for months after, the Vlasovite leaders persisted in their efforts to obtain U. S. sponsorship of a continued Soviet anti-Stalin unit. This was particularly true of General Meandrov, then acting as chief of staff of the KONR Army. (We shall come to General Trukhin's fate presently.) The U. S. authorities had long since clearly indicated the hopelessness of the situation. They had also, by their actions and by individual hints, implied that they would not resist a wholesale scattering from the very loosely guarded prisoner-of-war camp that held the bulk of the Heuberg contingent of the KONR Army. But, a "solidarist" himself, Meandrov followed the NTS line and would not give up. He did, however, announce that all who wanted to could take advantage of the various opportunities to leave the KONR Army internment area. Many did, but a sizable percentage, including Meandrov himself, stayed on. From Landau the group of die-hards was transferred, early in the fall of 1945, to Regensberg, and later, in the same winter, to Plattling, a Bavarian town near the Donau, and not far from Regensberg.

It was at Plattling that the last, lingering Soviet opposition hopes were extinguished by an abrupt and bitter stroke. Here, on a Sunday in February 1946, the bulk of some three thousand ex-Soviet veterans of the KONR Army were turned over to Soviet authorities by the U. S. camp administration. The blow fell at six in the morning, completely by surprise, the prisoners having been previously assured by U. S. officers on the spot that no forced repatriation was contemplated. It was accompanied by considerable violence on the part of the American troops involved. Whether or not this picture of what happened is accurate, it is more than certain that the tragedy of Plattling, its violence, its many suicide attempts, the dual role of American authorities, are deeply etched in the memory of surviving Vlasovites.

The Plattling incident — forced American repatriation of Soviet defectors into Soviet hands — was repeated at Kempton, Landshut, and elsewhere, usually on a smaller scale. It is probably this background that explains why an assumption has been made about the fate of the KONR leaders which in several instances is not correct, and which reflects unfavorably on the perpetrators of Plattling, the U. S. authorities. The fact of the matter is that, contrary to general opinion, a number of KONR leaders were *not* repatriated by the West.

Two accounts in Russian émigré journals, both quoting eyewitnesses, paint slightly differing pictures of precisely how General Vlasov, the leader of the wartime Soviet opposition movement, fell into Soviet hands. One account, that of a young woman interpreter who reportedly was with Vlasov to the moment of his seizure by the Soviets, states that the general left the castle near Schlüsselberg, where the First KONR Division was disbanding, to go to a U. S. Army headquarters to negotiate, and that he was recognized en route by a Soviet detachment. At this point the American personnel accompanying Vlasov in a jeep attempted to protect him. But an officer from another U. S. vehicle which had driven up announced that this was an internal Russian affair, and Vlasov was removed by the Soviet detachment.[12] Another account, quoting a KONR officer said to have been present, states that immediately after Vlasov's departure from Schlüsselburg on May 12, 1945, a Soviet car sped away in the same direction. Then, three kilometers out of town, two heavily loaded Red Army vehicles stopped Vlasov's car, demanding his surrender. In this account, Vlasov was accompanied by four U. S. Army tanks, whose commander — a gum-chewing American colonel — witnessed the scene neutrally and in the end commented: "This is not my territory, take him away." [13] A third account, by a German author, states that after rescuing Vlasov from one capture before reaching Schlüsselburg, the local U. S. Army unit inadvertently let him fall into Soviet hands while attempting to sneak him, disguised as an American, from the castle to a higher American headquarters.[14]

Despite their divergence in detail, one conclusion appears valid from these accounts. It seems that Vaslov's seizure occurred without premeditation on the part of U. S. authorities. This does not mean that the same authorities were not at that moment contemplating such a formal turning over. Nor does it mean that their dispatch of Vlasov into Soviet-frequented Czech territory was not either extremely naïve or actually intended to rid themselves of him. But as far as the record indicates to date, Vlasov was not formally turned over by the West to the USSR.

As for Vlasov's deputy, General Malyshkin, he was left in Füssen, the Bavarian town that was the KONR's last organizational center, to be overrun by Allied units. With him was Captain Strikfeldt, who in this critical moment was again near the Vlasov Movement after his late 1944 removal by the SS. The purpose was to enter into negotiations with U. S. officials — a mission that failed. Soon thereafter Malyshkin was interned in the American camp at Augsburg.

The Vlasov Movement's propaganda chief, Zhilenkov, was seen in the Augsburg camp. As in the case of Malyshkin, U. S. authorities turned him, too, over to Soviet officers, after transferring him to the Mannheim camp.

According to all accounts, General Trukhin, chief of staff of the KONR army, was seized on May 6 near the Czech town of Pribran by pro-Soviet Czech partisans while en route to establish contact in the Prague area with the First Division and above all with Vlasov himself, whose absence at this juncture slowed or even precluded essential decisions. On the next day Trukhin was transported eastward into Soviet hands. The same fate befell Trukhin's deputy, General Boyarsky, who preceded him in attempting to reach Prague. But the latter was killed on the spot by partisans on May 5.

General Zakutnyi reportedly was in Füssen on VE Day. Summoned to the local U. S. headquarters, he there encountered Soviet officers waiting for him, and was taken into custody by them.

As to what happened to General Blagoveshchenskii, who, of the participating Soviet generals, was most skeptical regarding the wartime opposition movement, I have a categorical but unverified account by a former KONR official who had occupied the apartment adjoining Blagoveshchenskii's in Marienbad, part of the KONR concentration around the Czech resort of Karlsbad. This official stated to me that during May 1945 Blagoveshchenskii had been repeatedly visited by Soviet officials bringing food and liquor for extensive festivities. Then, in the following month, he was shown by the general a striking document indicating that the Soviet government had named Blagoveshchenskii Soviet repatriation chief for the western part of Czechoslovakia. After commenting that the general had sought, unsuccessfully, to persuade him to return to the USSR, my source continued that the general himself never did tour the internment camps as he had expected to do, but instead disappeared to Pilsen shortly thereafter, following another festive occasion with visiting Soviet officers. This account suggests that Blagoveshchenskii was one of those not repatriated to the Soviets by Western authorities.

Two other KONR generals — both former Red Army colonels — should be mentioned here. One of them, Meandrov, attempted to commit suicide during one of the forced-repatriation incidents but failed. A similar suicide attempt was made by Maltsev, the colorful chief of the KONR Air Brigade, and, until World War II, a veteran Soviet Communist and Red Army career officer. According to one account, Maltsev was seized in the U. S. Zone of Germany in September 1945, and then, for reasons yet to be explained, was mysteriously spirited away to Paris. There, after his suicide attempt, he was nursed in a separate Soviet military hospital unit. Following a second suicide attempt, and despite the possibility of his not surviving the trip, Maltsev was sent back to the USSR.[15]

Our information regarding the capture of these Vlasovite leaders is neither as extensive nor as authoritative as we could wish. It does, however, appear that, of the six former Soviet generals, only three — Malyshkin, Zhilenkov, and Zakutnyi — were deliberately turned over to the Soviets by the West. The other three were not. Vlasov fell into Soviet hands by what might well be described as a trick of fate. Trukhin was captured before VE Day by pro-Soviet Czech partisans, while Blagoveshchenskii evidently offered his services to the Soviet government voluntarily. Contrary to a widespread impression, Western authorities did not turn over more than half of the top leaders of KONR. Moreover, for those other Vlasovites who could be persuaded to scatter, they created several opportunities to do so. Nevertheless, forced repatriations to the USSR were extensive. They represent an indelible blot on the West's tradition of ready asylum for political exiles.

If our picture of the events leading up to the KONR leaders' return to the USSR is sketchy and somewhat blurred, the same cannot be said of their eventual fate upon arrival there. In the August 2, 1946 issue of *Pravda* an announcement appeared. Albeit wholly opaque, it was the first mention of the Vlasov Movement in *Pravda*. It was relegated to the lower left-hand corner of the last (fourth) page, but its import was stark, incisive, and final. It marks the end of the Vlasov Movement:

## ANNOUNCEMENT BY THE MILITARY BOARD OF
## THE SUPREME COURT OF THE USSR

A few days ago, the Military Board of the Supreme Court of the USSR considered the case against *A. A. Vlasov, V. F. Malyshkin, G. N. Zhilenkov, F. I. Trukhin, D. E. Zakutnyi, I. A. Blagoveshchenskii, M. A. Meandrov, G. A. Zverev, V. D. Korbukov,* and *N. S. Shatov* for treason to the motherland and that they being agents of German intelligence, carried out active espionage-diversionary and terrorist activity against the Soviet Union, i.e. for crimes covered by articles 58–1 "b," 58–8, 58–9, 58–10 and 58–11 of the Criminal Code of the RSFSR. All accused admitted their guilt in the charges made against them.

In accordance with point 1 of the Order of the Presidium of the Supreme Soviet of the USSR, dated April 19, 1943, the Military Board of the Supreme Court of the USSR sentenced the accused *Vlasov, Malyshkin, Zhilenkov, Trukhin, Zakutnyi, Blagoveshchenskii, Meandrov, Maltsev, Buniachenko, Zverev, Korbukov,* and *Shatov* to death through hanging.

The sentence has been executed.[16]

Soviet Opposition and
The Soviet System

In making conclusions and generalizations regarding the over-all problem of Soviet opposition to Stalin, three major aspects stand out: the likelihood of opposition, the forms of opposition, and the ideology of opposition. In the following chapters, the Vlasov Movement will be analyzed in terms of these major aspects of Soviet opposition.

As to the likelihood itself of opposition, the concept of Inertness was advanced early in this study as the outstanding factor.

In the USSR, Inertness, the exclusion of individual initiative in anything in the least related to politics, has become the central feature in the political behavior of the individual.

A major explanation for this trademark of Soviet individuals is, of course, the impact of the totalitarian regime in the USSR. A system in which modern technology is combined with a wholly authoritarian leadership and ideology will inevitably lead to such a reaction. The minute supervision of most actions within the USSR, together with the extremely brutal punishment for even slight and innocent deviations, actually leaves the Soviet-bred individual little if any alternative to Inertness. Terror must be posited here as a prime method of Soviet as of any other modern totalitarian system.[1]

It would, however, be a crude and wholly false oversimplification to limit an over-all discussion of the Inertness of the Soviet citizen to its dependence on totalitarian terror. In a totalitarian system, and specifically in the Soviet regime, there are at least four other contributory causes for Inertness. There is, first, that major weapon of all totalitarian systems, propaganda. It is difficult for an inhabitant of a free or even relatively free country to imagine just how absolute the intensity and the scope of propaganda can be in a modern totalitarian state. Here propaganda is not only as universal in scope as mass communications are in other societies. It has one basic difference: it is monolithic. This precludes the circulation of other opinions and ideologies. It also cuts off the circulation of unwanted elementary facts that by themselves might or might not crystallize into opinion.

The result is that information not officially approved either is not circulated at all among the population, or is circulated only under the greatest obstacles, risk, and hesitation. An individual exposed so completely and continuously to one source of information and opinion, and one source only, is apt to become subject to it. This is so even when it runs contrary to all prescriptions of logic or abstract principles of behavior, when a particular individual should be wholly immunized either by persecution or by his origin. Thus it would be a grave error to underestimate the very real impact of internal Soviet propaganda. Inertness is fostered not exclusively by terror, but also by propaganda; favorable to making peace with the regime, it is at the same time confusing as well as stultifying to continued retention of opposition ideas and ideals.

A factor in Soviet Inertness that is close to propaganda is genuine conviction. Both wishful thinking and the often embellished testimony of ex-Communists encourage the hope and the belief that the number of Soviet citizens genuinely loyal to the system has been reduced over the years to a small percentage. This may, of course, be so. But if the at least partial effectiveness of Soviet propaganda is conceded, a perhaps regrettable corollary is that such propaganda must result in a considerable number of faithful adherents to the regime. Just as propaganda contributes to the more willing acceptance of Inertness, so does genuine conviction, simplifying and smoothing the adjustment.

In the efforts of the outside world to comprehend the attitude of the Soviet citizen to his government, one element is at times underestimated. This is the nature and the extent of rationalization in all human situations. Man on the whole is not a rebel, nor is he innately a martyr. When, as in the USSR, he is faced with a situation that objectively may be deemed alien and uncomfortable for him, the average person will rationalize his fate far more than is generally assumed. For example, the exiling of one member of a Soviet family is believed certain to embitter its remaining members. But the powers of rationalization may well induce many a Soviet individual to repress the unpleasantness of this fact by stressing the actual or potential benefits that may accrue to himself or other family members from the same regime that has been cruel to one of them.

In short, if man everywhere often adjusts to situations that in abstract terms he could be expected to reject, why should he not be expected to do the same in the USSR — where the penalties for not doing so, for not rationalizing away inclinations toward conscious resentment or even revolt, are ever so much more severe than they are in similar human situations elsewhere?

The vast weight on the individual Soviet citizen of rationalization, and thus of Inertness, has been described by a recent U. S. Naval Attaché to Moscow, Admiral Stevens: "But the truth in any case is that most Russians do not regard themselves as being badly treated. They know that dark things continue to happen under the Soviets to the individual, to whole communities and classes. But, fed on their fat diet of government propaganda, they believe that such things, although hard on the individual, are for the common good. In the absence of any means of information but the word of mouth, each person, each community, knows very little about what happens to other Soviet citizens, or why it happens. They know only that it is not healthy to be insistently curious. And the universal human feeling that 'it can't happen to me' — either because one is too clever or because one's conscience is clear — prevails among the Russians, lulling even the most fearful." [2]

Perhaps the most important single factor, along with terror, in explaining the Soviet individual's Inertness is the factor of social integration. It covers the whole gamut of ties, loyalties, associations, and identifications that the individual is bound to develop in *any* society. For the Soviet citizen the USSR is not only the place where he and his ancestors have been born and brought up. It is the place that he knows best, and where he has experienced not only sorrows but not a few personal joys. It is the place where he expects for better or for worse to spend his own life, where he will work and marry and raise a family. It is the country whose literature and customs and holidays and excitements he feels closest to, all such things in any other country being infinitely "foreign" to any but the most cosmopolitan of all of us.

Not only contemporary sociological theory, but the investigations for this study suggest that the centripetal forces of social integration are operative in the USSR almost if not quite as much as elsewhere in the world. In turn, the impact of such social integration, the identification with his own environment and society, is bound to increase the likelihood of conformity to the Inertness pattern.

The interconnection in Soviet Inertness between the negative factor — terror — and the positive one is also emphasized by the directors of the large-scale Refugee Interview Project of the Harvard Russian Research Center, Alex Inkeles and Raymond A. Bauer. Writing in the *New York Times Magazine*, they say of the Soviet exiles interviewed: "Coupled with their helplessness in the face of a ruthlessly oppressive regime was their affection for their homeland, family, work, status, and the whole way of life to which they were accustomed. Confronted with these circumstances, they accommodated as best they could to those things they disliked, in order not to lose what little was left of that which they cherished."

On a broader plane, one of the most thoughtful Western observers of the USSR, writing pseudonymously as O. Utis in *Foreign Affairs*, concludes: "The governed [in the USSR], a passive, frightened herd, may be deeply cynical in their own fashion, and progressively brutalized, but so long as the 'line' pursues a zigzag path, allowing for breathing spells as well as the terrible daily treadmill, they will, for all the suffering it brings, be able to find their lives just — if only just — sufficiently bearable to continue to exist and toil and enjoy pleasures. It is difficult for the inhabitants of Western countries to conceive conditions in which human beings in Eastern Europe or the Soviet Union (or for that matter India or China) not merely can survive but, being surrounded by others in no better plight, and with no alternative forms of life visible through the Curtain to attract and discontent the imagination, adapt themselves to conditions, look on them as normal, contrive to make arrangements like soldiers in an unending campaign, or prisoners or shipwrecked mariners. Such arrangements may seem intolerable to the average citizen of a civilized country, yet because, if not liberty, then fraternity and equality, are born of common suffering, a human life can be lived — with moments of gaiety and enthusiasm, and of actual happiness — under the most appalling and degrading conditions." [3]

The ever more widely accepted Western image of the USSR divides its population into those who favor the Stalin regime and those who oppose it. The chain of reasoning just presented suggests that this popular image is far from correct. Rather, the Soviet citizen, terrorized and otherwise impelled into a state of political Inertness in relation to the regime, at the same time develops numerous links to this regime. Moreover, his total isolation from the outside, together with both his intellectual primitivization and the inevitable impact of official propaganda, saps the capacity of the Soviet individual to act spontaneously on most matters. They minimize his ability to reason and react in consciously independent terms, and above all in matters having any relation to politics.

Inertness, as pictured here, leads to an unmistakable conclusion regarding the likelihood of Soviet opposition. This conclusion is that Inertness makes such native opposition considerably less probable than is widely believed outside the USSR. But this is far from meaning that the picture is one of black and white simplicity.

For instance, neither Inertness nor its opposite (spontaneity and independent thinking on all matters affecting political behavior) can by any means be considered absolutes. This is certainly true of the USSR, where much deviation from Inertness may be discovered either in individual exceptions to the prevailing pattern or in areas of activity furthest removed from politics. Even more importantly, Inertness is certainly never wholly absent from even the freest Western societies. This is borne out, for one example, in the increasing conformism in the American counterpart to Soviet officialdom, the "new middle classes" of professionals and office workers in and out of government, as has been stressed recently in David Riesman's *The Lonely Crowd*, C. Wright Mills's *White Collar* and the much-discussed *Fortune* studies of "corporation wives" and American business.[4] Nor can it be claimed, by any means, that the average person in the United States does much independent thinking in the realm of politics, ideology, or fundamental social issues.

Just how ill-informed on major political matters the average American is in the midst of the most extensive and opulent network of mass communications the world has ever seen is underestimated in the United States itself.[5] This paradox may augur Inertness, for the complexity of these political questions combines here with the increasing unlikelihood of an individual's affecting them one way or the other even in as relatively vigorous a political democracy as the United States. Together, this combination encourages the average person to turn away from independent thinking and action. Although Samuel Lubell's *The Future of American Politics* bespeaks vigor and gusto on election day, a competing trend is thus what Erich Fromm has described as a mass "escape from freedom." The concomitant of this has been the "welfare state." As Isaiah Berlin, the Oxford historian and philosopher, has portrayed it, "Today the very virtues of the paternalistic state, its genuine anxiety to reduce destitution and disease and inequality, to penetrate all the neglected nooks and crannies of life which may stand in need of its justice and its bounty — its very success in those beneficent activities — has narrowed the area within which the individual may commit blunders, has curtailed his liberties in the interest (the very real interest) of his welfare or his sanity, his health, his security, his freedom from want and fear." [6]

Much as the Cold War may obscure this, the fundamental trends of the twentieth century are common to the USSR and the West. The ever important differences are emphasized by past history, by ideology and folkways, by the resulting national character and institutional structures. But it is the similarity in human and social relations which is furthered by the dominant features of the current technological stage of the Industrial Revolution: urbanization, mass communication, occupational specialization, and, above all, standardization in production, in management, in consumption, in culture. Therefore elements of Inertness are certainly present, although not as prevalent or as unrivaled, in nontotalitarian contemporary societies. This is as plausible as the reverse of Inertness is in some individuals and in some activities within the USSR.

On the other hand, Soviet Inertness cannot be considered solely a product of modern developments. The pre-1917 history of the USSR unquestionably has also played a role in the nature and the extent of Inertness. Precisely how great this pre-Soviet influence is, and what it is, remains one of the most controversial and yet also one of the most neglected aspects of Western analyses of the USSR.

This much appears clear. Although Russia's contact with Western democracy before 1917 was far more considerable than many realize today, this experience with democratic institutions and mentality was extremely limited. Still more importantly, the economic and social institutions of Tsarist Russia, even in its strikingly liberal period in the early twentieth century, did not develop the kind of class relation, values, and traditions that lay at the basis of what is considered Western parliamentary democracy. Parliamentary democracy is a system traceable to the rise since the Middle Ages of several social forces competing with and limiting the powers of central authority: nationalism and national monarchies against imperial dynasties, the urban bourgeoisie against royal absolutism, the new gentry against the feudal aristocracy, the Protestant Reformation against a centralized Catholic authority, capitalism for *laissez faire* and against state mercantilism, an urban prole-

tariat and the lower middle classes for political equality and social reform, the labor movement for industrial democracy and various forms of
socialism.

These are vast social forces indeed. Singly and in different alignments
they pressed the Western world toward parliamentary democracy, and
toward rationalism and individualism in thought and in action. It is
these forces that were either absent or muted in Russia. Instead, we see
there a constellation of social forces shaping habits and expectations in
the population which inevitably were different from the West: the
long centuries of paternalism — not always inept but indubitably
heavy-handed — by the Tsarist regime, its immense bureaucracy and
state church, the great financial and political dependence of Russian
capitalism on the state, the very slow decline in the parochial structure
of village life, the inefficiency and related political infantilism of a court-
oriented gentry, the lateness and incompleteness of the development of
an urban middle class and professional intelligentsia made inevitable by
these other social forces, the repressed and therefore radicalized labor,
socialist, and intellectual movements.

With this contrast between Western and Russian historical evolution,
it is no wonder that the average Russian had in his psychological and
ideological make-up far less resistance to authority, collectivism, state
paternalism than is true of Western democracy's citizenry at its best.
This is not to say, as is done far too often and too glibly in the West,
that in view of Russia's past the Soviet individual cannot and will not
either crave or understand liberty. Democracy — political, social, economic — is an ideal that has become universal today. It is an ideal re-
vered at least as much in areas of the world that have not yet enjoyed
democracy as in the West. All available evidence indicates that this is
in considerable measure applicable to the Soviet population. But the
Inertness of that population must be traced to Russia's pre-1917 history
as well as to the twentieth century. This remains true even though, as
George Orwell showed so memorably in *1984*,[7] modern society has developed appeals and techniques which, as of the middle of this century,
can produce near-total Inertness as effectively in England, the deeply
civilized "Mother of Parliaments," as in the USSR, heir to an authority-
oriented past.

It has already been noted that Inertness must inevitably take different
forms depending on the relation of the individual to the regime. Those
closer to it, either in the administrative or the technical elite, must manifest more active accommodation in their relations with the regime

through opportunistic careerism, together with varying degrees of genuine enthusiasm and active loyalty. The average Soviet national, on the other hand, is able to rely heavily on more (although *never* totally) passive accommodation, through apathy and evasion of political commitments. These are two different manifestations of the same Inertness: the more active one of the elite groups, and the more passive one of the rank and file. It is therefore apparent that internally, too, Inertness is not a uniform pattern of behavior. Moreover, Inertness has innumerable shadings between its elite and rank-and-file manifestations, and not merely these two manifestations. But regardless of shadings, Inertness does not equal ignorance of politics, nor complete passivity toward it. With the regime promulgating — for its own uses — a highly significant mass politicization, an attitude of naïveté or unconcern is the reverse of the unique adaptational skills which distinguish Inertness.

Inertness, then, is a highly complex factor in estimating the likelihood of Soviet opposition. Although it is presented here as the decisive factor, neither its complexity nor its various shadings can be overlooked. As specific illustrations of how Inertness exerts its decisive influence — and of its vast complexity — the evolution of the Soviet individual outside of his native habitat and the Soviet response in 1941 to the German invasion may be cited.

It is only *after* the average Soviet national finds himself outside the confines of Soviet power that he tends to reflect systematically upon the innumerable injustices, cruelties, offenses, discomforts that his native regime had brought upon him and his dear ones. It is only at this point, after the break is made, that the Soviet citizen changes radically. Now an exile, he develops an active and also violent, bitter, implacable opposition both to the regime itself and to practically all of its characteristic features. It is at this point, too, that he insists categorically that both his own active opposition and that of a majority of the Soviet population were operative all along. It is essential to recognize this. Together with our insistence that Soviet society, like all others, does possess elements of integration, loyalty, progress, this brings out a cardinal point. The exile's rejection, total and strident, is far rarer within the USSR — not because there is less cause for it inside the country, but because all the immense factors causing Inertness work against its development.

Unless the outside world clearly perceives this postbreak origin of the Soviet exile's clear-cut, black-and-white rejection of the USSR, it may greatly, and fatefully, misjudge the nature and the extent of the undoubtedly important potential of disaffection within the USSR. While

Soviet exiles are of the greatest significance in a number of ways, they reflect only partially the mood within their native land.

These Soviet exiles provide substantiation for the concept of Inertness in one other manner. Both during and since World War II, Soviet nationals who broke with the Stalin regime were characterized by a profound bewilderment with the outside world. This bewilderment, which at times takes on the proportions of infantilism, embraces every conceivable area: occupational, social, political, ethical, intellectual, cultural, personal. The Soviet exile, for decades held tightly within the narrow limits of Inertness and the confines of his native land, in fact has lost (or never acquired) the individual sense of orientation and self-confidence that is the by-product of a less controlled existence. As usual, there are numerous exceptions, individuals with political vigor, personal resourcefulness, and great capacity to adjust to a new environment without sheer opportunism. But on the whole the Soviet exiles — Vlasovite, "defector," "nonreturner" — substantiate rather than invalidate our portrait of Soviet Inertness.

Another clear manifestation of Inertness can be found in the way in which the Soviet governmental machinery reacted to the shock of the German invasion in 1941. Soviet totalitarianism had, to a striking degree, succeeded in choking off initiative and spontaneous assumption of responsibility, not only among the mass of the population, but also among its officials, great and small. The officialdom, trained to the marrow of its bones to adhere to an uninterrupted flow of minute instructions from higher up, was uniquely unsuited to reacting speedily to the surprise German onslaught.

When this onslaught understandably threw Stalin and his most intimate entourage into confusion, the chief result was that Moscow's all-encompassing guidance of activities throughout the USSR became halting and incomplete. For the Soviet official, military hardly less than civilian, such a state of affairs was wholly inadequate: by the time World War II broke out, this Soviet official — if still in circulation — had been thoroughly cured of most habits of independence and initiative. Needless to say, there were exceptions. But only when orders from Moscow started flowing more smoothly again did the Soviet armed forces and its economy rally. And then, as the world has witnessed, the USSR performed near miracles of heroism and production.

But how different the situation was in the interim period, in the weeks and months before the top Soviet leaders regained full control of themselves and of the myriad reins of government. The totalitarian-imbued reaction of officialdom to this lapse was chaos, a chaos throughout the USSR and particularly in the areas nearest to the front. It was a chaos evidently indescribable in its extent and intensity, a chaos in the army, in transportation, in supply, and in administration.

An outsider should not underestimate the effects of a surprise attack on a major industrialized power. No other such power of comparable size has been exposed to a similar attack. Most particularly the United States, geographically the most protected of modern powers, has yet to pass the test. Nevertheless, one conclusion may be drawn regarding the stupendous and universal chaos that appears to have marked the USSR after June 22, 1941. It is traceable as much, if not more, to the deformities in the officialdom, in turn caused by Soviet totalitarianism, as to the inevitable dislocations under similar circumstances of any major industrial power.

In turn, this chaos must explain many of the military debacles which again and again befell the Red Army during the early phase. And it is these debacles that point to yet another development which, though it appears eminently logical once propounded, has also not been given due emphasis.

This last in a chain of factors is the widespread — some eyewitnesses say universal — conviction in the USSR, and particularly in the areas closest to the *Wehrmacht's* advance, that early German victory was for all practical purposes a certainty. The fact that this conviction was so widespread was attested to by all Soviet "nonreturners" whom I questioned at length in Germany. In view of the over-all hypothesis presented in this chapter, there seems to be ample reason to accept it as a logical consequence. If totalitarianism has limited severely the Soviet-bred person's capacity for independent action, and if this swiftly led to devastating chaos, is it not only reasonable to assume that a likely consequence would be a belief that all was lost? that the system which until the attack was omnipresent and omnipotent, but which now had evidently lost its grip, could not possibly regain this decisive hold?

It appears from the above that the initial Soviet reverses must be explained in a manner differing from the "surprise attack" and the "revolt" schools. Though granting anti-Stalinism as an element, it is reduced from the key to a subsidiary role. It was the Inertness of Soviet officialdom, its inability to respond spontaneously to a radically changed situation, that was primarily responsible for the catastrophic extent of the chaos that followed the surprise attack. And it is the Inertness of the mass of the Soviet population that accounts for a still more fundamental difference between this and the other interpretations. The "surprise attack" and the "revolt" schools have stressed, in opposite ways, the political factor. But if it is plausible that many a Soviet citizen may well have become incapable, at least at first, of spontaneous individual thought and action, this deeply ingrained Inertness appears largely to exclude the political as *the* deciding factor. The prevailing feeling during the months immediately following the German invasion was neither political devotion nor political disaffection, but apolitical Inertness.

This picture is unorthodox not only in comparison with prevailing American views but also as far as the outlook of most Soviet exiles is concerned. In what has been the most widely argued postwar controversy among the thousands of exiles from the USSR, the "new" émigrés point to the 1941–1942 period as proof that their own step was ideologically motivated, and that active American support to anti-Stalin activities could produce similar results. Just how sharp the attacks and emotions have been is not easy for a nonexile to imagine. The central personages in this controversy are discussed in the notes to this chapter.[8]

But if on 1941 this study differs sharply from prevailing American and émigré theories, there can again be no black-and-white simplicity in its picture regarding 1941 any more than there was on Inertness.

For example, it should not be overlooked that between 1939 and 1941 the German war machine, the world's finest to date, had seized with equal if not greater ease territories other than the USSR. In some instances, such as Western Europe and Czechoslovakia, the countries involved had enjoyed decades of democratic liberties. In no other country overrun by the German blitzkrieg, moreover, can one find even nearly as much totalitarian-engendered Inertness as we have ascribed to the Soviet population.

Moreover, if Inertness overshadows political disaffection within the USSR as the predominant source of Soviet behavior, in general and specifically in 1941, anti-Stalinism also remains a crucial factor. That it is repressed, deformed, atrophied, changes but does not eliminate it. This came very much to the fore in 1941. Then, as has been seen, it was Inertness that was decisive. Yet if politics were totally absent, Inertness would never have been as effective. Without the modicum of political disaffection, Inertness in the U. S. Army would have failed in causing chaos, defeatism, surrender, collaboration with the foe, and does fail to the extent that it exists. Likewise, it was doomed to failure in the Red Army had it not been for disaffection within the USSR. Different from crystallized political attitude as it was, this political disaffection is widespread in the Soviet population. It is this amorphous, itself inert, anti-Stalinism that made Inertness decisive in 1941.

Even given Inertness, it is probable that the USSR's resistance would have been greater had official propaganda in preceding months and years attacked the enemy with all the venom and monopoly at its command, rather than remaining benevolently neutral as did Soviet statements on Hitler Germany between 1939 and 1941. This point has more than merely historical significance. For while in 1941 the population had not been bombarded by such propaganda against the likely enemy, the same is certainly the opposite today: almost since the end of World War II, Soviet officialdom has poured a stream of anti-American propaganda into the eyes and ears of every Soviet citizen. And while it took well nigh a year for the Soviet population to become thoroughly aware of the meaning of German occupation, a similar process of wartime disenchantment may be reduced to a matter of days in a World War III if the opponent resorts to mass atomic bombing of major population centers.

As already suggested, a full-scale land invasion such as the 1941 German attack on the USSR has not been experienced by any comparable modern industrial power. Such a power is unique in its near-absolute dependence on elaborate communications, technology, supply services. It therefore remains to be seen just how, and to what extent, a highly complex and urbanized society will respond to a *surprise* attack, *on land*, and on a *very extended* front line akin to that of 1941.

Inertness is not equivalent to total passivity and lack of resourcefulness on the part of the Soviet individual. He can exhibit much vigor and independence in personal and technical matters. But the concept of Inertness does represent the withdrawal of *Homo Sovieticus* from things political. With it comes the basic trait of political behavior in the USSR —a lessening, if not the disappearance, of personal spontaneity, self-reliance, resourcefulness.

What, then, may be concluded regarding the likelihood of native opposition in the USSR?

The foremost role of Inertness in shaping the political behavior of the Soviet population leads to a rather definite conclusion. Although this conclusion is subject to a variety of qualifications, it is strongly confirmed by Soviet actions in 1941. This conclusion is that effective Soviet opposition to Stalin is rather unlikely. The conclusion is valid as long as Inertness, and the contributing factors both of terror and of social and emotional accommodation, remain nearly universal.

The small likelihood at present of effective Soviet opposition, the conclusion reached in the preceding chapter, does not in any way obviate a parallel fact. Even if it is not apt to be effective in the foreseeable future, native opposition to the Soviet regime has been present uninterruptedly since 1917. Past opposition, and also any occurring in the future, may be divided into three different forms:

1. Passive disaffection;
2. Individual defection;
3. Organized opposition.

By far the largest part of Soviet opposition so far falls into the first category. Beginning with the Civil War, passive disaffection has been continuous. As has been emphasized throughout this study, it is quite widespread within the restrictive, paralyzing confines of mass political inertness. Precisely what the content and the manifestations of passive disaffection are cannot be judged adequately from the outside. But all of Soviet policy, the content of its pronouncements, the pleading and threatening tenor of its propaganda, the extent and intensity of its terror — all these are aimed in large measure at the widespread passive disaffection of the Soviet population.

Individual defection, the second form of opposition, is manifested most visibly by Soviet citizens who become "nonreturners," who sever their ties with the USSR once they find themselves outside of its borders. A study of the Vlasov Movement provides considerable insight into individual defection. Born on alien soil in the midst of general war, the

Vlasov Movement was made up entirely of Soviet citizens whose path to opposition had been through individual defection. Thus an analysis of the first step, the act of defection that during World War II led Soviet citizens to collaborate with Hitler Germany, is of special interest.

Just as the "revolt" school accounts for the enormous total of the Soviet prisoners who fell into German hands by the anti-Stalin sentiments of these soldiers, so it attributes the wartime defectors' first step to this same political motivation. Again we disagree with the "revolt" school. It is our contention that in a large fraction of instances the first step of the Soviet defector-collaborators was motivated by the most elementary and essentially apolitical desire imaginable, that for sheer physical survival. As usual, such a statement needs qualification. Clearly, other motives played a role, a different one in each instance. But with many, and most likely a majority, of the Soviet defector-collaborators involved, survival was the motivation that decided them to take the first step.

This contention is based on the descriptions presented earlier of the murderous policy of starvation and neglect that was adopted by the German authorities with respect to hundreds of thousands of Soviet soldiers captured during the first year of *Wehrmacht* triumphs. These Soviet prisoners of war were massed together in vast concentrations, often in the open air, and malnutrition, disease, and total exhaustion rivaled each other in the death toll of these camps. Is it any wonder then — or an act that an outsider can blithely condemn — that many thousands of Soviet prisoners of war chose collaboration in preference to such miserable and seemingly certain death? And how many outsiders can affirm — from the bottom of their hearts and not in polemic or casual judgment — that they would have lived up to the proud injunction uttered by the Communist woman leader, La Passionaria (Dolores Ibaruri), during the Civil War in Spain: "It is better to die on your feet than to live on your knees"? Some can truly answer that they would have followed La Passionaria's injunction, and not a few of these Soviet prisoners of war indeed did. But it is important to raise this profoundly human problem of civic courage. It stands out as a key problem not only of this study but in general of our time — a time of increasing crisis, when civic courage is, alas, a standard intensely difficult to act by.

It should thus be kept ever in view that everywhere in the world man in the vast majority of cases is a creature neither heroic nor addicted to martyrdom. It is of such "average" men, then, that we speak when explaining the first step by the elemental instinct for sheer physical survival.

A reasonable question may be raised on the score that the worst forms of German maltreatment in Soviet prisoner-of-war camps were alleviated after the first year of the Soviet-German conflict, particularly following the nightmarish winter of 1941–1942. The answer is that the bulk of what subsequently evolved into the Soviet opposition movement was drawn from just the mass of early Soviet prisoners of war.

The first step toward collaboration with Hitler's Germany took vastly differing forms. But in a survey of the leaders' first steps — of which more is known than of the others — much can be posited on the first steps of the followers. For a minority of the Soviet nationals under German control was in fact motivated by anti-Stalin political convictions, convictions even more important than their secondary role in the majority's first step. Most of the key figures of the Vlasov Movement can be placed in this politically motivated anti-Stalin vanguard. Zykov, for example, seems to have been a brilliant intellectual, consistently and knowledgeably concerned with all major ideological problems. His earlier association with Bukharin, his arrest and exile, help to substantiate the genuineness of his anti-Stalinism. Moreover, Zykov reputedly retained clearly formulated political convictions with a frankly Marxian though "right-wing oppositionist" tinge. If Zykov was indeed Jewish, the problem of how a Jew could bring himself to collaborate with Hitler Germany remains puzzling. One not implausible explanation is that in the initial period of the war (Zykov was captured in the summer of 1942) the haziness of Soviet nationals regarding Hitler's *Ostpolitik* may well have been paralleled by an ignorance of just what National Socialism had in mind for Jews. Another explanation seems more applicable to Zykov, a brilliant, facile, cynical propagandist. Like Vlasov and his other associates, he was prepared to enter into this most repugnant "marriage of convenience" in order to make use of Hitler Germany to attain his own ends, the overthrow of Stalin.

Pent-up personal and professional resentment can engender strong antagonisms even more frequently than ideological differences. The Great Purges, in which Malyshkin himself was implicated, had deprived the Red Army of many of its trained officers. The conditions of chaos, disorder, demoralization, and incompetent leadership so stressed in Vlasov's "official" biography must have formed the bitter last image in the eyes of these career military men as they were captured by the *Wehrmacht*. It was also important that high-ranking Soviet officers were rarely subjected to the extreme brutalities meted out to many Soviet war prisoners in 1941 and 1942. Vlasov, for instance, was well treated. His chief German contacts and well-wishers were Hilger and Strikfeldt, both stanch Other Germany adherents. And in their eagerness to further the Other Germany cause, these German officials undoubtedly tended to impart to the wavering captured generals — even despite pessimistic utterances — a far more optimistic picture of the chances for a relatively independent anti-Stalin struggle than was in fact true.

What conclusions can be drawn as to the first step of the leaders of the Vlasov Movement, a specific group more easily identifiable than others and in many ways most important?

To begin with, even our scanty knowledge of these leaders indicates that their crystallized anti-Stalinism, as distinct from their probably universal particular resentments within the USSR, appears in each case except Zykov's to have been of very recent origin. Specifically, we know that Vlasov publicly and privately recounted how he made up his mind to oppose Stalin only in the weeks and months before his capture.

Secondly, there is little doubt that — again excepting Zykov — the anti-Stalinism of the Vlasovite leaders was of a highly unsophisticated and inarticulate kind. The two uppermost desires in their minds were a fanatical zeal to crusade against Stalin, and to do so, even if amorally, not wholly as quislings and mercenaries for Hitler Germany.

A third conclusion seems to be that none of these leaders came from the top layer of Soviet officialdom or even from the next one. Vlasov and Zhilenkov were the two well on the way up, but neither had really seen or tasted large-scale power.

Fourthly, it should be noted that all six of the Vlasovite leaders were of "Great" Russian origin. This statement remains correct, in essence, even if Zykov was in fact of Jewish ancestry, for both his family and party background suggest total assimilation, as does the act of German collaboration itself. This particular conclusion has several implications. For one, although most people in the USSR seem less intensely aroused about the nationality problem than exiles from the country, the all-Russian leadership of the Vlasov Movement will explain some of its nationality policies, and the separatist opposition to it. Moreover, this fact tends to belie the Russophobe contentions of some émigrés that other Soviet nationalities are distinctly more anti-Stalin than the Russians: non-Russian Soviet officials did not emerge anywhere as outstanding opposition leaders either during or after World War II, although secondary leaders may be cited among Ukrainians, Tartars, Caucasians. (The rather Russified — and rather low-ranking — Victor Kravchenko, who is of Ukrainian origin, is an exception that only confirms this observation.)

A fifth conclusion pertains to the problem of how to classify the Vlasovite leaders. On a moderate scale, Vlasov himself was evidently a true leader of men, a military figure with charismatic appeal. General Malyshkin, his organizational deputy, and General Trukhin, the military deputy, were both reportedly grayish, even-tempered, competent, and devoted. General Blagoveshchenskii was aging, crabby, skeptical. Zhilenkov, the "Soviet *barin*," was slick, amoral, and opportunist. Zykov, also slick but a moralist, by his brilliance, cynicism, and haughtiness begs comparison to Karl Radek, the ill-fated Kremlin contributor, in the 1930's, to many a Stalin speech and many an anti-Stalin joke.

These figures, so different in personality, fall into different opposition categories, too. Four of the leaders — Vlasov, Malyshkin, Blagoveshchenskii, and Trukhin — clearly belong to the military group, and Zykov to a deviationist party alignment. It is Zhilenkov who defies classification. As far as we know, he was not even, like Malyshkin and Zykov, a persecutee, or, like Vlasov, Trukhin, and Zykov, of questionable social origin, or, again like Zykov, a high-grade intellectual. In times of flux and chaos such as war, the enumerated sources of opposition will inevitably be augmented by an important addition. These are the many unclassifiable others who — like Zhilenkov — out of opportunism, latent conviction, or both, will join those already involved with one of the opposition currents.

And as a sixth conclusion it is important to note how accidental, how confused, and how halting each leader's path toward active wartime opposition seems to have been. Although this may contradict many current American notions, there is little ground for assuming that, given another set of circumstances (for Vlasov, for instance, no capture and no Other Germany proselytizers like Strikfeldt), all the generals involved would not have continued to serve the Soviet regime. *None* of the key Vlasov figures surrendered to the Germans voluntarily; all were captured. And it is a remarkable and important phenomenon that of a reported total of some fifty Soviet generals captured by Germany only about ten actively joined the wartime anti-Stalin opposition. The rejoinder may be made that Hitlerian *Ostpolitik* precluded greater defection. But both during and since World War II opportunities outside the USSR have not been few for Soviet generals and other high officials to ·

defect and to form opposition movements abroad. Although it is known that some were on the verge of doing so, extremely few actually did.

All of these conclusions serve to emphasize again that even the leaders of wartime opposition were at first confused and inarticulate in their anti-Stalinist position. They were accidental in their active opposition roles, and of distinctly no more than middling prominence in the USSR.

Finally, one more basic feature should be noted. If the top leadership of wartime opposition was dominated by military figures, with party intellectuals like Zykov and Zhilenkov completing the list, the picture is very different on the next power level. Here is where much if not most of the activities and ideas of the whole movement were originated and also translated into action. And here the predominant group was one that is an ever more important one in the USSR itself — the technical intelligentsia: engineers, architects, economists, scientists. From this category, which was nonpolitical in function, although far from always nonparty, the wartime opposition movement built up most of its actual central apparatus (much of it also in uniform in wartime). It was this category that lent the movement as much of its coloration as any single group. The military category, the other one that is outstanding, is in many ways close to the technical intelligentsia, not least because of the professional overlap in a number of technological areas. It is hazardous indeed to predict the future of Soviet opposition from its past. The Vlasov Movement, in particular, was a mutation as far as likely movements within the USSR are concerned. Yet if this wartime opposition may in any way be taken as a guide, it is in the ranks of the technical intelligentsia, together with the military, that potential leadership is to be expected.

Another explanation for the first step of both leaders and followers is the subtle universal logic of compromise. The experience of well-nigh all Western "fellow travellers" of the USSR is as complete an illustration of the logic of compromise as is that of the first step taken by wartime Soviet defectors. The logic of all compromises contains the conviction that if shortcomings, particularly grave shortcomings, are discovered, they are to be considered as exceptions to the rule.

In the German areas in which the Soviet defectors found themselves in 1941 and 1942, in the dislocation and totalitarian control of the sources of information that prevailed there, information was not readily available on what was actually happening even in nearby concentrations of

German-held Soviet citizens. If his own situation was different, the Soviet citizen concerned may well have remained in relative ignorance of the great maltreatment of his compatriots by the German authorities.

Furthermore, both Soviet propaganda and the mass Inertness in the USSR led to a poverty of individual thinking and information. This makes it less implausible that a Soviet citizen would not have a clear view of the doctrines of Hitler, of *Mein Kampf* or the National Socialist regime. Finally, there is the role that hope always plays in the logic of compromise. Particularly in the case of the convinced anti-Stalinist vanguard, there was a powerful desire to believe that if German policy was abominable at the moment, it was bound to improve. Indeed, throughout World War II the Soviet opposition movement remained a hotbed not only of such speculation but also of the wildest rumors, reflecting eternal faith in a change for the better. Each month, each week, probably each day, new theories and new rumors were eagerly propounded and circulated on which hope could feed. New German appointments, new official declarations, changes of heart in high places were conjured up in generous quantities. In part this was done — a not insignificant feature — by those German officials who for reasons sincere or not sought to bolster up the hope.

Fear of official Soviet reprisals was perhaps the common denominator among Soviet defectors, particularly the higher-ranking ones. Even at the very outset of the Soviet-German conflict, even in its most critical phase for the USSR, Stalin issued categorical orders against surrenders. He threatened soldiers, and particularly officers, with dire consequences if they fell into German captivity. Surrender was considered an act tantamount to unwillingness to fight to the last drop of blood. Therefore it was treason, in accordance with the deep-seated Communist conviction that there is no ground whatsoever between *active* loyalty and *active* opposition.

Nor was return to the USSR made more attractive by the defector's last image before capture. In that last image, two factors stood out above all else: the vast chaos and the conviction that German victory was assured. Both these factors receded before the first year of the Soviet-German conflict ended. But, particularly to the leading Soviet defectors, the last image of the USSR was this grim universal chaos and the initial certainty of German triumph. Such a memory could be highly conducive to taking the first step.

To begin with, it is far easier to decide to help overthrow one's native regime if its early demise seems assured anyway. And not in all instances need this help imply cowardice or opportunism, though certainly these were involved in some instances. Some defectors, although they would be unwilling to ally themselves with Hitler Germany in a drawn-out struggle involving great dependence on this ally, also hoped to remain more independent of their German "ally" if the Soviet regime was overthrown speedily.

As part of their last image of the USSR, many defectors were deeply shaken and disaffected by the inability of the Soviet apparatus, and particularly of the top leaders, to meet the initial attack effectively. To them this failing of the government apparatus was as much an eye opener as anything else that occurred at the time. This, they said, was particularly so since for years the Soviet regime had urged great effort and even greater sacrifices upon the population to prepare them for an outside attack.

The final explanation of the first step is one that permeates all the others. It is that outstanding trademark of the Soviet citizen, the well-nigh completely instinctive, nonspontaneous adjustment to the "party line" of the moment: Inertness. Inertness had made the Soviet national, politically disoriented, bewildered and far from self-reliant, maximally susceptible to an action like collaboration with the Hitler regime. And as the effect of Inertness was as a rule nearly complete within the USSR, so now the emancipation from the external symptoms of Inertness was striking and rapid. This great sense of vacuum and their search for new affiliation explain the swiftness with which the Soviet soldiers, only recently paralyzed by Inertness, now enlisted in German undertakings and embraced new anti-Stalin doctrines.

Once the shell of Inertness dissolves, the Soviet individual readily becomes intensely, even fanatically, resentful of the extreme oppression that pervades all Soviet life, oppression that Inertness had adapted him to while within the USSR. It is therefore a striking feat of backward projection that many a Soviet exile will bitterly deny and resent any suggestion that his present anti-Stalinism was not full-blown within the USSR and also perhaps not generally shared there. Closer questioning by this writer on many occasions revealed that only following German capture did coherent and compelling anti-Stalin emotions become crystallized. Resentments and ill memories of course existed all along. The abuses and cruelties of the Soviet system are far too universal to spare any of its populace. But only the loosening of Soviet-imposed external passivity gave free rein to these ever-present anti-Stalin potentials.

In summary, the leaders' first steps toward Nazi collaboration is a compound of political anti-Stalinism, professional and personal resentment, and the impact of Inertness and of the Other Germany. In the case of the rank-and-file Soviet defector, the drive to survive Nazi atrocities in the prisoner-of-war camp must be added, and the factors enumerated in this case tend to a reverse order of importance.

So devastating has been the impact of totalitarianism on the individual, so extensive and basic have been the inroads of the regime into his psyche and mores, that this first step, endlessly alien and complex though it appears, is typical rather than atypical for the Soviet citizen. Even if a future upheaval should be vastly different from World War II, the Soviet national's act of defection will inevitably be far more complex, far more alien, and far less predictable than many an American today hopes.

To repeat, individual defection occurs not primarily because of political anti-Stalinism. This is borne out not only by an analysis of the first step of wartime "nonreturners" but also by the trickle of postwar "defectors" out of the Soviet zones of Germany and Austria. Here, too, the essentially nonpolitical consideration of survival — fear of arrest for past misdeeds or present ties with German women — stands out. This does not mean that the nonpolitical impetus for individual defection is not exchanged for strong political motivation after the break with Soviet life — or that postwar defectors would not have been more numerous but for increasingly draconic Soviet reprisals and travel restrictions, and the lingering memory of the United States returning to the Soviet authorities the wartime and postwar defectors seeking asylum in the West. But as matters stand, the initial source of individual defection during both periods appears to have been nonpolitical.

What, then, of the third major form of native anti-Stalinism, organized opposition?

In terms of the world's preoccupation with the Soviet regime, and particularly with its strength and its future, few topics can be of more immediate interest than organized opposition to Stalin. What are the sources of such Soviet opposition?

Aside from speculation, our sole clue lies in the past record of opposition. This is one of the most secret and least studied phases of Soviet history. Our knowledge of it is severely limited. The two major sources are official Soviet material and the testimony and activities outside the USSR of key figures such as Trotsky, General Krivitsky, and Vlasov.

If all thirty-five years of the Soviet regime are surveyed, the following major sources of organized opposition may be surmised. First, there are those whose opposition was of pre-Soviet origin. In addition to the "White" partisans of the Tsarist regime, this includes the partisans of the February Revolution, the active adherents to the Russian Orthodox Church, the pre-Soviet intelligentsia, and those individuals whose social and economic origins were suspect in the eyes of the Soviets. Pre-Soviet opposition has declined progressively, especially after the Bolshevik victory in the Civil War.

Far more pertinent is the opposition that has arisen since the Soviet regime came to power. Here one can specifically identify two groups. One of these came from within the government. Such leading Communist Party figures as Trotsky, Kamenev, Zinoviev, and Bukharin clashed with Stalin on ideological grounds. An indeterminate number of lesser party members opposed the regime for ideological reasons or because of intraparty rivalries and power struggles. Outstanding figures like the suddenly executed Marshal Tukhachevsky suggest the Red Army as a source of opposition. The second post-1917 group is that outside the government. Dissent arose within the ranks of the technical and professional intelligentsia trained after 1917. Some national minority groupings are clearly an opposition source, as is the peasantry. So in general is that body of persecutees, Communist and non-Communist alike, who were arrested or otherwise repressed without prior participation in any opposition alignments.

But beyond such general observations, the whole subject remains shrouded in mystery. Whatever unrest or uprisings have taken place, the Soviet government has been highly successful at keeping the facts from the outside world. The exceptions, including the famous sailors' uprising at Kronstadt and the wave of unrest which in the 1930's accompanied rural collectivization, merely serve to underscore how little is known. And these known instances are pathetically few and pathetically unsuccessful. It is important to add that to date all available evidence speaks against widespread organization among the groups affected by the Great Purges of the late 1930's. Passive disaffection there was. Individual defection occurred. And unquestionably groups within the Communist Party and also within the Red Army and the nationality sphere considered organized opposition. But such consideration evidently did not pass the initial stage of discussion and tentative planning. If in some instances organized opposition reached a more advanced stage, these instances must have been tragically few and tragically unsuccessful. Neither the Soviet trial proceedings nor the testimony of Soviet "nonreturners" offers evidence to the contrary.

This means that organized opposition did exist, to the extent both of local unrest — notably during collectivization and in nationality areas — and of informal preliminary discussion among high and middling party, military, and nationality leaders. But in neither instance did organized opposition reach any significant proportions before being wiped out by the Soviet government.

It may be concluded that the Vlasov Movement in World War II was the outstanding single instance of Soviet opposition, at least since the Civil War ended in the early 1920's. Its considerable organizational and propaganda cadre, the 50,000 Soviet citizens in its last-minute military formation, the minimum of half a million and the possible maximum of over a million armed Soviet citizens who but for outside interference might have vastly swelled its ranks — all this makes the Vlasov Movement a unique instance of organized opposition against Stalin.

Having noted this, the next step is to inquire into the implications of the Vlasov Movement's unrivaled place in Soviet history. To begin with, the Vlasov Movement was made possible by a general war. Moreover, both its leadership and a major portion of its mass base originated at that stage of the general war when the Soviet government had lost control, and its defeat looked distinctly feasible. This fact, and earlier deductions from Inertness and the first step, lead to a crucial consideration.

As in 1941, the Stalin regime is apt to disintegrate only if so hard a blow is struck that its hold over the country is relaxed for a significant period. No grouping within the USSR has emerged to date that is likely, in case of Stalin's death, to compete effectively with his official heirs. Therefore such a decisive blow would perforce be a World War III. This study suggests that only when the opponent's military forces pierce the Soviet heartland as deeply, or as surprisingly, as did the Nazi blitz in 1941 can the shock be expected to be genuinely effective. Short of such a deep territorial — that is, land, not air — incision, little if anything is likely to suffice to create the kind of governmental paralysis that in turn releases the Inertness-bound populace from the official hold. This leads to a not irrelevant reminder. America's wartime strategic position with respect to the USSR would be far less proximate than that of Germany, which in 1941 bordered on the USSR proper from the Baltic to the Black Sea. Major military victories on the enemy's own territory would be immeasurably more difficult.

A second conclusion to be drawn from the Vlasov Movement's unique place in Soviet history is its relation to Hitler Germany. Its collaboration with Nazism was as essential in making the Vlasov Movement possible as were the initial Soviet reverses. This consideration was emphasized repeatedly by Vlasov and his associates. They felt that after Soviet opposition had failed for decades to organize itself successfully within the USSR, this must now be done outside the country. In the context of World War II and the moral and intellectual debilitation within the USSR, this reasoning led to the Vlasovite "marriage of convenience" with Germany.

In this union, in its own aspirations and decisions, the Vlasov Movement sought (subjectively) to remain independent and non-Nazi. In this it largely succeeded, despite pitfalls dictated by both its prewar Soviet context and its wartime German one. But in terms of its external record (objectively), the picture is wholly different. Its leaders and intellectuals functioned as German propagandists and its followers as German mercenaries. In retrospect, some have stressed the subjectively worthy aspirations and even actions of the Vlasov Movement. Others have concentrated on its objective record as that of a quisling tool of fascism. The whole history of the Vlasov Movement is the tragic dichotomy between its subjective and objective roles. The Western world may continue to frown at this "marriage of convenience," despite its tragic life and its tragic death. But without it there would have been no organized opposition to Stalin during World War II.

Today, too, thousands of Vlasovite survivors and postwar Soviet defectors are eager to launch organized opposition from abroad, this time with the United States as the ally. But their bitter internal cleavages, the vast technical obstacles, and above all their inevitably increasing psychological and ideological estrangement from the Soviet citizens now within the USSR — all these make the exiles a doubtful stimulant source for internal opposition.

Unless history goes counter to the precedent of three decades, organized opposition in the future will also fully develop only as the Vlasov Movement did: after Soviet reverses in general war, and through collaboration with an anti-Soviet power. Whatever limited opposition does survive within the USSR will probably be passive disaffection and individual defection, and not organized anti-Stalin movements.

Neither government practices nor political behavior in the USSR — highlighted by Inertness — make successful opposition likely in the foreseeable future. As to forms of whatever opposition does arise, the same factors make passive disaffection and individual defection appear more feasible than effective organized opposition. This leaves one major question: what light does the Vlasov Movement throw on the aspirations of Soviet opposition to Stalin?

During World War II, Vlasovite ideology — the articulated form of future aspirations — developed along three different currents. The main stream, most numerous and also least crystallized or formal, was flanked by a left and a right current.

At the "right" of the Vlasov Movement, and in control of the nonmilitary part of Dabendorf's School for ROA propagandists, was NTS. This was the old-émigré group that was founded in 1930 in Belgrade by the Tsarist emigration's second generation. After several changes, it had during World War II settled on the name of National Alliance of Russian Solidarists (*Natsionalno-Trudovoi Soiuz*). One of the most characteristic features of NTS was a trait not unlike that of some key Russian intellectuals of the latter nineteenth century. From the outset, NTS was imbued with a particular zeal for evolving and then recording in great detail, and with elaborate terminology, its position on a vast variety of historical, philosophical, political, and organizational questions. To this characteristic we owe the far more extensive record of prewar and wartime NTS positions than we have for the much less prolific and theoretical-minded wartime Soviet defectors.[1] The NTS ideology is discussed in the notes to this chapter.[2] In summary, its "solidarism" may be best compared to Russian nineteenth-century "Slavophilism." "Solidarism" may be described as "Neo-Slavophilism." The "solidarists," like the Slavophils, placed a central emphasis on intense nationalism, anti-rationalism, and Russia's unique mission. The sharpest division occurs over the methods advocated to achieve the harmonious society that both of the groups envisioned. The nineteenth-century Slavophil concept of "conciliarity" showed preference for a kind monarch ruling benevolently over an apolitical populace. This scheme of nineteenth-century Slavophils is revealingly less illiberal than elitism and corporatism, the NTS concepts of twentieth-century Neo-Slavophils.

Along with these profoundly illiberal views, along with its benevolent neutrality and actual sympathy for Franco's Spain, Hitler's Germany, and Mussolini's Italy,[3] NTS frequently emphasized something else — its concern for a society in which the individual could live in complete harmony with others and with society as a whole. This yearning for social justice and individual self-realization, together with its patriotism, made NTS palatable and even attractive to the wartime Soviet defectors. But its other ideological features placed this old-émigré group clearly in a "right-wing" camp.

The substance of NTS ideology, and the elaborate, phrase-mongering manner of presenting it, were throughout accompanied by two features: a vitalistic faith in action and self-sacrifice, and the use of centralized, streamlined methods of organization and proselytizing. This helps explain much of its wartime and postwar organizational successes.

Still further to the right in Vlasovite affairs is a fourth grouping, one that shared the NTS extremes of nationalism and conservatism without accepting its streamlining social outlook. This fourth grouping, made up of old émigrés, did not play nearly as important a role as the others within the Vlasov Movement. But it was the closest to Nazi officials and through this link sought systematically to influence the Vlasov Movement and its ideology.

The "left" current within the Vlasov Movement centers around Milentii A. Zykov. He is the brilliant ex-Soviet party journalist who first became Vlasov's ghost writer, and subsequently edited the early publications of the Vlasov Movement, *Zaria* and *Dobrovolets*. Though Zykov's disappearance in the summer of 1944 excluded him from direct participation in the composition of the Prague Manifesto, there is little doubt that his earlier influence did play a role. Whereas NTS was always highly conscious of ideology and of its extensive blueprints for a future Russia, Zykov was far more inclined to sneer at theory and to immerse himself in the grim daily activities of the anti-Stalin crusade. This does not mean that Zykov had become less intellectual or ideology-conscious. But he placed less emphasis than NTS on defining and recording his long-range ideological position. Another reason may well have been Zykov's apprehension that his "left" views could be used against him by his opponents, both German and within the Vlasov Movement.

Postwar testimony speaks of Zykov as a Marxist. Zykov often referred back to the moderate, Menshevik type of Marxism that he had heard in the home of his father, and also even more often to Bukharin's "right-wing" opposition within the Communist Party to which he had belonged in the 1930's. His "left" grouping within the Vlasov Movement had one central characteristic: a greater than average willingness to concede the necessity and constructiveness both of the Bolshevik revolution and of a number of major Soviet practices, such as state planning and even the kolkhoz system. NTS considered Marxism and socialism in general the epitome of the atheism and materialist philosophy that were fast ruining Western society. Contrary to this, Zykov and the less clearly identifiable group around him were willing to defend major premises of socialism even if, out of caution or conviction, they did not identify themselves wholly as disciples of Marx. This is illustrated by a panegyrical article that was published in the *Zaria* of July 26, 1943, on Russia's outstanding pre-Marxian socialist, Chernyshevsky.

To what extent, it may now be asked, was the Prague Manifesto influenced ideologically by the "left" and the "right" wings of the Vlasov Movement? In its identification with the early stages of the October Revolution and specifically with NEP, there is a definite proximity to the Zykov "left." In its nationalism, and in its anti-Marxism it leans toward the NTS "right." Indeed, although this is not made clear in the Manifesto, the Vlasov Movement in many ways inclined toward the same mystical and often illiberal doctrines typical of NTS. The suspicion of Western liberal institutions might also be attributed to NTS. But this suspicion was often as great with the main Soviet-bred current of the Vlasov Movement as it was in its old-émigré "right" deviant.

In general, one may look with skepticism on claims from either "right" or "left" regarding their dominance over the ideology of the Vlasov Movement. It was not a clear-cut ideology, but an amalgam of fluctuating, far from crystallized ideas and loyalties. Naturally, any current within the movement possessing either set ideas (such as NTS) or set predilections (such as those of the Zykov grouping) was bound to play a probably disproportionate role in the evolution and even in the phrasing of ideological pronouncements. Typically, the Prague Manifesto was a synthesis of three different drafts prepared by key adherents of each of the major ideological groupings: Zykov's former aide, an NTS leader who was chief instructor at Dabendorf, and an editor of *Dobrovolets* close to the Vlasovite leaders. However — and this is the basic point — the ideology of the Vlasov Movement is above all a reflection of the past and temper of its leaders and, to a lesser degree, its members, the Soviet citizens who found themselves under German control after two dozen years of Soviet existence. And it is the amorphous outlook of this intermediate grouping, intent on *non-party unity* within the Vlasov Movement far more than either NTS or the Zykov grouping, that has perforce been designated here as *the* ideology of the Vlasov Movement.

The waning of the earlier post-1917 zeal, the savage and extensive purges, the increasing monolithic routinization of life, the ever more blatantly propagandistic nature of Communist party doctrine — all these have made it increasingly difficult in recent years for many Soviet citizens to feel a positive political enthusiasm for their regime. In the Soviet defectors, these factors furthered a violent repudiation of the entire regime. Yet the system had a most profound political impact upon the populace. The ideology of the Vlasov Movement was a striking reflection of the generation within the USSR that the Soviet defectors represented. It also illustrates the remarkable extent to which the Soviet heritage is present in the Vlasov Movement.

What, specifically, are the elements in Vlasovite political thinking that might represent thinking within the USSR, and in particular the aspirations of Soviet opposition?

First of all, there is an increasing tendency abroad to disassociate progressive and libertarian inclinations in the Soviet population from the Soviet system. In doing this, some writers emphasize instead the continuing appeal of the February Revolution of 1917, which used Western democratic methods and slogans. Others concentrate on the powerful appeal to Soviet citizens of current Western ideas, material welfare, policies. Still others point to unique religious or sociological

features in the Russian past. The ideology of the Vlasov Movement indicates that although all of this may have played a role, it is the
decades under the Soviet regime that were decisive.

At a time when the USSR has surpassed all known forms of despotism, mass murder, and universal oppression, it may appear macabre
and ludicrous to contend that its political system could be the source
of genuine progressive and libertarian impulses within native opposition. And yet the Vlasov Movement suggests precisely that. How can
this be explained?

To begin with, the Bolshevik revolution in 1917 let loose a driving
surge of emotion toward liberty, equality, and fraternity. Although
subsequent governmental actions and governmental propaganda have
done much to negate and blunt its impact, the emotional surge itself
has left a deep imprint on most adult Soviet citizens. Even if to a West-
erner the passions of 1917 in retrospect may seem laden with the seeds
of present-day totalitarianism, to a Soviet citizen it strongly nourishes
his yearning for precisely the utopian New Society — with liberty,
equality, and fraternity for all — that the early Bolshevik slogans managed so well to dramatize and popularize.

Another basic consideration is that there was one period of Soviet
history which in the minds of Soviet citizens embodied much of their
image of the 1917 slogans. This is the period of NEP, Lenin's New
Economic Policy of the early 1920's. At that time, governmental re-
straints in economic life were minimized, and private activities were
given considerable independence. To a populace which, as already
noted, had largely accepted the Bolshevik revolution itself, it is this
post-1917 "liberal" period that stands out rather than either the Tsarist
era or the confused and unsuccessful tenure of the Provisional Government.

While the NEP period embodies the antistatist, *laissez-faire* aspirations of many a Soviet citizen, all of Soviet history has contributed
another basic tenet. This is a belief in the fundamental Soviet social
changes. Included here are state initiative in industrializing and controlling the nation's economy, its large-scale extension of education,
and above all its dominant role in social security, health, and welfare
— social changes which to millions even today, despite increasing
stratification and favoritism, imply an exciting upward social mobility,
a "career open to talent." This acceptance even by Soviet opposition of
the regime's basic social changes is accompanied by rejection of the
cruelties and shortcomings involved and by the desire to make a num-

ber of alterations. Nevertheless, this particular aspiration of opposition elements could conceivably facilitate post-Stalin statism. At the same time, however, it champions, at least in part, the kind of progressive social and humanitarian institutions that are also a central goal of contemporary Western democracy.

Many a Soviet citizen, accepting both the Bolshevik revolution and basic social reforms, has been either introduced by the regime to the antiauthoritarian classics of nineteenth-century Russian literature or confirmed in his interest in them. For it is one of the most striking phenomena of present-day Soviet life that, in the midst of extreme totalitarianism, the government has continued to pay homage to the great and freedom-minded works of Pushkin, Lermantov, Gogol, Turgenev, Chekhov, Tolstoy, as well as Herzen, Belinsky, even Bakunin. In doing so, the Soviet government is motivated by its propaganda considerations. It believes that the harnessing of these nineteenth-century giants of Russian culture for Soviet didactic purposes is both feasible and preferable to attempting their total prohibition. Nevertheless, the continued great popularity and accessibility of pre-Soviet Russian culture means that distinctly nonauthoritarian notions and ideals filter into the minds and hearts of millions of Soviet citizens.

Paradoxical though this may appear, it is thus the Soviet regime itself that provides Soviet opposition with its libertarian impulses and slogans. But the Soviet regime determines opposition ideology in another way, a far more negative one. If the Vlasov Movement is at all typical — and in this instance it may be assumed to be wholly so — the Soviet heritage leaves a large element of authoritarianism in the ideology of opposition.

Specifically, the authoritarianism in opposition ideology manifests itself above all in its attitude toward central authority, toward the government. This attitude is one of investing it with a maximum of power. Checks and balances, pluralism, nongovernmental centers of political power (parties, trade unions, and so on) and of economic power (private ownership of other than minor trade and manufacture) enjoy little confidence. This means that the Soviet heritage makes a political organization other than statism well-nigh inconceivable to most Soviet citizens — including those in opposition and those with genuinely libertarian yearnings.

Authoritarianism in opposition ideology may also be observed in the intolerance and impatience — and benign ignorance — of other viewpoints. This attitude has typified the Vlasov Movement and also the entire political life of the postwar exile community. Again, this authoritarian trait prevails among these same anti-Stalinists who very genuinely dream of a libertarian freedom for each individual in a post-Soviet society.

Lastly, authoritarianism took one other familiar form in the case of the Vlasov Movement: extreme nationalism. Some of this nationalism stems from the inevitable homesickness of exiles. Another source is the strikingly strong pride not only in the homeland itself but also in the industrial and the social and educational achievements of the Soviet period. Something else is crucial here, as it has been throughout the world in the past century. This is a defense mechanism against Western Europe (and now the United States), its pace, its leadership, its ever alien ways. Ambivalent and yet strident, this attitude marked the old Russian intelligentsia no less than it did Vlasovite ideology.

In general, its potentially or actually illiberal attitudes and blueprints emanated almost as much from the Soviet-bred "left" and the main stream of the Vlasov Movement as from its frankly elitist and corporatist émigré group, NTS. What else should be expected from citizens of so authoritarian a social system as the totalitarian USSR? Authoritarian practices, authoritarian morality, authoritarian intolerance — and authoritarian ignorance and sense of superiority over things foreign or otherwise alien — this Soviet heritage could not but leave its mark. Present-day Soviet exiles usually cannot themselves perceive this, and angrily resent and deny it, but an ugly heritage it nevertheless is. Thus in the nationalism of the Vlasov Movement too easily and too often its deep patriotism, its unswerving loyalty to the cause of the liberation of their peoples were twisted into chauvinism. At times, Vlasovite nationalism degenerated into xenophobia and anti-Semitism. Anti-Semitism is one of the more serious charges lodged against the Vlasov Movement, though it has as often been as vigorously denied. A detailed recital of the postwar charges and rebuttals by key polemicists such as the Mensheviks Aronson and Nicolaevsky [4] is omitted, but the nature and the degree of anti-Semitism existing in the Vlasov Movement are discussed in the notes to this chapter on the basis of extant issues of *Dobrovolets* [5] and other wartime data.[6] In brief, an analysis leads to the following conclusion: despite anti-Semitic references, there is nothing in the public pronouncements of the Vlasov Movement to indicate that anti-Semitism was an *integral* part of Vlasovite ideology. This is borne out by the fact that every non-Nazi wartime German official close to the Vlasov Movement whom I interviewed stated that the movement, by and large, was not anti-Semitic. For important contemporary corroboration, we have a striking complaint made in 1945 by Dr. Taubert of the Propaganda Ministry: "The Vlasov Movement is not National Socialist. . . The Vlasov Movement is a thin tincture of liberal and Bolshevik ideologies. Also important is that it does not fight against Jewry and in general does not recognize the Jewish question." [7]

Gradually a pattern emerges from the Prague Manifesto, from aspirations expressed or implicit in the Vlasov Movement's actions and pronouncements. At least in broad outline, it represents the ideological position to be expected of Soviet opposition.

On the one hand there is authoritarianism. This is in line with both the aspirations and the authoritarian features of the Vlasovite ideology. Here advocacy of the state as the holder of most power — political, economic, and social — combines with the skepticism and intolerance toward alternate views and schemes. On the other hand, we find here a problem unsolved so far by the Western parliamentary democracies. This is the psychological and emotional problem of making the individual feel a meaningful part of a free community.

This preoccupation was uppermost in Vlasovite thinking on the future. It was the ever more universal preoccupation with the welfare state. As elsewhere in the world, the Vlasovites' welfare state foresaw a government responsible for measures and institutions guaranteeing the social and economic welfare of the population.

The customary rubrics of capitalism and socialism are not applicable here. Today the welfare state is cutting across capitalism-socialism frontiers, a major reason why both terms are increasingly debilitated. For the welfare state refers to the *social controls* over a nation's economy and not to the *forms of ownership*. That is why to date the welfare state has been fairly compatible with both private-ownership capitalism and nationalized-economy socialism, although in fact modifying both. At the same time, the traditional features of nineteenth-century parliamentary democracy — individualism, institutional pluralism, libertarianism — are increasingly socialized under governments predominantly capitalist (the United States) as well as socialist (Great Britain after World War II). And Soviet defectors show little attachment for either of the terms. The Soviet heritage makes much in capitalism seem cruel, materialistic, hypocritical. The same heritage, by linking the terms "Socialism" and "Marxism" to the Soviet regime, have made both concepts (and also the concept of class warfare) repugnant. It is the welfare-state features of capitalism and socialism, in their contemporary state forms, that find strong backing. The libertarian features of both are frequently, although far from universally, misunderstood, questioned, cast aside.

What emerges in the Vlasov Movement's ideology is a mixture. Taking our definitions from the *Oxford English Dictionary*, democracy, "a social state in which all have equal rights," is here combined with authoritarianism, or being "favorable to the principle of authority."

A heady mixture this, and perhaps seemingly nonsensical. And yet it is an all-important mixture, not only for the present analysis of Vlasovite ideology but for many areas of the world today. Everywhere, one great question hangs over the immediate future. Which element will prevail in the inevitable mixture between traditional parliamentary democracy and the welfare state: authoritarianism or democracy?

The Vlasov Movement reflects the Soviet-bred predilection for a non-Western form of the welfare state. From this fact, and from parallel manifestations of intolerance, dependence on authority, and chauvinism, a conclusion is warranted. The Vlasov Movement's welfare-state blueprints showed a greater authoritarian than libertarian tendency.

Whether a similar authoritarian tendency will prevail in future opposition movements cannot be hazarded. The common Soviet heritage, the decades of Soviet totalitarianism favor such a conclusion. This heritage may be at least partially reversed if anti-Stalin currents within the USSR are accompanied by vigorous, and yet understanding, libertarianism in the outside world. To what extent such a libertarianism will exist (or how successfully it will have adjusted to the apparently unavoidable spread of the welfare state), and what effect it will have on a Soviet-bred generation of anti-Stalinists, must remain a subject for prayerful hope and speculation. But the Vlasov Movement suggests that future opposition ideology will continue to combine libertarian aspirations with authoritarian impulses, both focused on the welfare state. In this combination, the ideology of opposition reflects almost completely the values and experience of Soviet life.

No elaborate rhetoric is required to emphasize the grim, possibly tragic urgency to the United States, and to the whole non-Soviet world, of the problem treated in this book. If World War III does not come upon us in the next few years, this will be so in large measure because of Soviet opposition to Stalin, and the understanding of this opposition both by Stalin and by the non-Soviet world. If war does come, its outcome will depend to a considerable extent on the same precise understanding by both sides of just what opposition is likely to arise within the USSR, and under what circumstances. Lastly, whether a post-Stalin Soviet area will evolve toward freedom or will instead degenerate into more dictatorship or a bloody, chaotic Time of Troubles — this, too, will be immensely affected by the world's understanding of its aspirations, problems, and currents.

It is therefore highly desirable, in conclusion, to inquire what the present case study of World War II and of the Vlasov Movement suggests regarding the relation to Soviet opposition of the United States, as the leader of the free world.

Since World War II, official American policy and operations on Soviet opposition have been channeled increasingly through the U. S. Government's ever-growing program of anti-Soviet propaganda — Psychological Warfare.[1] In the spring of 1952, the Secretary of State went to the extent of declaring that the "campaign of truth [a synonym for Psychological War-

Chapter XIII
Soviet Opposition
and
the United States

fare] is the central part of our foreign policy today." [2] Psychological Warfare is generally defined as propaganda adapted to war and to the special wartime audiences: enemy, homefront, neutrals, allies. [3] In turn, the purpose of propaganda remains "to influence mass attitudes on controversial issues." [4] During and since World War II, Psychological Warfare has become the domain of three rapidly growing and also increasingly overlapping American groups. These are the Psychological Warfare personnel of the U. S. Government, the practitioners of mass communication (writers, publishing and broadcasting executives, and specialists in public relations and advertising) and lastly the analysts of mass communication: academicians in the areas of sociology, political science, and psychology, and commercial specialists in market research and public-opinion measurement. [5] Today, U. S. Government propaganda abroad is carried out principally — but far from exclusively — by the Departments of State and Defense and the Central Intelligence Agency. To coördinate these agencies, the Psychological Strategy Board was established in 1951. It operates under the President's top-level National Security Council. [6]

Two international organizations, established to counter similar Communist ventures, are also part of the Psychological Warfare picture. One of these is the International Confederation of Free Trade Unions, in Brussels, formed to oppose the Communist-controlled World Federation of Trade Unions. The other is the Congress for Cultural Freedom, with main offices in Paris. It was founded after the 1950 conference in Berlin of anti-Communist intellectuals, to combat Soviet "peace" campaigns and also the "neutralism" among West European and Asian intellectuals. A key role in American propaganda among Soviet satellites in Eastern Europe is played by the National Committee for a Free Europe. It is the parent body of the Crusade for Freedom and of Radio Free Europe. Its lesser-known sister organizations are the Committee for a Free Asia and the American Committee for the Liberation of the Peoples of Russia. The latter was activated in 1951 to support propaganda activities by Soviet exile anti-Stalinists, and the same year sponsored three conferences in Western Germany (Füssen, Stuttgart, Wiesbaden) to bring together the key émigré political organizations. Early in 1952, the chairmanship of the American Committee for the Liberation of the Peoples of Russia was assumed by Admiral Alan G. Kirk, until then U. S. Ambassador to the USSR. [7]

In terms of the United States and of its present policies, this study suggests two basic conclusions on Soviet opposition itself which are of most immediate concern. Both of these basic conclusions differ considerably from prevailing American opinion, official and otherwise. The first conclusion emphasizes a striking phenomenon: the great ambivalence of attitudes toward the world's principal antagonists, the USSR and the United States.

The vastly complex attitude of native opposition to the Soviet system may be broken down into four component parts. The most articulated one is rejection of terror, of the Soviet police state. But as important in the total picture is another component part. This is the continuing impact of the ideas and aspirations of the Bolshevik revolution of 1917: its humanitarian idealism, its craving for fundamental (and anticapitalist) social reorganization, for equality and — a paradox today — liberty for all. In many ways this aspect of Soviet opposition, the urge for a new social system built around a noncapitalist welfare state, makes anti-Stalinists feel closer to the otherwise abhorred Soviet regime than to the capitalist, antirevolutionary West. The same is true of another component part. This is the strong nationalism, a self-conscious pride and sensitivity regarding the international status of their homeland. Lastly, much of Soviet opposition appears to share with the regime its body of authoritarian political mores. This again deepens the gap between Soviet anti-Stalinists and the still largely individualistic parliamentary West.

It would therefore be a cardinal error if Americans continued to assume — as probably most do today — that the aspirations and attitudes of Soviet opposition were wholly against the regime, and wholly — or even predominantly — on the side of the anti-Soviet bloc. This counsels against the United States' relying on propaganda weapons which, although currently in use and perhaps successful elsewhere, are alien to Soviet anti-Stalinists and the population in general. Among such questionable weapons are exclusively American conceptions of Communism, capitalism, and democracy. So are many of the exile anti-Stalinists from the USSR. Although these exiles will vehemently deny it, ever-increasing estrangement from their homeland is becoming a prevailing characteristic. Inexorably, this estrangement followed the years and even decades of absence, the bitter frustrations and unreal passions of exile existence. And even the trickle of current defectors undergoes a rapid transformation in the same direction. Even more bewildered than the nineteenth-century peasant immigrants of Oscar Handlin's *The Uprooted*, lonelier still than the nineteenth-century exile intellectuals of Alexander Herzen's *My Past and Thoughts*, their thoughts are soon channeled and articulated anew. All too often this is done not by themselves, however, but by the still alien terms and theories of the exile world and of the anti-Soviet world.[8]

As questionable for reaching the Soviet population may be appeals centered around Russia's democratic February Revolution of 1917. A recent example of such appeals is the one issued on its thirty-fifth anniversary by seventy-five prominent Americans, ranging from United States Senators to Herbert Hoover and Norman Thomas.[9] The February Revolution, superseded after only half a year by the Bolshevik *coup d'état*, inevitably remains an attractive symbol to the free world. But the years following the French Revolution and even those after the Nazi period have shown conclusively that lengthy and basic upheavals — not excluding the Soviet regime — become accepted by the native population. Throughout modern history, such mass acceptance has been with reservations and modifications, rather than wholesale. Nevertheless, past symbols such as the February Revolution are not likely to have the living meaning and attraction to the present-day Soviet population that many an American believes.

An obverse warning regarding the content of U. S. Psychological Warfare, its message to the USSR, is contained in the case of Zykov, the Soviet ex-party journalist and Red Army commissar who in World War II became General Vlasov's brilliant political aide. In his activities under Nazi aegis, Zykov remained clearly close to Soviet ideology. His was the Communism, Marxism, Leninism of Bukharin's right-wing opposition in the Soviet Communist Party of the 1920's and 1930's. In present-day terminology, Zykov was akin to a Titoist: a Communist anti-Stalinist. Yet in wartime Germany a number of both Nazi and non-Nazi officials perceived the desirability of anti-Soviet propaganda being conducted — at least in part — from a vantage point as close to the Soviet as Zykov's. Part of the German approach was undoubtedly cynicism about all ideology. Another component was the empirical shrewdness of propaganda practitioners like Goebbels. Yet a further element must have been the Nazis' own radicalism toward non-authoritarian Western society. This anti-democratic radicalism, and the traditional Hitlerian use of the term Socialism — they, too, made it easier for German officialdom to use freely and extensively a man of Zykov's outlook — and of his haughty, non-servile temperament. In contrast, America's current propaganda appears reluctant to give even limited scope to a Zykov-like approach. It is highly questionable whether today Zykov would be allowed to spread his Communist brand of anti-Stalinism.

Also doubtful, in its present form, is the new Cold War interest in the many nationalities of the USSR. This American interest, growing rapidly in the last years, centers around the nationalities as a prime source of centrifugal, separatist opposition — and hence as a promising focus for Psychological Warfare. The nationality problem, long neglected by Western specialists, is one of the most complex and subtle in the USSR. In brief, the heart of the nationality problem may be described as a double paradox

It is a paradox, for one thing, that the Soviet régime has at the same time immeasurably weakened and immeasurably strengthened the development of the national components of the country. In the weakening of the evolution of Soviet nationalities, the forced post-1917 absorption and Bolshevization of nascent independent republics was only the first step. Since then, the pattern has been one of recurrent purging of local leaders and intellectuals, together with a resettlement, education, and employment policy which has scattered thousands and even millions far from their native area. This in turn furthered at least partial assimilation and new cultural attachments in predominantly Great Russian areas. As a concomitant, the government's efforts toward both industrialization and greater central control through importing specialists of Great Russian origin have accelerated the pre-1917 trend which made the cities of the non-Russian areas predominantly Great Russian in population. When the purges and the two-way resettlements are combined with a governmental policy which ignored or actively worked against the possible economic self-sufficiency within national areas, then it is clear that the capacity of Soviet nationalities to either seek or sustain independence has been seriously sapped. But now we come to the paradox. It is also the Soviet government which largely brought about the considerable national self-consciousness which remains in evidence. It accomplished this in part through the much-heralded cultural autonomy of Soviet nationalities. This is true although strict limitations on content reduced this to national dances, costumes, music, and selected epics — in effect, folklore autonomy rather than cultural autonomy. As important has been the Soviet government's continuing organization of its administrative districts in terms of its national areas. Although such a structuring has been accompanied by repeated removals of local leaders and populations, as well as increasing replacement by Great Russians, the effect has nevertheless been to maintain and reinforce extensive national self-consciousness.

The other paradox is this. During and since World War II, centrifugal anti-Stalin movements of Soviet nationalities found leadership, ideology, and material support from the outside. Aside from the Moslem underbelly of the USSR, in Central Asia and parts of the Caucasus, Soviet defectors on the whole did not manifest any decisive separatist sentiments at the time of leaving Soviet control. The initiative came either from post-1917 émigrés or, in the case of the Ukraine and Byelorussia, from intellectuals of the smaller Western areas held by Poland until 1939. It is these non-Soviet leaders who had the driving conviction in separation — total, unconditional, and without plebiscite — from a post-Stalin USSR. This conviction was usually combined with near-racial antipathy toward all Great Russians. It is significant that initially the Soviet-bred defectors did not manifest either the separatism or the Russophobia. But it is no less significant that so completely had the act of defection stripped them of reference points by which to live, so much of their remaining values (and also outside material support) was in terms of their nationality, that these Soviet defectors in large numbers accepted the outside separatist leadership. Another reason is that the non-Soviet leaders had monopolized much of émigré politics during and after World War II. The alternatives, too, were either unpalatable (Great Russian nationalists such as NTS, Kerensky, or the monarchist *Rossiia*) or (as in the case of the wartime Vlasov Movement) shortlived and discouraged by the authorities.

The history of the Vlasov Movement itself contributes to a middle-ground formulation regarding separatist sentiment among Soviet defectors. The picture has of course been greatly confused by the German and Vlasovite propaganda which identified the Vlasov Movement with the nonexistent ROA Army and the scattered half million to a million *Osttruppen* of all Soviet nationalities who in theory (and at times in apparel) made up this huge phantom "Vlasov Army." Many wartime German sources added to the confusion when they spoke of "Vlasov's Cossack Army." After the war, Western descriptions often either repeated the Cossack theme, or spoke of the "Vlasov Army" as being a Ukrainian one. Both descriptions are completely erroneous. No statistics are available on the national composition of Vlasov's small KONR Army. But eyewitness testimony suggests a make-up akin to that of the USSR itself: approximately 50 percent each of Great Russians and various categories of non-Russians.

Totally apart from the KONR Army, Ukrainian, Caucasian, Cossack, and Turkmen military formations existed under usually intensely separatist tutelage. While the Vlasov Movement stood for a *post-victory* settling of the issue *inside* the USSR, the separatists groupings insisted on *immediate* recognition of their native area's post-Stalin independence. But this is not conclusive regarding the composition of either the KONR Army or the separatist formations. Assignments to both, as well as to the remaining bulk of mixed *Ostbattailone*, were decided by German authorities and rarely by the Soviet defectors themselves. Many of the non-Russians in the Vlasov Movement were of the assimilated type, the partially or completely Russified, which is becoming widespread within the USSR. On the other hand, a considerable segment of the Soviet nationals embraced the outlook of the non-Soviet separatists. Thus the history of the Vlasov Movement and of the parallel German-sponsored units indicates the presence among non-Russian defectors from the USSR of *both* separatist and nonseparatist tendencies.

In turn, our second paradox brings out an important point. Even though today citizens inside the USSR are probably passive on the nationality issue or in the process of Great Russian assimilation, the same need not remain true in time of upheaval, chaos, general war. World War II shows that at such a time the bewilderment and vacuum caused by the dissolution of Soviet authority may well impel individuals toward that which is least unfamiliar even if long dormant: nationalism. With it come the centrifugal urges of separatism. This suggests that Americans should neither underestimate the Soviet nationalities' potential explosiveness nor, on the other hand, exaggerate it — and misplace it in time. It would be as erroneous to count on articulated separatist sentiments in time of peace as it would be to preclude their swift flowering in time of upheaval. Meanwhile, at least as much attention is warranted by "Soviet patriotism," the spread of nonparticularized nationalist bonds to the USSR as a whole. To repeat, one form this Soviet patriotism is likely to take is extreme self-consciousness (and pride) regarding the standing of the USSR in world affairs.

The Soviet population's intense national sensitivity — even among anti-Stalinists — also casts serious doubt on an interpretation of World War II that has gained in popularity in Germany as well as in the United States. According to this interpretation, Germany would have triumphed in 1941–1942 if Hitler had followed the more moderate *Ostpolitik* toward the Soviet population of his non-Nazi diplomats and military. If only Hitler had made a clear-cut distinction between the people and the regime, if he had not forced the people into the arms of the regime — then the Soviet population would have backed even Hitler against Stalin. In the course of the war, however, Soviet citizens on both sides of the front — including Vlasov — opposed and resented hardly less than Hitler these Utilitarian dissenters from official *Ostpolitik*. The reason is that, like Hitler, the Utilitarians were not willing — or able — to pay the high price for Soviet mass support. They, too, revealed little concern and even less sympathy for the aspirations and real independence of a post-Soviet area. They, too, preferred not the relatively stubborn, uncoöperative collaborators like Vlasov but the careerists and mercenaries among old émigrés and the recent defectors from the USSR. Aside from momentary and partial support, such an externally subtler approach holds little more promise than Hitler's *Untermensch* extremes. It was Hitler himself who insisted on this at the revealing 1943 conference on Soviet defection. Recalling that Pilsudsky had established his country's independence in World War I after collaborating with Imperial Germany, Hitler rejected Vlasov outright as a similarly independence-minded collaborator. For unlike the Utilitarians. Hitler perceived at least in part (and in his own manner acted upon) what is this study's first basic conclusion: the population of the USSR is profoundly nationalist and no less Sovietized, and therefore exceptionally unreceptive to Germany's New Order (or the American Way of Life.) [10]

This study has detailed the amorphousness, the amorality, the opportunistic dexterity to be found in the wartime Vlasov Movement. But alongside — and beneath — these Soviet-bred traits, these concomitants of the individual political atrophying of Inertness, there looms large in the USSR a national self-consciousness and a tangible, even if not articulated, body of basic aspirations. Indeed, what is in fact illustrated by the German experience in World War II is the opposite from the currently popular interpretation. It shows conclusively that neither the smoothest outside propagandists — many Utilitarians were such — nor the most powerful war machine can afford to slight these national attachments and basic aspirations. Hence to persist in the prevailing belief that it was principally Hitler's atrocities which prevented German triumph, rather than near-universal disregard by German officialdom of the Soviet population's own aspirations, is to court serious American misjudgments on how Soviet citizens can and should be approached.

The second basic conclusion also runs counter to the view generally accepted in the United States. Contrary to the widespread American faith in the extent of Soviet opposition, potential if not actual, it is its weaknesses that this study's findings emphasize again and again. So does the entire history of the Vlasov Movement and of related World War II manifestations. To be sure, the presently opaque and muted Soviet opposition — and especially passive disaffection — remains a key factor in the USSR and hence in world affairs. But the second basic conclusion of this study is that in the foreseeable future, organized anti-Stalin movements — the decisive form of Soviet opposition — will not displace the present regime in time of peace. For its success, the opposition requires major Soviet reverses (on Soviet soil) in a general war, together with large-scale and politically skillful support from the military opponent.

This conclusion grew out of our reëxamination of the Soviet response to the German invasion of 1941. Contrary to the prevailing American interpretation, the principal cause of the vast initial Soviet retreats and surrenders was not anti-Stalin sentiment but the invader's seeming dissolution of Soviet authority. It was the resulting chaos, magnified by the all-important paralyzing Inertness of the Soviet populace and officialdom, which explains the German triumphs. And only after such triumphs, and not before, could Soviet opposition to Stalin have become an active and perhaps decisive factor. Today, however, the situation is radically altered. Even if solution of the Soviet-American conflict is sought through a major war — an approach which in the past has aggravated innumerably more problems than it resolved — there can be no assurance of what is the Soviet opposition's foremost prerequisite: a *successful* invasion *on land* into *major* areas of the USSR. For at present the USSR is far better geared not only militarily but also geographically and propaganda-wise than it was against the German surprise attack of 1941. The Soviet system, too, appears distinctly more stable and more viable than is generally believed in the United States. As long as this is so, internal opposition to the Soviet regime will remain of only secondary importance.

In peace and in war, the American public and the U. S. Government cannot ignore the great significance and desirability to the free world of Soviet opposition to Stalin. But it is equally important not to overestimate or oversimplify its potentials — and its rejection of the Soviet system.

# Appendixes

# Appendix I

# GENERAL VLASOV'S OFFICIAL BIOGRAPHY [1]

It is the unknown Russian soldier, who voluntarily took up arms against Bolshevism, and who finally decided to give vent in armed struggle to the hatred which for twenty-five years had been accumulating against the bloody Stalin regime, who laid the foundation of the Russian Liberation Movement.

It arose spontaneously; spontaneously because it ripened at the bottom, because it was the natural answer of the people to the whole policy of Bolshevism. Force can be opposed only by force. Many understood this, and as soon as an opportunity presented itself, millions of Russian people, deliberately withdrawing from the war, surrendered as prisoners, and hundreds of thousands enrolled as volunteers to fight against Bolshevism. But this was only the first stage.

To strengthen and furnish a foundation to this spontaneously arisen movement, it was essential to cement it ideologically, to give it a banner. It was essential to enter upon the second stage.

Against Bolshevism, but for what? Against collective farms, but perhaps for the landlords? Against the inhuman penal system of Bolshevik state capitalism, but perhaps for the factory owners? A more or less precise answer to this question had to be given; the outlines of the coming New Russia had to be sketched. On December 27, 1942, Lieutenant General Andrei A. Vlasov issued an appeal, in which he clearly defined the aims and problems of the struggle of Russian men and women against Bolshevism.

From this moment on, the name of General Vlasov was indissolubly linked to the Russian Liberation Movement. Any movement, of whatever size or in whatever field it may originate — be it in the field of politics, art, or technology — is always connected with a name or with several names. These names always carry the masses along with them, become banners for them. That is what the name of General Vlasov became. And this proved

[1] Osokin, *Andrei Andreevich Vlasov*, 1944. A note on the inside back cover, typical of Soviet publications, states that the work was published in 3000 copies, in the month of August. V. Osokin is the *nom de guerre* of a former Red Army officer who became Vlasov's aide-de-camp in Germany and now lives in South America. For an earlier English translation, see Fischer, "General Vlasov's Official Biography." For a copy of this publication, I am indebted to B. A. Yakovlev, Director of the Institute for the Study of the History and Institutions of the USSR in Munich, Germany, and co-editor of the volume of biographical essays by World War II exiles from the USSR, *Thirteen Who Fled* (New York: Harper, 1949).

that the Russian Liberation Movement had become stronger, that it had become an ideologically integrated, a purposeful, movement.

In the complicated and confused political situation of today, millions of Russians who find themselves on this side of the front have discovered a name with which they can identify their fate, their hopes for the future. To define their position, these people say: "I am a Vlasovite." Vlasovite — this one word enables them to come to an understanding with each other.

Disputes flare up around the name of Vlasov. By all possible means Soviet propaganda strives to blacken his name, tries to stamp it with the infamous stigma of traitor, and labels him German spy and hireling. In the Red Army, lectures are given on the subject: "General Vlasov — traitor to the Motherland." On this side of the front rumors circulate among Russians in labor camps, in volunteer units, in service units of the German Army, often clumsy, often provocative, often contradictory. It is said that Vlasov is a stooge for Stalin, that ROA is a Bolshevik Fifth Column, that Vlasov has long ago been flown to Moscow, that he has been killed by Bolshevik agents; — and finally, that Vlasov is the person on whom God has laid the task of saving the Russian people from Bolshevism, and that services are being held in Russian churches for the preservation of Vlasov's life and the victory of his cause.

Who, then, is Vlasov? How does it happen that a former Soviet general has taken the path of open struggle against Bolshevism and become the leader of this struggle?

Andrei Andreevich Vlasov was born on September 1, 1900, in the family of a peasant of the village Lomakino in the province of Nizhni Novgorod. His grandfather was a serf. Vlasov's father sought to give his children an education.

"Learning is not something to carry on your back — it's real wealth, to be made use of," he was fond of saying.

As soon as the eldest son Ivan was old enough, his father enrolled him in school, and afterwards sent him to a teachers' seminary in Nizhni Novgorod. This, however, was a strain on the household's limited means. The family increased in number (Andrei was the youngest, the thirteenth child), and the tailoring in which the father was engaged failed to alleviate the situation. Andrei was able to enter school, and later a theological seminary, only because his brother Ivan provided for him. Upon completing his course at the seminary, Ivan had become the first village teacher of peasant origin in a district of 300 kilometers. With the aid of Ivan, Andrei completed school and the theological seminary. But he still had to pursue his studies on a scanty subsistence, living a hand-to-mouth existence in a corner which he rented from the family of a hack driver on the outskirts of Nizhni Novgorod. While enrolled in the upper classes at the seminary, Andrei started to earn money by giving lessons, tutoring children of petty officials and the poorer merchants.

The February revolution and the October *coup d'état* found Vlasov a
student in the fourth year of the theological seminary. Like the overwhelming majority of the people, he at that time did not envisage clearly the
platform and program of the Bolsheviks. The Bolsheviks promised peace,
land, freedom; they promised to abolish the obstacles to education; they
brought with them the destruction of class distinctions, of caste rigidity
which had made Andrei suffer so much in school and in the seminary.
Could one say that this was bad?

In 1918, Vlasov entered the first-year course of the Agricultural School
at Nizhni Novgorod University. But the times were not right for studying.
The young Soviet Republic was living through difficult days. In the East,
the army of Kolchak had captured Perm and threatened Viatka; in the
South, the Volunteer Army had surrounded Tsaritsyn, aiming to cut off
wheat and oil from Red Moscow; in the West, Yudenich was gathering
forces; in the North, the British were landing. Inside the country, surrounded on all sides, reigned the policy of War Communism. Everything
was concentrated in the hands of the state. Without permission from the
government it was impossible to get housing and it was unthinkable to
travel by railroad. In the villages, the food-requisitioning detachments were
carrying on, taking from the peasants bread for which they paid with
worthless currency. On the roads, road-block detachments were catching
smugglers and speculators. The last economic resources were being used,
the last human reserves were being mobilized.

In the spring of 1919, Andrei Vlasov was drafted into the 27th Volga
Infantry Regiment, but he did not stay there long. In a few weeks he was
sent from the regiment to the first officers' school of the Red Army. The
course was short. In four months Vlasov was sent to the Southern front as
a lieutenant.

In this period the army of Denikin, having suffered a decisive defeat near
Orel and Voronezh in the latter part of October 1919, was rapidly rolling
back South. The headquarters of the Southern front, located at that time
in Kharkov, sent Vlasov to one of the regiments of the 2nd Don Division,
which had participated in the operations on the rivers Don and Manych.
Here, under combat conditions, Andrei A. Vlasov carried out in practice
his military knowledge. There also he found the way to the Russian
soldier's heart: a warm, tender word toward a subordinate, concern about
his living quarters, food, and clothing, the desire to give the soldier even
the smallest pleasure, but along with this, the severest requirements and
harshness toward those who showed even the least neglect and carelessness
toward duty. This method always made Vlasov the favorite commanding
officer, and the unit which he commanded became the most exemplary
unit.

Early in 1920, the whole of the Ukraine and the Northern Caucasus were
cleared of the White Army, but clouds hung again over the young Soviet

Republic. In the Crimea, Wrangel was gathering strength; in the West, Poland began military action. The 2nd Don Division was transferred to the Northern Caucasus, to the Wrangel front.

At this time, Vlasov was already a company commander, but he did not stay long on this assignment. In a few months he was transferred to the headquarters of the division and became Deputy Chief of Staff for Operations.

This work was not to the liking of the young, energetic officer. After some time, he found himself in charge of the cavalry and infantry reconnaissance of one of the division's regiments.

In November 1920, the Red Army conquered the Crimea. The liquidation of the Wrangel front ended for Vlasov the period of combat action in the Civil War. It is true that in the Ukraine armed groups of bandits frequently continued to exist and operate in units until 1922. Action against them was already of an episodic character and was carried out by separate detachments. Vlasov was a commander of one of these detachments, fighting the bands of Makhno.

During the Civil War, Andrei A. Vlasov had devoted all his energy and strength to the struggle against the White movement. In that period he deeply believed that the Bolsheviks were bringing happiness, freedom, and bread to the Russian people, and that the Soviet government would give Russia advanced legislation and universal education. It is true that rumors were reaching him of the Kronstadt rebellion, of the unrest among peasants opposing the policy of War Communism, of the terror of the Cheka, but nevertheless, at that time he found justification for the policy. It seemed to him that the country was waging a cruel war, that all means had to be used to achieve victory, that rigid authority must be maintained, and that afterward everything would be settled more to everyone's liking.

In the period from 1921 to 1923, the Red Army shrank from 6,000,000 to 600,000. Officers were demoted from the command of regiments to command of companies, divisions were reduced to regiments, and regiments to battalions. Vlasov, who, by this time, had come to love the military profession dearly, decided to devote all his life to it. He was named a company commander.

Under Andrei A. Vlasov's leadership his company soon became outstanding. The Chief of Staff of the Red Army, Pavel P. Lebedev, while inspecting the North Causcasian military district and attending parade practice, personally thanked Vlasov for the excellent training he had given his men.

Soon thereafter, Vlasov, on the day of the fifth anniversary of the Red Army, received an inscribed silver watch, and in 1924 was named commanding officer of the regimental school of the 26th Infantry Regiment. He remained at this post for four years. In 1928, he was sent to Moscow to the Advanced School of Infantry Tactics, for Red Army officers' training. In 1929, after completion of the course, he again returned to the regiment, in the capacity of battalion commander. In 1930, he left his regiment and took up duties as tactical instructor in the Leningrad Refresher School for Red Army officers.

In 1930 Vlasov also joined the Communist Party of the Soviet Union. In the same year he was appointed to the Advanced School for Military Schools' Instructors, organized by the Central Administration of Military Training Establishments. The method of teaching tactics used by Vlasov at the Advanced School was highly appreciated by the director of the training establishments of the Red Army, Kazansky. Having returned to Leningrad with commendations he again took up his work in the School as deputy to the director of the training section. Soon, however, he was transferred to the mobilization department of the Headquarters of the Leningrad military district. Here he remained until 1933.

But this work did not satisfy Vlasov. He still felt drawn to the line units, to more active work with people. In 1935, he was transferred to the post of deputy director for combat training in the Leningrad military district. To him this work was much more interesting. While inspecting the district together with the Deputy Commander of the Leningrad military district, General Primakov, they discovered that the 11th Infantry Regiment of the 4th Turkestan Division had been very inadequately trained. The commanding general, to straighten out the combat schooling of the regiment, named Vlasov as regimental commander. After the regiment was brought into top shape, Vlasov was given command of the 137th Infantry Regiment, which soon occupied the first place in the Kiev military district. Following this, Vlasov was named Deputy Commander of the 73rd Division.

In 1938, Timoshenko, at the time commanding the Kiev military district, drew Colonel Vlasov into work in the headquarters of the district. Vlasov became the director of the department of combat training. But he worked only briefly on this assignment. In the fall of 1938, he was called to Moscow and was appointed Chief of Staff to the military advisor in China, General Cherepanov.

The Soviet Union was following a dual policy in China. On the one hand, by supporting Chiang Kai-shek with arms, and sending its military specialists to his army, the Soviet Union strengthened the side fighting Japan and thereby its own position in the East. On the other hand, the Soviet Union, by supporting the Communist elements and by leaning on the Chinese Red Army (Chu-Teh and others), was kindling a struggle inside China, seeking to sovietize it. The increasing threat on the part of Japan forced the Soviet government to alter somewhat its policy in China in the direction of increased military aid for Chiang Kai-shek. It was just in this period that Vlasov arrived in China.

The Chief of Staff of the military advisor had the task of lecturing to the commanding group of the Chinese army on the foundations of operational tactics. Andrei A. Vlasov carried out this task and some time afterwards was assigned the extremely responsible position of military advisor to General Yen Hsi-shan.

About this general, who was governor (in fact the unlimited ruler) of two gigantic provinces in Northern China, Shansi and Suiyuan, there was a saying in China: "Nobody can count money in China like Yen Hsi-shan." Sly, calculating, a subtle diplomat, Yen Hsi-shan, having formally recognized the supremacy of Chiang Kai-shek, actually failed to carry out his orders, and, hiding out in the mountains, preserved his forces. Vlasov was given the difficult task of forcing Yen Hsi-shan to take part in the offensive which Chiang Kai-shek was at the time intending to undertake.

Vlasov spent four months with Yen Hsi-shan. Under incredibly difficult conditions, he confronted Yen Hsi-shan with the necessity of joining in the operations against the Japanese army. By using great diplomatic ingenuity and displaying all his effervescent energy, he obtained from Yen Hsi-shan permission to visit his regiments and divisions.

After the recall of General Cherepanov to Moscow, Andrei A. Vlasov performed the duties of chief military advisor to Chiang Kai-shek. In November 1939, after the arrival of the new advisor, General Kachanov, Vlasov was recalled to the Soviet Union. For his good work in forging together the Chinese army, Chiang Kai-shek decorated Vlasov with the Golden Order of the Dragon.

In this period the Soviet Union was living through tense days. The Bolsheviks made a sharp about-face in their foreign policy. After futile negotiations with the Anglo-French delegation, a treaty of friendship and non-aggression was concluded with National-Socialist Germany in August 1939. The war in the West which began shortly after this created favorable conditions for increasing Bolshevik influence. The Bolsheviks threw off the mask of love of peace, and showed their true face — the face of Red Imperialism. Taking advantage of the fact that the Polish army had actually ceased to exist after the decisive blow inflicted on it by Germany, the Soviet Union occupied Western Ukraine and Western Byelorussia. After this began the "working over" of the Baltics, and the conflict with Finland ripened.

The Soviet Union had to enter the war. But all was not well with the Red Army. The Yezhov purges (*Yezhovshchina*), which had rolled over the land, had a detrimental impact on the army, hitting hardest the highest commanding personnel. The Red Army was in effect beheaded.

Involuntarily, doubts crept in: were all these commanders really enemies of the people? Would all the gigantic efforts, the incredible deprivations which the Russian people had undergone and were undergoing prove to be for nothing — all because of the Stalin regime? Perhaps the grandiose international ideas, for the sake of which the Russian people were suffering, were not a necessity to them?

The Russian people had sacrificed much, very much, and from this Andrei A. Vlasov drew the following conclusion: whether these international ideas would prove themselves lasting or not, the Russian people would live on and must be strong. Therefore, the Motherland must prepare to the utmost for the impending war, and then the Russian people could take a vote of their own. With this in mind, Vlasov went all out in the work of strengthening the organization and combat training of the Red Army.

In December 1939, Vlasov was named commander of the 99th Infantry Division. This was a frontier division (in the Peremyshl area) and was therefore rapidly brought up to wartime strength. The composition of the division was not homogeneous; suffice it to say that it contained representatives of forty-four nationalities. It was difficult to fuse these elements, but under the guidance of Vlasov the division soon improved its fighting qualities sharply. This was aided strongly by the fact that, after the pitiful experience of the Finnish war, the Red Army introduced a number of measures aimed at increasing discipline and strengthening the authority of the commander. For the first time in all his long years of service in the Red Army, Vlasov was in sole charge of a unit.

In order to familiarize the soldiers and officers of his division with combat conditions, Vlasov undertook numerous marches with the division, and in all weather conditions carried out firing exercises after the marches.

In the fall of 1940, inspections of divisions were made in military districts throughout the Soviet Union to determine the best-trained division of the Red Army. The 99th Infantry Division was recognized as the best in the Kiev military district. The People's Commissar of Defense, Marshal Timoshenko, who was in the district at the time, after getting acquainted with the combat training of the 99th Division, found that this division was also the best in the whole Red Army. The division was awarded simultaneously three challenge banners of the Red Army: for the best infantry regiment, the best artillery regiment, and the best division as a whole. Vlasov himself was decorated with an inscribed gold watch by Timoshenko, and with the Order of Lenin by the government.

In December 1940, Vlasov was called to Moscow. The General Staff of the Red Army had called a meeting of the highest commanding personnel, at which meeting General Meretskov, at the time Chief of the General Staff, was to present a report on the tasks for the coming year in the army's combat training. Andrei A. Vlasov was to report along with Meretskov. He was to tell of his experiences in the combat training of his division, the best in the Red Army. In his report he made an appeal to rear the soldiers in the spirit of Suvorov, pointing out that it was essential to make use of the age-old experience of the Russian army, while taking into consideration contemporary developments.

In January 1941, Vlasov was named commander of the 4th Tank Corps (Lwow). By this time it was absolutely clear that the coming war would be, to a large extent, a war of tanks. Despite the fact that the Soviet Union had been the first country to introduce major tank detachments into its army, the Red Army at this time found itself lagging in this field. (This was because General Kulik, upon returning from Spain, had been able to convince Voroshilov, and through him Stalin, of the uselessness of large tank detachments, and these had been disbanded.) The experience of the fighting in Poland, and later in France, proved the importance of large tank detachments, and their reëstablishment in the Red Army was begun at high speed. The war found Vlasov commander of the 4th Tank Corps. In the first days of the war it became clear that the Red Army was not prepared, despite the fact that it readied itself for war for twenty-three years.

Vlasov's corps on the Ukrainian front received the first blows of the enemy. It was soon greatly weakened, however. By order of the front commander, General Kirponos, Corps Commissar Vashugin, a member of the War Council, removed from the corps one and a half tank divisions, intending with this group to strike a counterblow. Owing, however, to his incompetent leadership the tank group wandered into a swamp, where all tanks had to be abandoned. Vashugin shot himself.

Vlasov, with the remnants of his corps, under the blows of the mailed fists of German armored-tank units, fought his way out of encirclement to Berdichev. The corps was in a very poor condition. There was a shortage of fuel, there were no spare parts, and as a result expensive tanks had to be left behind owing to minor disrepair. On the 16th of July, Vlasov with the remnants of his corps reached Berdichev, having by this time fought up to twenty heavy battles with the enemy's first-class forces.

On the 17th of July, Budenny called Vlasov to Kiev. Vlasov was given the assignment of commanding the 37th Army and the Kiev fortified area, as well as the garrison. In conditions of total disorder and demoralization, Andrei A. Vlasov defended Kiev during August and September. Only after Kiev found itself in a solid encirclement, out of which there was little hope to escape, did Vlasov send a radiogram to the Kremlin, pointing out the uselessness of further defense. From Stalin he received the order to withdraw.

The retreat was a difficult one. For 550 kilometers, all the way to Kursk, they battled through the encirclement. In Voronezh, Vlasov was received by the commander of the Southwest sector, Marshal Timoshenko, and by Khrushchev, member of the War Council. He was named deputy service chief of the Southwest sector. In this work he came face to face with the chaos and disorder reigning behind the front. There was no army clothing, there was a shortage of ammunition and of vehicles. And all this after one of the richest countries in the world had for twenty-four years prepared for the war, after 170 million people worked only for defense during that time. Whose fault was this? In Vlasov's mind the answer gradually ripened, terrible in its certitude: the Bolshevik regime alone was to blame.

In November 1941, Vlasov was called back to Moscow. There was panic in the capital: factories and organizations were being evacuated, old men and students were hurriedly herded together to dig trenches and antitank ditches. Under such conditions Vlasov was faced with the difficult task of forming the 20th Army and defending Moscow. With his army Vlasov was able to stop the enemy and push him back from the approaches of Moscow to Rzhev. For this operation he was decorated by the Soviet government with the Order of the Red Banner and promoted to the rank of Lieutenant General.

In March 1942, Vlasov was named deputy commander of the Volkhov front. General Meretskov was commanding the front.

A shock army had been created for the liberation of encircled and starving Leningrad, but this army was itself soon surrounded and cut off from the rest of the front. For the alleviation of the resulting difficult situation, Vlasov flew to the surrounded army in an airplane. Assuming command of the army from General Klykov, he was able to break the German ring and form a narrow corridor (three kilometers in width), connecting the army with the rest of the front. But he lacked the forces to widen the breach and to evacuate the army. General Meretskov did not come to the rescue. The corridor was again cut off, and the ring around the besieged army tightened even more.

Vlasov saw that the hungry army (Red Army men were receiving 50 grams of bread a day), encircled in forests and swamps, was doomed to perish. Here, among the starving Red Army men, who were rotting alive in the swamps, the same question which had agitated him before came to him with particular sharpness: What for? Why were Russian people perishing?

If in the first days of the war it was still possible to explain the panic and disorder in the army by the unexpectedness of the military blow, one thing was now perfectly clear to Vlasov: the Russian people did not want to fight and die for Stalin and Bolshevism. For the first time in their history the Russian people surrendered into captivity and deserted *en masse*, using any trick to remain in the areas occupied by the German army.

Thus the people voted for the Soviet regime. . .

During all his earlier work in the Red Army, Vlasov did not separate himself from the interests of the people. In the Civil War he had defended the Bolsheviks because he believed that they would give the people a happy life; in peacetime he had actively helped to build and fortify the Red Army because he believed that the only country with a Dictatorship of the Proletariat needed a strong army, needed a force able to defend its gigantic, unprecedented construction.

But now to continue his previous work meant to go against the interests of the people. Fighting under such conditions became useless, unnecessary, even harmful.

Andrei A. Vlasov together with the remnants of his army was captured. Many ideas were thought over in captivity, much received a different evaluation, and the conviction that Bolshevism was the worst enemy of the Russian people, that it must be torn out by the roots from the soil of Russia became hardened and crystallized. If Bolshevism dies, then the Russian people will live; if Bolshevism survives, then the Russian people will die out, will cease to exist. Either — or. There was no third choice.

Many ordinary Russians had already begun an armed struggle against Bolshevism. They were pointing the way, they were setting an example.

In December 1942, Andrei Andreevich Vlasov placed himself at the head of the Russian Committee, organized by him, and thereby became the head of the spontaneously conceived Russian Liberation Movement.

Around Andrei A. Vlasov Russian patriots are drawing together, people who have set as their life's aim the destruction of Bolshevism and the creation of a new free Russia. The process of gathering strength is taking place, and cadres are assembling.

The time will come when the Russian Liberation Army, thoroughly prepared, will strike a blow at Stalin, at Bolshevism. And this blow will be supported by the multimillion masses of the Russian people on the other side of the front.

The Bolshevik period was a bloody dead end in the history of Russia. The Russian people in huge numbers have already understood this. But they do not desire a return to the past, they want to complete the people's revolution begun in 1917.

Against Bolshevism, but not for the old regime, not for the reëstablishment of autocracy, but for the New Russia.

For a Russia without Bolsheviks and capitalists!

To the peasants — liberation from the kolkhoz slavery!

To the workers — a normal working day and an income guaranteeing not only a minimum living wage, but also the satisfaction of the cultural demands of modern man!

To the intelligentsia — freedom of creative endeavor!

To the peoples of Russia — the freedom of developing their national cultures, and self-determination!

To yourself, your family, and your Motherland, freedom of labor and creative effort!

Such is the will of the people.

The Russian Liberation Movement expresses this will. That is why, repeating the words of Andrei Andreevich Vlasov, we say:

"Russia is ours!
Russia's past is ours!
Russia's future is ours!"

# Appendix II

# HITLER ON SOVIET DEFECTION [1]

Conference of the Führer with Field Marshal Keitel and
General Zeitzler, on June 8, 1943, in Berghof

*Present:* The Führer
Field Marshal Keitel [2]
General Zeitzler [3]
Lieutenant General Schmundt [4]
Colonel Scherff [5]

*Started:* 12:45 o'clock

*Keitel:* From the general perspective, the question of policy toward war prisoners who enter the Volunteer Helpers' (*Hilfswillige*) units and the national detachments on the Eastern front, my view is the following. General Zeitzler can make corrections if I err. The propaganda which Vlasov is developing on his own has offered a possible foundation for our large-scale propaganda, at present under way under the code name "Silver Stripe." To encourage desertion we have issued leaflets which were coordinated word for word with Reich Minister Rosenberg.[6] He approved and authorized them. In May the campaign therefore got started at full speed. After they come over, they are now being given special treatment. That is the policy-setting Order 13, which is being used as a leaflet.

*Führer:* I've seen that leaflet.

*Keitel:* It has been provided that deserters be received in special camps, treated particularly decently.

---

[1] *Besprechung des Führers mit General Feldmarshal Keitel und General Zeitzler am 8. 6. 1943 auf dem Berghof* (Conference of the Führer with Field Marshal Keitel and General Zeitzler, June 8, 1943, in the Berghof). For the full German text, see Fischer, "Vlasov and Hitler." The text is reproduced in Russian in Dvinov, *Vlasovskoe Dvizhenie* pp. 89–102. Three brief extracts in English may be found in *Nazi Conspiracy and Aggression*, III, pp. 959–960. The 22-page typed German original was kindly made available to me by Boris L. Gourevitsch, a Russian émigré writer, from the New York Library of the World Jewish Congress.

[2] Field Marshal Wilhelm Keitel, Chief of the Supreme Command of the German Armed Forces (*Wehrmacht*) throughout World War II.

[3] General Kurt Zeitzler, Chief of the General Staff of the German Army.

[4] Lieutenant General Rudolf Schmundt, Senior *Wehrmacht* adjutant to Hitler.

[5] Colonel Walter Scherff, official historian of World War II in Hitler's headquarters.

[6] Alfred Rosenberg, Minister for Eastern (Soviet) Occupied Territories and NSDAP *Reichleiter* for ideological indoctrination.

*Führer:* That is all right.

*Keitel:* And that they be able afterwards to apply for various possibilities, firstly as plain laborers, secondly as Volunteer Helpers, and thirdly also for the national detachments (*landeseigene Verbände*).

*Führer:* That we don't have in it.

*Zeitzler:* No, not in leaflet 13.

*Keitel:* That was mentioned afterwards in the implementation orders. They are to be transferred after a given time. The General of the Eastern Troops (*Osttruppen*) [7] has announced this, I have learned. If they have proven themselves during a probationary period they may apply for such employment and in some cases will be employed accordingly, that is, as Volunteer Helpers as well as in the national detachments.

Now, this large-scale propaganda is based on leaflets signed by the National Committee or the Russian National Committee. In them we say a number of customary things: "You will get good care, will be treated decently, will get work, will get back to your homeland" — and as regards the future — "The German Reich will not maintain the system of Bolshevism later, will not retain the land confiscation, etc." But the decisive factor in these leaflets, so important that I must report it to you once more, is that we also say: "Come over — if you come over, you can enter the Russian Army of Liberation." It actually says that in the leaflet.

*Führer:* That leaflet should have been shown to me earlier.

*Keitel:* We have to correct it in that respect now. That is one of the points which was not decisive for those people but which has played a role nevertheless.

*Führer:* That's not so tragic, either. In all of it I see only one thing today, and it is the deciding thing for me: We must avoid creating a false conception on our own side. A differentiation must be made between the propaganda which I make in Russia and what we ourselves will do in the end.

*Keitel:* That is, what we do behind our front.

*Führer:* And, above all, what we believe. We must avoid the spread, even in the slightest, of the notion on our side that in this way we could really find a compromise solution, somehow akin to, say, East Asia with its "free" or "national" China. We have people who have some such vague idea. On this, I have to point out that this "national" China has up to now not furnished a single useful soldier.

In this field we already received a tragic lesson in the world war, with Poland, as I've already pointed out recently. This business, too, got started there originally through the Polish legionnaires, who at first seemed entirely

[7] General of Eastern Troops; supervised Soviet volunteers serving in the *Wehrmacht*. In 1943, Lieutenant General Ernst Köstring, Moscow-born ex-German military attaché to the USSR, was named to the post, which was redesignated "General of Volunteer Units."

harmless. But the situation suddenly reversed itself. We must also realize one thing: I have always found that there are only a very few people who keep a completely clear head throughout a war and who don't follow some sort of illusions. The saying that a drowning man will grasp at a straw is unfortunately only too true. This holds true not only for the drowning man but for all men who are endangered. A great proportion of men who are endangered, then see things no longer in their true light.

Here I could refer to memoranda which I got from Berndt [8] at the time of the retreat, when people suddenly abandoned reality and, immediately after the landing of the Americans and the English in North Africa, embraced a vision: "That's where our salvation lies, that's where we must march." Sheer madness, against which at that time I defended myself so strongly, but which suddenly befogged and beclouded people entirely. In the gradual spread among us of something like this — in that alone I see a danger.

We have plenty of these people. There's a multitude of them in the Rosenberg shop. But unfortunately we have them in the armies also. They are former Baltic nobles and other Baltic Germans. But they are also earlier Ukrainian émigrés, who have meanwhile become assimilated in Germany, sadly enough in part were even made citizens, and who naturally are happy to see the German liberation campaign. But in the back of their minds are not our vital national aspirations but their own goals.

That's how it was in 1915–1916. When the great crises occurred in 1916 — in the West the Verdun miscarriage, the Somme battle, the Brusilov offensive in the East, Roumania attacking us, etc. — at that time too everyone unquestionably lost his head, unfortunately even the soldiers. The only man who at that time opposed this was Bethman-Hollweg, who tried constantly to swim against the stream. But he was simply crushed by the military arguments. Ludendorff said later: "I was also informed through military channels that I would get 500,000 men. This was wrong. Unfortunately I was misinformed." Every thinking person would have said immediately: You will get not 500,000 men for the fight against Russia, but rather an army established by the Poles to proceed against Germany and Austria and to liberate Poland, if the opportunity presents itself. For every nation thinks of itself and of nothing else. All these émigrés and advisors only want positions for later on.

*Keitel:* On that, I can report that when the Polish state stood against us, German officers — like one regimental commander of a cavalry regiment, who had been in the German army and fought for four years — went over to Poland to take over the leadership of a detachment: old Polish nobility.

*Führer:* The danger is today exactly the same. Order 13 is in any case completely out of the question. The other things, too, can only be done

---

[8] Alfred Ingomar Berndt, young German journalist who rose rapidly as protégé of Goebbels' Propaganda Ministry.

under one condition: that not the slightest practical consequences will ensue; and, above all, that we avoid the extension of an outlook such as I have unfortunately already encountered in several gentlemen. Even from Kluge [9] I have heard several times: "We can do it immensely more easily if we build up a Russian army." I can only say this: We will never build up a Russian army, that's a phantom of the first order. Before we do that, it is much simpler that I get the Russians to Germany as workers. That is much more decisive. I don't need a Russian army, for in any case I would have to maintain a German cadre.

If instead I get Russian workers, it will be of more help to me. Then I can release Germans, and then I can reschool Russians. The best thing is to utilize the Russian laborer for work in Germany. Naturally we'll have to provide for him differently if we assign to him more exacting tasks.

The only decisive thing is that we don't evolve an outlook which says: "Perhaps, one day, when we are badly off, all we'll have to do is found a Ukrainian state. Then everything will be in order, then we'll get a million soldiers." We'll get nothing, not one man. That's an illusion just as it was in the other war. That way we would be committing the greatest lunacy. From the outset, we would be abandoning the whole objective of the war.

Only the other day I told Zeitzler that I had a conference with Rosenberg and Koch.[10] There I could establish only one thing, that naturally there exist tremendous differences between these two. Rosenberg has his political underworld crowd from his own former émigré days. Now naturally we were quite sympathetic toward these émigrés in 1919–1922, because it was said that perhaps there'll be an overturn in Russia. It turned out that all this was illusion, too. The émigrés have accomplished nothing. They have lived off us in Germany and were fed by us. As early as 1921 I had a disagreement with Rosenberg about it and told him, "Rosenberg, remember one thing: revolutions are made by people who are inside a state, not by people who are outside it." It was at that time that the Ukrainian Hetman presented himself. So I said, "Rosenberg, what do you expect from this man?" "Well, he is organizing the revolution." So I said, "Then he should be in Russia. People who make a revolution must be inside the state. It's exactly as if I were in Switzerland and said: I am organizing a revolution in Germany from Switzerland. That's downright childish. How do you visualize this?" So his answer was, "Lenin." So I said, "Lenin didn't do it. Rather it was we who ruined and smashed Russia; and it was into this shattered Russia that we brought Lenin, who could then be inside it. But one simply cannot make a revolution from outside. At that time the Tsar had been overthrown. First the Kerensky revolution had taken place. Russia

[9] Field Marshal Günther von Kluge, commander of the Central sector of the Eastern Front.

[10] Ernst Koch, Gauleiter for East Prussia and *Reichskommissar* for the occupied Ukraine.

was first ruined on the battlefield, and only then did the inner collapse follow." I tried to make this clear to Rosenberg. He has that crowd this time too.

Something else: Rosenberg is one of the keenest thinkers in all *Weltanschauung* questions. It's just this preoccupation with *Weltanschauung* questions that has given him very little contact with everyday problems.

The *Weltanschauung* problems and the everyday problems are therefore not easily reconciled. Now, naturally, both exponents came to me, the one of *Weltanschauung* questions and of grand strategy, and the other concerned with everyday problems — Koch. Koch told Rosenberg to his face: "*Parteigenosse* Rosenberg, what you are telling me is certainly very simple. But there's one thing you must admit: only if I give these people a sphere of action can I carry out the policy which you want — establishment of universities, creation of national committees, etc. If I don't give them a sphere of action then the entire work which you are doing is nothing but the storing up of revolutionary energy which must one day be unleashed against us."

Then Koch said: "It's like this — Backe [11] comes to me, and behind Backe there's the *Wehrmacht*. The *Wehrmacht* doesn't say, dear Backe, shall we negotiate whether you can provide the rations? Instead the *Wehrmacht* demands it. And at home the German people say: we also demand it. And Backe comes to me and says: you must deliver to me 5.7 million tons of grain. No one cares where I get it from, whether I get it for love or not. No one cares what I give the other fellow for it. I've got nothing to give. I have nothing to offer in return, I must simply take it. But then it is said: We need 10,000 horses and 100,000 tons of meat, and this and that. Then we just have to buy."

I have a similar case in the *General Gouvernement* [occupied Poland]. It was quite clear — the gentlemen there also had to admit that I was right. The gentlemen said, there is no economic order( *Wirtschaftsordnung*) in the *General Gouvernement*. How should there be economic order in a country where there are 120 people to a square kilometer — the French can't feed 80 people to the square kilometer. Instead, they have a pigsty in their country where all the junk from the Reich is sent in and all that is good is extracted. Everyone decides that he won't have this, that he'll buy his own stuff. Thus, the Four Year Plan buys, the *Luftwaffe* buys, the quartermasters of the separate armies buy, Speer [12] buys, and each overbids the other, pays too much, and thereby undermines the currency. Why should a Polish farmer deliver something for 12 *zlotys* if he can get 4–5 Reichsmarks for it? We've given the workers there salaries which are just laughable. In the factories they are paid in *zlotys*. With these few *zlotys* the

[11] Herbert Backe, head of the Food Ministry.

[12] Professor Albert Speer, Minister of Munitions and subsequently also Director of War Production.

workers are then supposed to buy something from a farmer, who gets ten times as much for it in marks from a lot of German government agencies. Every outfit immediately yells at you: You can't do that! What, then, should be done? Furthermore, Frank [13] says: "Besides, I have only 11,000 policemen in a land of about 147,000 square kilometers with something over 16½ million people. I need all the policemen to maintain order in Krakow, Warsaw, and a few other places. How am I to do that? Those are problems which are insoluble."

So Koch says, in turn: "Tell me, *Parteigenosse* Rosenberg, what am I to do? Should I tell Backe, I'm sorry, *Parteigenosse* Backe, I must build up an orderly, clean Ukrainian state, so I can't give you 5.7 million tons of grain. I only have 2 million or 1 million tons, and that's all there's to it. My task here is to build up the state." To that Rosenberg had no reply either. Koch said, "My dear Rosenberg, you live in the Eastern Ministry, in the beautiful world of territory organizing. I, on the other hand, am confronted every day with the task of satisfying a thousand requests. To me, my job means trying to satisfy these requests. I was put here to do that. There's nothing else I can do, either. How should I do it otherwise?"

He said: "Here I'm losing 500,000 Jews. I have to remove them, because the Jews are the element of unrest. But in my territory it was actually the Jews who were all the craftsmen. You want to establish universities and high schools now, so that people will fight against Russia. I'm not even in the position to let the worker who has to work here get his boots repaired. I can't do that, because there are no craftsmen since the Jews are all gone. What's more important, that I teach the Ukrainian to repair boots, or that I send him to the university so that you build up the Ukrainian state?"

Of course, the tremendous danger lies in this — that we will be egged on by the émigrés, who naturally look upon this as their life's task, to the point of losing the ground under our feet. Then the thing keeps slipping in this manner till in the end power is suddenly in the hands of people who don't have any political insight and who don't know what really goes on in the world.

I have experienced one thing. Among others, the reproach that partisans were active in his territory was made against Koch. To this, Koch replied: "How do you come to make me a reproach on this? Show me the army area where there've been no partisans. What do my police forces amount to? Give me enough police, then I'll do away with the partisans. Take the troops out of one army area, then you'll see whether there are partisans there or not. I am in the northern area, where there have always been bands anyway, not in the fertile area. The army too is constantly forced to make campaigns against the partisans in the army areas, as much as 50 kilometers behind the front. I on the other hand am hundreds of kilometers

---

[13] Hanns Frank, Governor General of occupied Poland (*General Gouvernement*).

behind the front and moreover have no people. With whom am I supposed to accomplish that?"

All that is theorizing, in the nebulous never-never land. That's even aside from the fact that on this we shouldn't make a commitment for the future at all. I cannot make any commitment for the future which will confront me with independent states or autonomous states. For one starts out with an "associated" state à la Poland and ends up with an independent state. It's quite clear, that would be the end of the song.

Therefore, to make sure that no wrong notions arise on our side, this matter must be handled more unequivocally. General Zeitzler has already said that it would be important for me to state my position on this to the key officers, especially the generals and fieldmarshals.

*Keitel:* Lammers [14] is putting down your views in a short memorandum. He has already spoken with me about it. I have asked him for it urgently, since it is so difficult to make this clear to our generals. I can say it with certainty since I know it from Küchler [15] and Kluge themselves. In the establishment of so-called national units and in their arming they see a relief from the unrest in the rear areas.

*Führer:* Now Zeitzler says this: There are undoubtedly such detachments which could not simply be eliminated today because they would have to be replaced by something else.

*Zeitzler:* In all, we have 78 battalions, 1 regiment, and 122 companies. Of the 78 battalions, only 47 are with the Fieldmarshal in the Ostland, Ukraine, and in the BdE. [16] Therefore, there aren't really many at the front, and they are all very much scattered in so far as they are at the front.

Then there is still a category of 60,000 men. Those are a sort of guard outfits, organized in very small units.

*Führer:* That's necessary. One can't do without such units.

*Zeitzler:* And the Volunteer Helpers are about 220,000 men. These are among the troops, almost up to "Kanonier 4, 5." One can't remove them.

*Keitel:* In the Volunteer Helpers I see neither a political nor a propagandistic nor any other problem. The thing is more dangerous in the national detachments, because they are organized in bigger units.

*Zeitzler:* There is only one single regiment. The rest are all battalions. That isn't dangerous either.

*Führer:* In my eyes the decisive thing is not the existence of such a detachment. Rather, the decisive thing is that we must not fool ourselves about what may be expected or what we will be able to concede to the other side. We must not get into a state of mind in which one day the military will again come, as in 1916, and say: "Now it's up to politics to do

---

[14] Dr. Hans Heinrich Lammers, chief of Hitler's chancellery on government affairs.

[15] Field Marshal Georg von Küchler, commander of the Northern sector of the Eastern Front.

[16] BdE: *Befehlshaber der Einsatztruppen* (Commander of Reserve Troops).

something, to create a Ukrainian state, just as a Polish state was established then." Afterwards Ludendorff was forced to say: "If I had only been told that earlier . . . my specialists, my experts told me that I would get 500,000 to 700,000 men, and this was the cause for it." For Ludendorff was blamed for the founding of the Polish state. And he couldn't shrug this off. But he alibied for it: "I did it during the crisis, because I was told that I would get soldiers."

*Keitel:* Then it may be said that we look upon the Russian Committee, the originator of the propaganda leaflets signed by Vlasov, as purely a propaganda weapon.

*Zeitzler:* There must be a strict distinction made between what goes to the enemy, where anything can be said, and what is done in the interior.

*Keitel:* I put this question specifically to Rosenberg once again: "What are your plans regarding the Russian Committee? On our part they are being used for propaganda for this desertion action." Answer — "I agree both to the consolidation of these Volunteer Helpers (as he calls them), and members of the Russian, Ukrainian, Caucasian, Tartar, etc., combat units (as he calls them), under the designation, 'Russian, Ukrainian Liberation Army,' as well as to the propaganda utilization of this measure." That means, not only utilization for propaganda, but also consolidation. And that's what the Führer doesn't want.

*Zeitzler:* We're not doing that, either. The most we could do, in order to reward the people serving with us, and in order to keep them with us, is to invent something of positive value, whether it be money or a promise that they'll get something afterwards. I consider consolidation completely erroneous, and especially to the division level. Battalions are still workable — one can keep them in hand. But it must in no case go above that, except for the Cossack division, which is supposed to be very stable.

*Führer:* I would say, that once we were successfully in the Caucasus, we could surely get units, not from the Georgians, but from the small Turkic peoples.

*Keitel:* We except those, because they are the strongest opponents of Bolshevism. These Turkic legions which are only national detachments stand outside the discussion. I may mention once again that last year, in early September, we said on this score: The national detachments which have especially proved themselves in the repression of bands — that is, the companies —

*Führer:* They existed then already.

*Keitel:* — insofar as they are composed of absolutely reliable elements on a voluntary basis, are to be maintained and even enlarged. That's what we said then.

*Führer:* The enlarging is already dangerous.

*Zeitzler:* It was getting to be too much already.

*Führer:* But the enlarging must now naturally be restrained somehow since such "enlarging" has no limits. It can be interpreted one way by some people and another way by others.

*Keitel:* The General of the *Osttruppen* is also in favor of the enlarging.

*Zeitzler:* No, I'll be able to keep him in hand. Battalion will be the maximum.

*Keitel:* Now further: Their utilization for fighting at the front, or the employment of émigrés or leaders of the former intelligentsia, remains most strictly forbidden. This was specifically stated at that time. Such people must not be allowed to get in, and we have ejected them, too. I myself have conducted such an action in the Central sector (*Heeresgruppe Mitte*). There, émigrés had, through interpreter jobs, actually penetrated into leading positions, and we threw them out.

*Schmundt:* It isn't that Colonel General Lindemann [17] is wild on setting up detachments. Rather he says: "We must distinguish between propaganda to the enemy, where anything goes, and the rear areas." He says, "We have now managed to release our soldiers for the front through the fact that I alone in my harvesting district have 47,000 Volunteer Helpers. These, for example, handle my whole railroad for me; and this in return for food and lodging."

*Keitel:* Volunteer Helpers or national detachments?

*Schmundt:* Volunteer Helpers. But they are people who do these things for themselves, voluntarily, without supervision and without police. And the partisan warfare has died out. Until now, that could be done for bread and maintenance. Now Vlasov comes along and wanders around preaching national independence in the villages as well as to the Volunteer Helpers and the troops.

*Keitel:* I've already forbidden that.

*Schmundt:* Colonel General Lindemann doesn't say, as the Fieldmarshal thinks, that we want to build up on a large scale. Rather he says: "I am calling your attention to the danger. Because now the people are already asking, What is Germany's counter offer to us? Now Vlasov has whipped up in them the idea of independence. But he also has undoubtedly fought even more against the partisan warfare." But now comes the counterquestion and Lindemann says: "The moment has come when we must do one of two things. Either we make a promise to Vlasov that he will eventually get this and that — even if we don't intend to honor it — or we terminate the affair completely. Otherwise it can hit us from the rear. The people will be dissatisfied and will suddenly start, for instance, sabotaging the railroad instead of serving it."

*Führer:* I don't need General Vlasov at all in the occupied area.

*Schmundt:* But that's what he does.

---

[17] Colonel General Georg Lindemann, commander of the 18th Army on the Eastern Front.

*Führer:* That must be stopped. I need him only at the front.

*Schmundt:* The army leaders want to have this decision.

*Keitel:* It's been taken.

*Führer:* Zeitzler, we're clear about it, in the rear we don't need Vlasov. He will function only across, to the other side.

*Zeitzler:* Only across, with his name and the pictures.

*Keitel:* May I at the same time raise a question which has been urgently submitted by the *Heeresgruppe Nord* through the general staff of the Army: They request that Estonians, Latvians, and Lithuanians be put into German units as volunteers and, specifically, as German soldiers and that the vacancies may be filled that way.

*Führer:* We can't do that so generally.

*Zeitzler:* There's also the Latvian SS brigade.

*Führer:* Those are single units. But one can't do that on a mass scale.

*Keitel:* Incorporated in the frame of the army. They are not to be organized in special units as volunteers on the basis of the work-duty law, but used to fill in the existing gaps in German troop formations.

*Führer:* No, under no circumstances. That would lead to my making these units completely unsafe in the end. In that case they would have to be really hand-picked and well-trained, too.

*Keitel:* That's done in any case.

*Führer:* But if you put these people normally into a troop, it can happen that they carry in with them a terrific poison. That can't be done quite so simply.

*Zeitzler:* It's only the one division, Niedermayer, where I had proposed that we establish a ratio of 1:1. There it's astounding. Now the Russian soldiers are really training our people for digging in and in terrain exploitation. They have a way of digging themselves in and lying down that's amazing.

*Keitel:* That's the Niedermayer division, it has Turkic people. It carries the number 162.

*Führer:* Where is it, anyway?

*Zeitzler:* It is in the *Gouvernement.* I thought it unsafe, too, although Niedermayer wanted it that way. So I proposed 1:1, and it is now undergoing reorganization.

*Führer:* One thing is quite clear: we have put these units into action seriously at only a few places, and there they do not measure up to the final test.

*Zeitzler:* No, not to the final test. In the one memorandum which I have with me, it also says: "Although they are with us for 1½ years they are still not reliable to the end."

*Führer:* One can't rely on that. That's why I must say again and again: We can make propaganda across, however we like. We can do all that. But it must be understood that this must not eventually become a vision such as we had in 1916. That must not be. Above all, one thing must not happen — we can't give these units to a third man who gets them into his hand and says: "Today you work with them, tomorrow you don't." One day we would get a sort of strike slogan. That will run along the entire front. Then, suddenly, they're organized and ready to start extorting.

*Keitel:* On that, I can only report that Vlasov has been recalled. He's no longer at the front. He has been forbidden any propaganda activity at the front as well as his own propaganda activity. The only decision that remains to be taken is whether we should let the appeal of the "Army of Liberation" continue to go across.

*Führer:* Yes, there you can do anything.

*Keitel:* I didn't consider that dangerous. For *we* are the Army of Liberation from Bolshevism.

*Führer:* I am convinced that the appeal of the Army of Liberation is effective to the other side because the people don't want to fight, they want peace.

*Zeitzler:* I've put the stress on the pictures, showing how it looks in the deserter camps. One gets further with that than with political things.

*Keitel:* Now, as for the utilization of people from the deserter camps.

*Führer:* There I stand on the point of view that we transport them off and put them to work in Germany. They are prisoners of war. If I could only spare about 30, 40, 50,000 men for the coal commissar. But one would have to treat them really decently then.

*Zeitzler:* I have set as a goal that they should become decent workers in Germany. At the front one can't do much with deserters. I can put in one or another as Volunteer Helpers where there are gaps. But the mass should go to Germany as workers, to release German people.

*Führer:* I can only say that if we don't get our coal situation in order, the moment will come when I can no longer make any munitions, any explosives, when we can't make any more submarines. So it will come to be in a hundred areas. It's idiocy, but this moment would then come. It's already tragic when the Italians come and ask why we don't deliver coal. We can't because we have too little of it. That's obviously a *Schlamperei*.

*Keitel:* Then I'll inform the Reich Minister Rosenberg of your decision: that it is out of the question that any practical effect behind our front is in any way intended in these matters; that we will continue the propaganda toward the enemy with these means; that we won't let Herr Vlasov work actively in the Russian territory any more. If he wants to get across —

*Führer:* It's not that way with the others, either. We don't allow that, for example, the young son of —— [18] should make propaganda in Germany. We're not just preaching to the winds, but are making propaganda across

---

[18] The name is omitted in the original official transcript.

to our opponents. I am convinced that the Russians, the other way around, would be making propaganda across to us. It must be avoided that false hopes are raised on our side.

*Keitel:* But it is really true that the generals, especially Kluge — I know it personally from him, I've spoken with him enough about it — would see a relief in it.

*Zeitzler:* There's simply a lack of a clear decision from above. It will just have to be stated from above once and for all.

*Keitel:* Now, may I express another request in a matter which is now being worked on. After the instructions for the Volunteer Helpers are issued, there arises the question of a general concept regarding the national detachments, their composition, training, and similar things. It would be good if again we could get it first and show it to the Führer. It is now still being worked on in your organizational section.

*Führer:* Perhaps with the aid of today's stenogram — today I have put down my ideas — Lammers can get the idea once more, and thereupon take care of the matter.

Furthermore, we could do something else. We could see how the affair proceeds. It would be possible, too, perhaps, to get together a part of our top commanders once more and for me to tell it to them personally.

*Schmundt:* That would be wonderful.

*Keitel:* That would be very good. I have seen that it's somewhat of a self-delusion: One hopes to receive some help and doesn't realize what sort of flea one gets into one's fur coat.

*Schmundt:* One could also tell them a part of what you, my Führer, told our allies in Klesscheim.

# Appendix III

## DABENDORF PROPAGANDA SCHOOL [1]

### OUTLINE OF COURSES

PART I: GERMANY

1. Historical survey of the development of Germany (until Versailles)

A short characterization of the period of the Middle Ages. The Empire of Otto I (the First Reich). The Reformation and the period of the Renaissance in Germany. The Thirty Years' War and its consequences. The rise of Prussia and its role in the unification of Germany. Germany and the invasion of Napoleon. The unification of Germany at the end of the nineteenth century (Second Reich). The distribution of forces in Germany at the end of the nineteenth century. The struggle of England against the growing might of unified Germany. The World War. The Versailles peace and its consequences.

2. The History of the National Socialist Movement.

The situation of Germany after the Versailles peace. The ruinous role of social democracy and Jewry. The renaissance of the German spirit through Adolf Hitler and his associates. The coming to power of the National Socialists. The renaissance and unification of Germany. Liberation from Versailles. The 25 points of Adolf Hitler and their fulfillment.

3. The Foundations of National Socialism

The foundations of the world outlook of National Socialism. The race theory. Measures for the protection of racial purity (Nuremberg Laws). The struggle with Jewry. The concepts of people and nation. "The common good is above the private good." Willingness to fight for the freedom and independence of the nation. Loyalty to the idea. The role of the state as a popular organism. The state — the holder of the highest political rights, the regulator of the economic life of the people. The meaning of the Führer system for the German people. The selection of the best for leadership. Responsibility before the leader. National unity — the basis of state might.

4. The Jewish Question

The peculiarities of the Jewish people. The Jews are alien to all peoples. They do not have a fatherland and did not sacrifice their blood for the

[1] *Biblioteka Propagandista No. 9*, pp. 5–9.

defense of a homeland. They are a people-parasite, demoralizing other peoples. The Jews are the inventors and carriers of destructive ideas. They aspire to world domination. They are war mongers.

5. The State and Public Structure of Germany

Adolf Hitler — the leader of the people, the party, and the Reich Chancellor of the state. The structure of the party and associated organizations: SA, SS, NSKK, NSF, and others. The structure of governmental organs. The organization of labor in Germany: the ministry of national economy, the ministry of labor, the Reich commissioner for labor, the head of an enterprise. The labor front. Private legal associations.

6. The Labor Question in Germany

Labor is the main value in Germany. Labor is activity for the benefit of society, it is the foundation of the well-being of a people. Any type of labor is honorable. The conditions of labor. Concern for the worker. Training of cadres.

7. Agriculture in Germany

The significance of agriculture in Germany. The peasantry — the source of the nation's strength. The situation of peasants until 1933. The increase of peasants' households after 1933. Inherited indivisible household. Measures for its protection and strengthening. The productivity of agriculture in Germany. The conditions of work in agriculture.

8. Social Relief in Germany

In Germany there are no propertyless compatriots. "The German people, help yourself." Relief organizations; social insurance, "*Winterhilfe*," "*Kraft durch Freude*," "Labor and Beauty," the German Red Cross, etc. Aid to the sick, the invalids of labor and war, orphans.

9. Family and the Education of Youth in Germany

The family is the foundation of a nation. The woman is the mother of a nation. The child — its future, its hope, its strength. Care for the woman, protection of labor. Aid to the mother, the family, and the child. The integration of school and family education. Moral, physical, and work education of youth. Youth organizations. Specialist training and the selection of the best.


Part II: Russia and Bolshevism

10–14. Brief familiarization with the many centuries of the history of the Russian people and the development of its statehood (*gosudarstvennost*).

15. Ideological Oppression in the USSR

The USSR is an ideocratic state. The ideas of world revolution, alien to the people, were inculcated in all layers of the population and all age groups. Ideological influences were transmitted through children's organizations, in school, in the army, at work, in everyday life. These influences revealed themselves in literature, music, painting, sculpture, architecture, theater, and movies, and were augmented by direct terror. The results of ideological oppression and the necessity for the spiritual emancipation of the Soviet individual.

16. The Land Policy of the Soviet Regime

The importance of the land question for Russia. The emancipation of peasants in 1861. The Stolypin reform — an attempt at a capitalist solution of the land question for the Russian people. In 1917 the Bolsheviks deceived the peasants, having promised them land. Concession to peasants during the NEP period. The rise in agriculture. The collectivization of agriculture is carried out in the interests of the International, against the will and desire of the Russian people. Losses in the process of collectivization. The unprofitability of sovkhoz and kolkhoz.

17. The Labor Question and *Stakhanovshchina*

Dictatorship of the party instead of dictatorship of the proletariat. Participation of labor in the management of the country. The solution of the labor question in the USSR. Low standard of living of the Soviet worker in comparison with the European. Exploitation and enslavement of workers. The sacrifices borne by the workers were used by Jews in the name of world revolution, an idea alien to the Russian people.

18. Soviet Intelligentsia and Culture

The destruction by the Bolsheviks of Russian culture. Social requisitions, censorship, supervision, and oppression in all forms of spiritual life. The creation of ideals saturated with an alien materialistic spirit. The influence of these ideals on the moral make-up of the Soviet individual. The concentration of Jews in cultural organizations.

19. Family, Youth, Upbringing, and Education in the USSR

The consequences of the civil war: *bezprizorniks*, impaired state of education. The leveling of the rights of women to men's, views on marriage and the family — the decomposition of the family. Communist education of children in school and in different organizations. Decline in population increase. Measures by the Soviet regime.

20. The Struggle of the Regime Against the Population

The ideas of Bolshevism are alien to the people. The struggle of the population against the Bolsheviks began in 1918 and continues until now.

All levels of the Russian people participate in the struggle. The methods of the regime's struggle against the population: lies, deceit, espionage, provocation, terror and physical elimination. The intelligentsia is subordinated to the power of the party bureaucracy and the Jewry that stands behind its back. The dictatorship of the proletariat means the oppression of the people and the use of its energies in the name of lifeless ideas.

21. Economic Policy of the Soviet Regime

The goal of industrialization — the creation of economic independence of the Soviet Union and its preparation for a war for world revolution. The building of industry solely with this aim and without consideration of the interests of the human being. Use of the labor of prisoners in the camps of NKVD. The price of creating the "giants of the five-year plans." Industrialization led to the enslavement of the people.

22. The Foreign Policy of the USSR.

The foreign policy of the USSR is aimed at the achievement of world revolution. In carrying out its foreign policy, the Soviet regime used the Commissariat for Foreign Affairs, the Comintern, NKVD, Peoples Commissariat for Foreign Trade, the Red Army. 1917–1924 — the struggle of the Soviets for existence and recognition. 1924–1935 — "peaceful coexistence" and preparation of revolutions in other countries. From 1935 — the aggressive policy of the Bolsheviks and, as the result, a bloody war unnecessary for the Russian people, for interests alien to it.

23. Jewry in Russia.

Jews in Russia. The negative attitude to them of the population. Spontaneous Jewish pogroms. Active participation of Jews in the political parties of Russia. Jews financed the Bolsheviks before the revolution of 1917. A majority of Jews in the Politburo during the seizure of power by the Bolsheviks. The carrying out of the Jewish program of revenge against the entire non-Jewish world — the destruction of religion, national Russian culture, the elimination of the best representatives of the people. The struggle against the Bolsheviks is inseparably linked to the struggle against Jewry.

24. Russia Under the Power of the Bolsheviks

The inevitability of the revolution of 1917. The Bolsheviks came to power fraudulently. Insolent deceit of the people. Characterization of Soviet economics. Industrialization and collectivization and their results. The complete pauperization and enslavement of the people. The economy is serving world revolution. The dictatorship of VKP(b) [2] and Stalin. The absence of political rights for the people. The terror of the Bolsheviks. Unconscion-

[2] The Communist Party of the Soviet Union (Bolsheviks).

able lying of the Bolsheviks. The Comintern and the idea of world revolution. Critique of the ideas of communism. Summarized evaluation of the Soviet regime. Bolshevism is the mortal enemy of the Russian people.

25. England — the Historical Enemy of Russia

The rivalry of England and Russia. The participation of England on the side of Russia's opponents in the Crimean War, in the Russo-Turkish and Russo-Japanese Wars. The mutual relations between England and Russia during the World War. "England will fight to the last Russian soldier." The mutual relation between England and the USSR were also hostile at the outset. The English were always contemptuous of the Russian people. The present war is being waged in the interests of England and world Jewry. England wants to weaken the Russian and the German peoples in order to enslave them.

26. The Russian People and the German People

Common traits in the development of the Russian and German peoples. The establishment of contacts between the two peoples: foreign relations, trade, arts and crafts, military science.

The turn of Russia westward: the era of Peter I. The Russians and Germans from Peter I to Soviet Russia: the most important events, diplomacy, commercial ties, social-political and cultural ties. The perspectives of their amity.

27. USSR and Germany

The policy of the USSR toward Germany in the period of the Versailles republic. Sharp enmity against National Socialism after its coming to power in 1933. Anti-German propaganda and hostile acts. The role of Jews as instigators of the hostility. Talk about friendship in 1939, but in fact efforts to seize territories while Germany was engaged in war. Preparation for a war with Germany begins in 1933. Stalin and the Bolshevism headed by him are guilty of the war.

Part III. The Russián Liberation Movement

28. The Foundations of the Russian Liberation Movement

Bolshevism and the Russian people are incompatible. The task of our people is the struggle against Bolshevism, in alliance with the German people.

The Thirteen Points of the Russian Committee are the slogans of the struggle of the Russian people, the final goal of which is the creation of the New Russia and the establishment of social justice.

The translation of the Thirteen Points into life is impossible without the creation of a popular lawful state, in which the laws will be inviolable both for the citizen and for the state itself. The basis of the economy of the new state must be private property and private initiative. The state will guide the economy.

The armed force that is essential for the struggle against Bolshevism and for the translation into life of the new regime, is ROA, which is being built on the principle of unity of all peoples of Russia for the struggle against Bolshevism.

## Appendix IV

## THE PRAGUE MANIFESTO [1]

### MANIFESTO OF THE COMMITTEE FOR THE LIBERATION OF THE PEOPLES OF RUSSIA

Countrymen! Brothers, and Sisters!

In this hour of great trials we must decide the fate of our homeland, our peoples, and our own fate.

Mankind is going through an era of the greatest upheavals. The present world war is a fight to the finish of opposing political systems.

It is fought by the powers of imperialism, led by the plutocrats of England and the USA, whose power is based on the suppression and exploitation of other countries and peoples. It is fought by the powers of internationalism, led by the Stalin clique, dreaming of world revolution and the destruction of the national independence of other countries and peoples. It is fought by freedom-loving nations, who thirst to live their own way of life, determined by their historical and national development.

There is no worse crime than the one Stalin commits, of destroying the countries and suppressing the peoples who strive to preserve the land of their forefathers and build their happiness by their own labor. There is no worse crime than to subjugate another people and force one's own will on it.

The forces of destruction and slavery camouflage their criminal aims by using slogans like defense of freedom, democracy, culture, and civilization. By defense of freedom they mean the conquest of other lands. By defense of democracy they mean to force other nations to accept their political system. By defense of culture and civilization they mean the destruction of monuments of culture and civilization, created by thousands of years of other nations' labor.

For what then do the peoples of Russia fight this war? Why are they doomed to incalculable sacrifices and suffering?

Two years ago Stalin was still able to deceive the peoples with words about the patriotic liberating nature of the war. But now the Red Army has crossed the state boundaries of the USSR, forced its way into Rumania, Bulgaria, Serbia, Croatia, and Hungary, and is flooding these foreign countries with blood. Now the real character of the Bolsheviks, who continue

---

[1] The translation of the Manifesto was made from the Russian original in issue No. 1 of *Volia Naroda* (Berlin), official organ of the Committee for the Liberation of the Peoples of Russia, November 15, 1944.

the war, becomes clear. It is their aim to strengthen still more the mastery of Stalin's tyranny over the peoples of the USSR, and to establish it all over the world.

For more than a quarter of a century the peoples of Russia have experienced the burden of Bolshevik tyranny.

In the Revolution of 1917 the peoples who inhabited the Russian Empire sought to realize their aspirations for justice, general welfare, and national freedom. They revolted against the spent regime of the Tsar, which did not and could not abolish the causes of social injustice, the remnants of serfdom, and the economic and cultural backwardness. But after the Tsarist empire was overthrown by the peoples of Russia in February 1917, the parties and leaders were unable to decide on bold and consequent reforms. With their ambiguous policy, their compromises and their unwillingness to assume responsibility before the future, they failed to justify themselves before the people. The people spontaneously followed those who promised them immediate peace, land, freedom, and bread, those who advanced the most radical slogans. The Bolshevik Party promised the people a social-order system, where the people could live happily and, for this, the people made incalculable sacrifices. It is not the fault of the people that this party, after seizing power, not only failed to realize the demands of the people but, strengthening their repressive organs more and more, robbed the people of the rights they had won, and forced the people into permanent misery, into lawlessness, and into the most unscrupulous exploitation.

The Bolsheviks robbed the peoples of Russia of the right to national independence, development, and distinct characteristics.

The Bolsheviks robbed the peoples of freedom of speech, freedom of political convictions, their personal liberties, free choice of domicile, and travel, freedom of profession, and the opportunity for everyone to take his place in society in accordance with his capabilities. They replaced these freedoms with terror, party privileges, and arbitrariness toward the individual.

The Bolsheviks took from the peasants the land they had conquered, they deprived them of their right to work on their land freely, and to use the proceeds of their labor as they wished. By chaining the peasants down by means of the kolkhoz system, they made them into coolies of the state, without any rights, the most exploited and oppressed ones.

The Bolsheviks robbed the workers of their right to choose freely their profession and place of work, to organize and fight for better working conditions and wages, and to influence production. They made the workers into slaves without any rights of state capitalism.

The Bolsheviks robbed the intellectual of the right of free creative work for the well-being of the people, and with violence, terror, and bribery they sought to make them a tool of their lying propaganda.

The Bolsheviks condemned the peoples of our homeland to permanent misery, hunger, and extinction, to spiritual and physical slavery, and, finally, they forced them into a criminal war for causes foreign to them.

All this is being camouflaged with the lie about the democratism of the Stalin constitution and the building of a socialist society. No other country in the world has or ever had such a low standard of living, while the material wealth of the country is so enormous. No other country has had such trammeling of rights and humiliation of the individual personality as there has been and remains under the Bolshevik system.

The peoples of Russia have lost forever their faith in Bolshevism, where the state is an all-devouring machine and the people have become impoverished slaves without any rights. They see the terrible danger that hovers over them. If Bolshevism should succeed in establishing itself on the blood and the bones of the nations of Europe — even if only tmporarily — then the fight of the peoples of Russia, carried on for years and taking an immense toll, would have been in vain. Then Bolshevism would take advantage of the nations' exhaustion in this war, and rob them totally of their ability to resist. Therefore the efforts of all peoples must be directed at the destruction of the monstrous Bolshevik machine and at giving every man the right to live and work freely in accordance with his capacity and capabilities, to establish an order that protects the individual from lawlessness and does not permit anyone, including the state, to deprive him of the fruits of his labor.

ON THE BASIS OF THIS, THE REPRESENTATIVES OF THE PEOPLES OF RUSSIA IN FULL RECOGNITION OF THEIR RESPONSIBILITY TO THEIR PEOPLES, TO HISTORY, AND TO THEIR DESCENDANTS, WITH THE AIM TO ORGANIZE A UNITED STRUGGLE AGAINST BOLSHEVISM, HAVE ESTABLISHED THE COMMITTEE FOR THE LIBERATION OF THE PEOPLES OF RUSSIA.

The Committee for the Liberation of the Peoples of Russia has as its aim:

(*a*) The overthrow of Stalin's tyranny, the liberation of the peoples of Russia from the Bolshevik system, and the restitution of those rights to the peoples of Russia which they fought for and won in the people's revolution of 1917;

(*b*) Discontinuation of the war and an honorable peace with Germany;

(*c*) Creation of a new free People's political system without Bolsheviks and exploiters.

As the basis for the new political system of the peoples of Russia the committee lays down the following main principles:

(1) Equality of all peoples of Russia and their real right for national development, self-determination, and state independence;

(2) Establishment of a (*natsionalno-trudovoi*) system where the interests

of the state are subordinated to the task of raising the welfare and the development of the nation;

(3) Maintenance of peace, establishment of friendly relations with all countries, and international coöperation to the greatest possible extent;

(4) Extensive government measures to strengthen family and marriage; real equality of rights for women;

(5) Liquidation of forced labor and guarantee to all laboring people of the right to free labor as the basis for their material well-being; determination of wages for all types of labor that provide for a civilized standard of living;

(6) Liquidation of the kolkhozes, and gratuitous turnover of the land to the peasants as their private property; free choice of forms of land use; freedom to dispose of the products of one's own labor, abolition of forced deliveries, and annulment of debts to the Soviet government;

(7) Establishment of inviolable private property earned by work; re-establishment of trade, crafts, artisan enterpirses, and furnishing to private initiative the right and opportunity to participate in the economic life of the country;

(8) Providing the intellectuals with the opportunity to create freely for the well-being of their people;

(9) The guarantee of social justice and protection for laboring people against any kind of exploitation, regardless of their origin and their former activity;

(10) Establishment for all, without exceptions, of a real right to free education, medical care, vacation, and old-age security;

(11) Destruction of the system of terror and tyranny; liquidation of forced resettlement and mass deportation; establishment of genuine freedom of religion, conscience, speech, assembly, and press; guarantee of inviolability of persons, their property, and homes: equality of all before the law, independence and public proceedings of the courts;

(12) Release of all political prisoners of Bolshevism, and the return home of those in the prisons and camps who suffered reprisals for their struggle against Bolshevism; no vengeance or persecution whatsoever of those who discontinue their fight for Stalin and Bolshevism, regardless of whether they fought from conviction or coercion;

(13) Rehabilitation of national property destroyed during the war — towns, villages, factories, and plants — at the expense of the government;

(14) Support of war invalids and their families by the state.

The destruction of Bolshevism is an urgent task of all progressive forces. The Committee for the Liberation of the Peoples of Russia is convinced that the united efforts of the peoples of Russia will receive support from all the freedom-loving nations of the world.

The Liberation Movement of the Peoples of Russia is the continuation of years of struggle against Bolshevism and for freedom, peace, and justice. The successful end of this fight is now insured:

(*a*) By the greater experience in struggle than in 1917;

(*b*) By the existence of growing and organizing armed forces — the Russian Army of Liberation, Ukrainian Liberation forces, Cossack troops, and national units;

(*c*) By the existence of anti-Bolshevist armed forces behind the Soviet lines;

(*d*) By the existence of growing opposition forces among the people, the government apparatus, and in the army of the USSR.

The Committee for the Liberation of the Peoples of Russia regards the UNIFICATION OF ALL NATIONAL FORCES AND THEIR SUB-ORDINATION TO THE COMMON CAUSE OF DESTROYING BOL-SHEVISM AS THE PREREQUISITE FOR VICTORY. Therefore, the Committee for the Liberation of the Peoples of Russia supports all revolutionary and opposition forces against Stalin and Bolshevism; at the same time it decisively rejects all reactionary projects connected with a limitation of the peoples' rights.

The Committee for the Liberation of the Peoples of Russia welcomes Germany's help under conditions which shall not impair the honor and independence of our country. This help is at this moment the only tangible opportunity to organize an armed struggle against the Stalin clique.

With our fight we have taken upon ourselves the responsibility for the fate of the peoples of Russia. With us are millions of the best sons of our country, who have taken up arms and have already shown their courage and willingness to sacrifice their lives for the liberation of the motherland from Bolshevism. With us are millions of people, who have left the USSR and are giving their labor to the struggle's common cause. With us are scores of millions of brothers and sisters, suffering under the yoke of Stalin's tyranny and awaiting the hour of liberation.

Officers and soldiers of the Liberation troops! The blood shed in a common struggle has welded together into comradeship of battle the soldiers of different nationalities. We have a common goal. Our efforts must also be joint. ONLY THE UNITY OF ALL ARMED ANTI-BOLSHEVIK FORCES OF THE PEOPLES OF RUSSIA WILL LEAD US TO VICTORY. Do not let the arms out of your hands, fight for unity, fight supremely against the enemy of the people — Bolshevism and its accomplices. Remember, the tortured peoples of Russia are awaiting you. Liberate them!

Countrymen, brothers, and sisters now in Europe! Only victory over Bolshevism will make possible your return to your country as full-fledged citizens. There are millions of you. The success of the struggle depends on you. Remember that you are working now for a common cause, for the heroic Liberation troops. Multiply your efforts and your work achievements! Officers and soldiers of the Red Army! Cease the criminal war which is aimed at oppressing the peoples of Europe. Turn your weapons against the Bolshevist usurpers, who enslaved the people of Russia and condemned them to hunger, misery, and absence of rights.

Brethren and sisters in our motherland! Intensify your struggle against Stalin's tyranny, against his war of conquest. Organize your forces for the decisive struggle for the rights of which you were robbed, for justice and well-being.

The Committee for the Liberation of the Peoples of Russia calls all of you to unity and to the fight for peace and freedom.

*Prague, November 14, 1944*

*Chairman of the Committee for the Liberation of the Peoples of Russia:* [2]

Lieutenant General A. Vlasov

*Members of the Committee:*

Lieutenant General F. Abramov
F. Alekseev, public figure
Professor S. Andreev
Professor G. Anufriev
Lieutenant General E. Balabin
Shamba Balinov, public figure
Professor F. Bogatyrchuk
S. Bolkhovskoi, actor
Colonel V. Boyarsky
G. Gordiyenko, worker
Lieutenant A. Dzhalalov
Lieutenant General G. Zhilenkov
Major General D. Zakutnyi
Captain D. Ziiablitsky
Y. Zherebkov, public figure
Colonel Buniachenko
Colonel M. Meandrov
A. Zaitsev, Dozent

Professor A. Karpinsky
Professor N. Kovalev
A. Lisovsky, journalist
Major General V. Malyshkin
Corporal I. Mamedov
Professor I. Moskvitinov
Y. Muzichenko, author
H. Podlaznik, worker
Professor S. Rudnev
Sergeant S. Saakian
E. Tenzorov, Dozent
Major General F. Trukhin
Professor A. Tsagol
Kh. Tsymbal, peasant
Captain I. Chanukh
Ebragim Chulik, M.D.
F. Shlippe, public figure
F. Yanushevskaia

---

[2] Of the persons whose names are listed here, Vlasov, Balabin, Bogatyrchuk, Zhilenkov, Zakutnyi, Malyshkin, Rudnev, and Trukhin were members of the original Presidium of the Committee for the Liberation of the Peoples of Russia, and Muzichenko was a candidate. In addition to those listed, N. N. Budzilovich was a member and Professor P. N. Ivanov was a candidate. (Source: *Volia Naroda*, No. 1).

*Candidates of the Committee:*

Lieutenant V. Dubovets
V. Yegorov, worker
A. Kazantsev, worker
P. Lumin, engineer
D. Levitsky, public figure
Y. Rodnyi, worker

P. Semenov, engineer
Professor L. Smirnov
Professor V. Stalmakov
Professor V. Tatarinov
A. Shcheglov, soldier

(The names of some Members and Candidates of the Committee for the Liberation of the Peoples of Russia are not published in view of their presence in the territory of the USSR or for reasons of personal safety.)

# References and Notes

For references that are not complete below, see the bibliographic section, Sources on the Vlasov Movement.

## Chapter I. The Context

[1] Stalin, *O Velikoi Otechestvennoi Voine Sovetskogo Soiuza* (On the Great Patriotic War of the Soviet Union), p. 352. See the firsthand accounts of the outbreak of the Soviet-German war by a Soviet general, now a refugee in the West: Alexei Markoff, "How Russia Almost Lost the War," *Saturday Evening Post*, May 13, 1950, pp. 31, 175–178; also Michel, *Es Begann Am Don* (It Began on the Don), and Erich Kern, *Dance of Death* (New York: Scribner, 1951).

[2] Carroll, "It Takes a Russian to Beat a Russian," p. 81.

[3] *Nazi Conspiracy and Aggression*, III, p. 127.

[4] Frederick L. Schuman, *Soviet Politics at Home and Abroad* (New York: Knopf, 1946).

[5] Stalin, *O Velikoi Voine*, pp. 15–20.

[6] Robert E. Sherwood, *Roosevelt and Hopkins* (New York: Harper, 1948), p. 335; Winston Churchill, *The Hinge of Fate* (Boston: Houghton, Mifflin, 1950), p. 493.

[7] Stalin, *O Velikoi Voine*, pp. 352, 353.

[8] Carroll, "It Takes a Russian," p. 81.

[9] Hanson W. Baldwin, "What Kind of a War," *Atlantic Monthly*, July 1949; Leopold Braun, "The Myth of the Mighty Red Army," *American Legion Magazine*, October 1951; Drew Pearson, "How We Can Crack the Iron Curtain," *Look*, July 17, 1951; Hubert Pryor, "Should We Wage Secret War on Russia?" *Look*, June 5, 1951.

[10] Boris Shub, *The Choice* (New York: Duell, Sloan and Pearce, 1950), p. 59.

[11] Adolf Hitler, *Mein Kampf*, pp. 152–153; English translation, pp. 179–182.

[12] *Ibid.*, German ed., pp. 742–743; American ed., pp. 950–952.

[13] *Ibid.*, German ed., pp. 751–752; American ed., pp. 960–961.

[14] *Trial of Major War Criminals*, XXVI, 329–332.

[15] *Ibid.*, XXXIX, 369–371.

[16] *Ibid.*, XXVIII, 6.

[17] *Der Untermensch* (Subhuman Being).

[18] The basic aspect of Germany's occupation policy was ruthless economic exploitation of the native population. How coolly and cynically this was planned for is revealed in the official notes of a conference of Undersecretaries held on May 2, 1941: "The war can be carried on only if in the third year of the war the entire *Wehrmacht* is fed by Russia. This means that undoubtedly several millions of people will starve to death, if we get out of the country what is needed for us" (*Trial of Major War Criminals*, XXXI, 84). How faithfully the policy was carried out is indicated by the fact that it was the completely ruthless veteran Nazi, Ernst Koch, who was selected for the key post of Reich Commissioner for the Ukraine, the area considered by Hitler to be most important. Koch himself provided a succinct summary of his position in a speech delivered to a Nazi party meeting in Kiev on March 5, 1943: "I will extract the last bit out of this country. I did not come here to spread bliss, I have come to help the Führer. The population must work, work, and again work. . . Now some people have gotten excited about the population perhaps not getting enough to eat. That the population cannot expect. . . We are a master race, which must remember that the least German laborer is racially and biologically a thousand times more valuable than the population here" (*Trial*, XXXVIII, 89, 90).

A second pertinent aspect of the German occupation of the USSR is the purging of the local population. In a detailed "Top Secret" report of Task Forces (*Einsatztruppen*) of the Security Police and the SD, this type of purge is described as "combatting Communists and criminals." Indeed, it does contain such entries as, "Three Communist officials and one *Politruk* were liquidated at Gorodnia." But this report of one of Gestapo Chief Heinrich Himmler's more famous units goes on to list: "In Minsk 632 and in Mogilew 836 persons were shot. . . The liquidations for the period covered by this report have reached a total of 37,180 persons" (*Nazi Conspiracy*, VIII, 100). As the "period covered" consisted of a single month, October 1941, and the area included only one subsector of occupied territory, Byelorussia, the report provides grim and eloquent testimony regarding the scale on which mass executions must have taken place.

Closely related is a third occupation policy: the suppression of partisan units. Here again, a few excerpts from official German documents leave no doubt about the treatment meted out. A public announcement by the German commandant of Kiev, dated November 29, 1941, begins: "A transmitter has been damaged in Kiev with evil intent. Since the culprit could not be detained, 400 men from Kiev were shot" (*Trial*, XXXIX, 477). Further evidence of the enormity of the methods used in dealing with the inhabitants of "guerilla-polluted areas" is shown in an order issued by Goering on October 26, 1942: "Simultaneously with the combatting of partisan groups and the combing of the areas polluted by them, the cattle present there are to be removed as well as food supplies, to ensure that they are no longer accessible to the group." Not only are these areas to be stripped of foodstuffs, they are to be stripped of their citizenry as well. "The entire male and female labor force, which can be considered in any way for the labor conscription, are to be compelled to report and then be transferred to the General Plenipotentiary for Manpower for use in rear areas or in the homeland" (*Trial*, XXVIII, 1–2).

This directive by Goering sheds light upon the second major area of official *Ostpolitik* we wish to consider briefly here: the manner of dealing with the *Ostarbeiter* — the Soviet laborers for Hitler Germany.

The specific policy for the "recruitment" of *Ostarbeiter* was set forth in a statement issued in the spring of 1942 by the Plenipotentiary of Labor Mobilization, Fritz Sauckel: "The recruitment of foreign labor takes place essentially on the basis of free choice." This praiseworthy attitude is, however, considerably qualified by the very next sentence. "Where in occupied areas the appeal of free choice does not suffice, conscription and removal must be undertaken under all circumstances" (*Trial*, XXXII, 202). What this meant in practice is bluntly described by a high official in the *Ostministerium* in the autumn of 1942: " 'Recruiting' methods were used which probably have their origin only in the blackest periods of the slave trade. A regular manhunt was inaugurated" (*Nazi Conspiracy*, III, 248). It may be assumed that even the most docile or anti-Stalin Soviet citizen conscripted through such methods would not be overly enthusiastic. Little can be found in their further treatment as members of the labor force to increase their zeal.

Precisely how low the *Ostarbeiter's* status was to be was foretold in an early statement by Goering: "The German skilled workers belong to the war industry; it is not their task to shovel and to break stones, the Russian is there for that. . . Furthermore, stronger utilization in agriculture; if machines are lacking, human hands have to produce what the Reich has to request from the agricultural sector of the East." As if to insure that no one should fail to identify the *Ostarbeiter* as workers of the lowest category, Goering adds an order: "The Russian free workers obtain a *badge* which makes them recognizable as such" (*Trial*, XXXII, 497–501, and *Nazi Conspiracy*, III, 834–837). The type of treatment accorded the *Ostarbeiter* may well be surmised from the "reforms" initiated early in 1942 by Sauckel. Responsible for production, he insisted that only if treated well could they perform well: "Not only did he ensure proper feeding, he also showed consideration for the emotional reaction of the Russians brought as laborers. For this reason it was his second demand that the 'barbed wire' be dropped." Instead, "the Russians will be put up in closed camps which will be guarded." And finally, "he considered as unfeasible the wage rates decreed until now" and obtained from the Reichmarshal the concession "that the Russians could earn up to half of the wage of the German worker" (*Trial*, XXVI, 312–313).

Here, then, is the picture of the lot of the *Ostarbeiter*: brought to Germany in huge droves and mainly by force, closely confined to guarded camps, assigned the severest and most menial tasks, denied the possibility of earning more than half the wage paid the lowest German worker, always identified as *Untermenschen* by the hated *Ost* patch. Yet it was in reference to these *Ostarbeiter* that Sauckel made the proud boast: "It has always been natural for us Germans to refrain from cruelty and mean chicaneries toward the beaten enemy, even if he had proven himself the most bestial and implacable enemy, and to treat him correctly and humanly" (*Nazi Conspiracy*, III, 57).

[19] *Nazi Conspiracy and Aggression*, III, 126–129.

[20] *Goebbels Diaries*, p. 185.

[21] For full text, see *Trial of Major War Criminals*, XXVI, 610–627. For background data on Alfred Rosenberg, see *Nazi Conspiracy and Aggression*, II, 593–624, and Rosenberg, *Memoirs of Alfred Rosenberg*. Also see Rosenberg, *Der Mythus des 20. Jahrhunderts* (The Myth of the 20th Century).

[22] *Nazi Conspiracy and Aggression*, III, 242, 249, and Supplement A, 335–336.

[23] *Nazi Conspiracy and Aggression*, III, 242–251.

[24] Fischer, "Vlasov and Hitler," pp. 65–66.

[25] Original text of document in *Trial of Major War Criminals*, XXVII, 275–283. Translation in *Nazi Conspiracy and Aggression*, IV, 59–65.

[26] *Nazi Conspiracy and Aggression*, III, 837.

[27] *Goebbels Diaries*, p. 52.

[28] *Ibid.*, p. 225.

[29] *Ibid.*, p. 348.

[30] *Ibid.*, p. 328.

[31] *Ibid.*, p. 225.

[32] *Ibid.*, pp. 378–379.

[33] *Ibid.*, p. 330.

[34] *Ibid.*, pp. 546–547.

[35] Specific data on German military organization are contained in three extensive sections in the Nuremberg Trial Series: "The General Staff and High Command of the Armed Forces," *Nazi Conspiracy and Aggression*, II, 316–415; "The German General Staff and High Command," *Nazi Conspiracy and Aggression*, VI, 625–635; "Biographical Index of Principal Persons Referred to in the Interrogations," *Nazi Conspiracy and Aggression*, Supplement B, 1679–1713. Other sources include "Organization Chart, Wehrmacht, 1938–1945," *Nazi Conspiracy and Aggression*, VIII, 776; an organizational chart of the German Armed Forces, *Trial of Major War Criminals*, XXXII, 463, translated into English in *Nazi Conspiracy and Aggression*, VI, 412; and Walter Görlitz, *Deutscher Generalstab* (German General Staff) (Frankfurt am Main: Frankfurter Hefte, 1951), p. 595, and Table IX, "General Staff Organization."

[36] *Nazi Conspiracy and Aggression*, III, 637–639; *Trial of Major War Criminals*, XXVI, 401–406; XXXVIII, 92; XXXIV, 502, English translation in, IV, 549; XXXV, 81–86, English translation in, IV, 459–461; and *Nazi Conspiracy and Aggression*, Supplement A, 826–828.

[37] Fischer, "Vlasov and Hitler," p. 69.

[38] *Goebbels Diaries*, p. 330.

## Chapter II. The Other Germany

[1] Carroll, "It Takes a Russian to Beat a Russian," p. 82.

[2] The nationality problem continues to be one of the most hotly fought over among exiles from the USSR. For milder-than-usual samples in English of émigré controversy

on this subject, see Reuben Darbinian, "America and the Russian Future," *Armenian Review*, Summer 1951; Lev E. Dobriansky, "The Political Policy of the Ukrainian Congress Committee of America," *Ukrainian Quarterly*, Winter 1951; Michael Karpovich, "Russian Imperialism or Communist Aggression?," *The New Leader*, June 4 and June 11, 1951; and Ivan Kurganov, "The National Problem in the Soviet Union," *Russian Review*, October 1951. See also Roman Smal-Stocki, *The Nationality Problem of the Soviet Union and Russian Communist Imperialism* (Milwaukee: Bruce, 1952).

[3] Demaree Bess, "They Want to Go to War Right Now," *Saturday Evening Post*, August 18, 1951.

[4] Bogdan Raditsa, "Beyond Containment to Liberation," *Commentary*, September 1951.

[5] Fischer, *Russian Emigré Politics*.

[6] A notable example of widespread American publicity for an émigré sensationalist is that of Constantine W. Boldyreff, son of a Tsarist General and an early old émigré member of the "solidarist" NTS. He is now American representative of the organization and also Professor of Russian in the School of Foreign Service at Georgetown University in Washington, D. C. Boldyreff's reputation rests to a large extent on his articles, placed prominently in major American publications: "The Story of One Russian Underground Organization Attempting to Overthrow Stalin," *Look*, October 26, 1948; "We Can Win the Cold War — in Russia," *Reader's Digest*, November 1950; "Only Human," *New York Daily Mirror*, June 11 and June 12, 1951; "How the Russian Underground is Fighting Stalin's Slavery," *American Federationist*, May 1951.

[7] Fevr, *Solntse Voskhodit na Zapade* (The Sun Rises in the West), pp. 20–21.

[8] Fischer, "Vlasov and Hitler," p. 64.

[9] For background material on the Ukrainian Nationalist Movement, see Simon Narizhnii, *Ukrainska Emigratsia* (The Ukrainian Emigration) (Prague, 1942); *Ukrainian Resistance, The Story of the Ukrainian National Liberation Movement in Modern Times* (New York: Ukrainian Congress Committee of America, 1949); Mikola Lebed, *UPA* ([Germany] Press Bureau of Ukrainian Supreme Liberation Council (UHVR), 1946) and N. Y. Hryhorijiv, *The War and Ukrainian Democracy*, (Toronto: Industrial and Educational Publishing Co., 1945).

[10] The existence and striking extent of the economic and occupational islands in the totalitarian sea of Hitler Germany are illustrated by the memoirs of key figures in the anti-Nazi opposition which culminated in the July 20, 1944 *Putsch*: Ulrich von Hassell, *Vom Andern Deutschland* (From the Other Germany) (Zurich: Atlantis Verlag, 1946); Rudolf Pechel, *Deutscher Widerstand* (German Resistance) (Erlenbach-Zurich: Eugen Rentsch Verlag, 1947); Hans Bernd Gisevius, *To the Bitter End* (Boston: Houghton, Mifflin, 1947); Fabian von Schlabrendorf, *Offiziere Gegen Hitler* (Officers Against Hitler) (Zurich: Europa Verlag, 1951).

## Chapter III. General Vlasov

[1] *Nazi Conspiracy and Aggression*, III, 247.

[2] Hilger, "Observations on General Vlasov," p. 2.

[3] Wladimirow, *Dokumente und Material*, p. 68.

[4] Rudnev, "Andrei Andreevich Vlasov."

[5] B. I. Nicolaevsky, "Porazhenchestvo," *Novy Zhurnal*, XVIII, p. 226.

[6] [Wlassow], "Die Tragödie eines Generales," p. 18.

[7] Kerr, *The Russian Army*, pp. 46, 59, 64.

[8] *New York Times*, December 19, 1941.

[9] Curie, *Journey Among Warriors*, p. 179.

[10] Kerr, *The Russian Army*, p. 5.

[11] Hilger, "Observations on General Vlasov," p. 1.

[12] Dvinov, *Vlasovskoe Dvizhiene*, pp. 78, 81.

[13] Originals of this leaflet, "480 RAB/IX. 42," as well as of leaflets "481 RAB/IX. 42" and "482 RAB/IX. 42" are at YIWO, Jewish Scientific Institute, New York.

[14] Leaflet "480 RAB/IX. 42."

[15] Dvinov, *Vlasovskoe Dvizhenie*, pp. 78, 81.

[16] Hilger, "Observations on General Vlasov," p. 2.

[17] Nicolaevsky, "Porazhenchestvo," *Novy Zhurnal*, XIX, p. 219.

[18] Carroll, "It Takes a Russian to Beat a Russian," p. 85.

[19] Petrov, *My Retreat from Russia*, p. 282.

[20] Wladimirow, *Dokumente und Material*, pp. 70–71.

[21] *Ibid.*, pp. 71–72.

[22] Nicolaevsky, "Porazhenchestvo," *Novy Zhurnal*, XVIII, p. 233; A. S. Kazantsev, *Tretia Sila*, June 25, 1950, p. 15.

[23] Kitaev, *Russkoe Osvoboditelnoe Dvizhenie*, pp. 23, 24.

[24] Nicolaevsky, "Porazhenchestvo," *Novy Zhurnal*, XVIII, p. 234; Kazantsev, *Tretia Sila*, June 25, 1950, p. 15.

## Chapter IV. ROA: Russian Army of Liberation

[1] Heinz Guderian, *Erinnerungen eines Soldaten*, pp. 322–323. See also Bor-Komorowski, *The Secret Army*, p. 235.

[2] Carroll, "It Takes a Russian to Beat a Russian," p. 81.

[3] *Nazi Conspiracy and Aggression*, III, p. 127.

[4] *Trial of Major War Criminals*, XXXVI, p. 108.

[5] *Ibid.*, XXXIX, pp. 515–516.

[6] *Nazi Conspiracy and Aggression*, III, p. 246.

[7] *Trial of Major War Criminals*, XXIX, p. 112.

[8] *Ibid.*, XXXVIII, p. 88.

[9] Nuremberg Trial, unpublished document NG-3534; Fischer, "Vlasov and Hitler," p. 67; Carroll, "It Takes a Russian to Beat a Russian," pp. 82, 85; Köstring, "Freiwilligenverbände," p. 2; and Kleist, *Zwischen Hitler und Stalin*, pp. 205f.

[10] *Nazi Conspiracy and Aggression*, III, p. 247.

[11] Nuremberg Trial, unpublished document NG-3534.

[12] Michel, *Ost und West*, pp. 48, 49, 45.

[13] Nuremberg Trial, unpublished document NG-3534.

[14] *Dobrovolets*, January 12, 1944; February 6, 1944; May 17, 1944; June 14, 1944.

[15] Nuremberg Trial, unpublished document NG-4301.

[16] Nuremberg Trial, unpublished document, identified by British classification "PWD 3 Aug. 44 Captured German Document."

[17] Buchardt, *Die Behandlung des Russischen Problems*, pp. 105–106.

[18] *Dobrovolets*, March 26, 1944.

[19] *Nazi Conspiracy and Aggression*, VI, p. 696.

[20] Nuremberg Trial, unpublished document NG-3534.

[21] Köstring, "Freiwilligenverbände," p. 3.

[22] Text of letter by Caucasian leaders is reproduced in Thorwald, *Einer von Ihnen War Wlassow*, p. 131.

[23] *Parizhskii Vestnik*, July 15, 1944.

[24] *Novoe Slovo*, June 21, 1944.

[25] *New York Times*, October 14, 1944.

[26] Nuremberg Trial, unpublished document NO-2544.

[27] Köstring, "Freiwilligenverbände," p. 5.

[28] *Dobrovolets*, January 2, 1944.

[29] *Dobrovolets*, January 19, 1944.

[20] *Novy Put* (Riga), No. 10 (30), 1943; and *Dobrovolets*, August 22, 1944.
[21] Unpublished German document, identified by British classification "PWD 3 Aug. 44 Captured German Document.
[22] *Otvety Redaktsii gazety "Dobrovolets,"* pp. 2–10.

## Chapter V. The Russian National Committee

[1] Nicolaevsky, "Porazhenchestvo," *Novy Zhurnal*, XIX, pp. 216–217. A summary of Vlasov's program appears in *Parizhskii Vestnik*, June 12, 1943.
[2] Carroll, "It Takes a Russian to Beat a Russian," p. 85.
[3] *Ibid.*
[4] *Novy Put* (Riga), No. 10 (30), 1943.
[5] *Zaria*, April 14, 1943; *Parizhskii Vestnik*, June 5, 1943.
[6] Wladimirow, *Dokumente und Material*, pp. 65–67; and *Parizhskii Vestnik*, June 5, 1943.
[7] *Zaria*, April 18, 1943; Wladimirow, *Dokumente und Material*, pp. 58–63.
[8] In his April 1943 speech, General Malyshkin touched first on the continuously explosive national question. Like Vlasov after the Smolensk Manifesto, he endorsed the middle position, that of post-Stalin self-determination: "We take the stand that the new Russia must realize national freedom, including self-determination to the extent of separation. But this goal can be achieved only after the main task — the overthrow of Bolshevism and the destruction of the Stalin tyranny — is completed."

Throwing light on "socialism" in a post-Soviet Russia, the speaker declared: "We take the position, furthermore, that all those industries which during the period of Bolshevism were erected at the expense of the blood and sweat of the whole people, must become the property of the state, national property. . . Should it appear preferable and be in the interests of the people, however, the state will raise no objections to the participation of private initiative. . . Private initiative will be made possible not only in peasant holdings and industry. . . We believe that private initiative must also participate in other facets of economic life, for instance in trade, handicrafts, artisan work. Only an unimpeded free private initiative can create those prerequisites which are essential for a favorable development of the welfare of the entire people."

One of the most revealing sections of this address deals with the attitude of this Soviet-bred opposition to the post-1917 "white" émigrés. "To all former participants of the White Movement we can say definitely the following: Anyone does not belong to us who believes in the restoration in Russia of nobles and large landowners, in the restoration of privileges based on origin, caste, or wealth, in the restoration of outlived governmental forms." To former Communists, however, Malyshkin is more hospitable. He offers the assurance that "everyone who renounces those ways of thinking, which he accepted actively or passively until now, will find an appropriate place in our ranks."

[9] *Goebbels Diaries*, p. 347.
[10] Carroll, "It Takes a Russian to Beat a Russian," p. 85.
[11] *Possev* (Limburg, Germany), May 7, 1950.
[12] *Trial of Major War Criminals*, XLI, p. 187.
[13] *Borba* (Munich), November–December 1950, pp. 19–20.
[14] *Biblioteka Propagandista No. 9*, pp. 3–9.
[15] Jolis, "When the Red Army Fought Stalin," pp. 11–12.

## Chapter VI. Vlasov and Himmler

[1] *Trial of Major War Criminals*, XXIX, pp. 122–123; English translation in *Nazi Conspiracy and Aggression*, IV, p. 559.

[2] *Trial of Major War Criminals*, XXIX, p. 20.

[3] *Ibid.*, XXIX, p. 118.

[4] *Ibid.*, XXXVII, p. 507.

[5] *Ibid.*, XLI, p. 186.

[6] Michel, *Ost und West*, pp. 251–253.

[7] D'Alquen's prominence in the SS is suggested not only by his post as editor of the SS organ, *Das Schwarze Korps*, but also by his authorship of an official history of the organization, *Die SS. Geschichte, Aufgabe und Organisation der Schutzstaffeln der NSDAP* (The SS, The History, Tasks, and Organization of the Security Troops of the NSDAP) (Berlin, 1939). Text reproduced in *Trial of Major War Criminals*, III, pp. 130–140. SS equivalents of German and U. S. military ranks are listed in *Nazi Conspiracy and Aggression*, II, p. 1099.

[8] Dvinov, *Vlasovskoe Dvizhenie*, p. 119.

[9] D'Alquen, Arlt, and Strikfeldt testimony in Thorwald, *Einer von Ihnen war Wlassow*, pp. 87–118.

[10] Rosenberg, *Memoirs*, p. 280.

[11] *Trial of Major War Criminals*, XLI, p. 187.

[12] Thorwald, *Einer von Ihnen war Wlassow*, pp. 105, 109–118.

[13] The concentration-camp experiences of one NTS leader are recounted in A. Nemirov, *Dorogi I Vstrechi* (Paths and Encounters) (Regensburg, 1947).

[14] *Trial of Major War Criminals*, XLI, pp. 186–194.

[15] Dvinov, *Vlasovskoe Dvizhenie*, pp. 109–110.

[16] "Aufzeichnung über den Besuch des Generals der Kav. Köstring, General der Freiwilligen-Verbände beim Herrn Reichsminister am 28.11.44" (Notes on the Visit of Cavalry General Köstring, General of Volunteer Units, to the Minister [of Occupied Eastern Territories] on November 28, 1944).

[17] "14-oe Noiabria 1944 Goda v Prage" (The 14th of November, 1944, in Prague), *Borba* (Munich), November 1948, pp. 18, 19.

[18] Dvinov, *Vlasovskoe Dvizhenie*, p. 110.

[19] *Trial of Major War Criminals*, XXIX, p. 118.

## Chapter VII. KONR: Committee for the Liberation of the Peoples of Russia

[1] Buchardt, *Die Behandlung des Russischen Problems*, pp. 289–291.

[2] "14-oe Noiabria 1944 Goda v Prage" (The 14th of November, 1944 in Prague), *Borba* (Munich), November 1948, pp. 18, 19; *Volia Naroda* (Dabendorf), November 15 and 19, 1944.

[3] *Volia Naroda*, November 18, 1944.

[4] *Ibid.*, November 15, 1944.

[5] Boldyreff, "The Story of One Russian-Underground Organization," p. 26.

[6] *Ibid.*, December 20, 1944.

[7] *Völkischer Beobachter* (Berlin), December 7, 1944.

[8] It is revealing that, like Vlasov, Shandruk — now also a Lieutenant General — was to head both the political and the military organization. Like Vlasov, too, Shandruk had fought against the *Wehrmacht* at the outset of World War II (with the Polish army) and had become a German prisoner of war. But unlike Vlasov, Shandruk was an old émigré. A career officer in the Tsarist army by World War I, he rose by 1920 to be Major General and Division Commander in Petliura's independent Ukrainian Republic. Between the wars, he was chief of the Ukrainian exile government's skeleton general staff in Warsaw. He remained a German prisoner of war from 1939 until November 1944, when he was called to Berlin. After the failure of the January 25, 1945 talks between Vlasov and Shandruk, the establishment of a German-sponsored Ukrainian body wholly independent of the KONR lay dormant. Only on March 17, 1945 did Germany's

desperate military situation and the proseparatist, anti-Vlasov efforts within the German government make possible a Weimar gathering of Ukrainian leaders, which named Shandruk head of the Ukrainian National Committee and the previously nonexistent Ukrainian National Army. The latter was to include *Osttruppen* of Ukrainian origin and the "Galicia" Division, also under German command, which, formerly called the *14. Grenadier-Division der Waffen-SS*, was now in its last days renamed the First Ukrainian Division of the Ukrainian National Army. As an attempt to give representation to the three Ukrainian groupings under German control, the Ukrainian National Committee had as its chairman an old émigré from the Eastern Ukraine (Shandruk) and as its two vice-chairmen a Galician (Western Ukrainian) leader, Professor Volodimir Kubiovich, and an Eastern Ukrainian of Soviet vintage, Olexander Semenenko, a Kharkov lawyer who earlier in World War II had served as German-sponsored mayor of his native city. See the March 1945 issue of *Ukrainskii Golos*, a Berlin newspaper which became the organ of the Ukrainian National Committee; Oleg Lisiak, ed., *Brodi, Zbirnik Statei u Narisiv* (Brodi, Collection of Articles and Sketches), (Munich: Brotherhood of Soldiers of the First Ukrainian Division of the Ukrainian National Army, 1951); Nikon Nalivaiko, "Legioni v Natsionalnykh Voinakh, Do Istorii Divizii 'Galichina' i 'Pershoi Ukrainskoi Divizii'" (Legions in National Wars, On the History of the "Galicia" Division and the "First Ukrainian Division"), *Narodna Volia* (Scranton), series of seven articles from October 6, 1949, to November 17, 1949.

[9] *Volia Naroda*, January 31, 1945.

[10] *Ibid.*, December 20, 1944.

[11] The first of KONR's four organizational components was its Administrative Department. It was headed by General Malyshkin, closest to Vlasov of all his associates. One of the tasks of Malyshkin's Department was to conduct the affairs of KONR itself. In view of this, and of the close personal relation, it is not surprising that at its last session KONR elected Malyshkin its Deputy Chairman.

A major activity of the Administrative Department was the conclusion of a formal financial agreement with the German government. On January 20, 1945, *Volia Naroda* published the following information bulletin from KONR: "On January 18, 1945, in Berlin, a credit agreement was signed between the Government of the Reich and the Committee for the Liberation of the Peoples of Russia. According to this agreement, which is in full accordance with the principles of the Prague Manifesto, the Government of the Reich is furnishing the necessary credit to the Committee. . . ." The same issue of the KONR organ also announced that the German Foreign Office had held a reception in honor of the signing of the agreement — a gesture to emphasize KONR's near-governmental status. The independence of KONR's position is stressed even more strongly in an editorial in the next issue of *Volia Naroda*, on January 24, 1945: "The credit agreement between the German government and the Committee for the Liberation of the Peoples of Russia once again underscores the political and legal independence of the Liberation Movement, which is acquiring an independent material basis just at the moment when the struggle against Bolshevism must become for us an unavoidable duty of the day." None of the announcements mentions any sums. Moreover, it may well be asked whether KONR was not protesting too much. That the situation of the Committee was in fact considerably less favorable than the editorial indicates is suggested by one German account. It states that the previously existing German 15-percent deduction from the wages of the *Ostarbeiter* was not to be eliminated, as had been requested by the Vlasov Movement. Rather, it would now be used to produce an estimated 100 million marks annually for the German government, to serve as part repayment for KONR credit (Buchardt, *Die Behandlung des Russischen Problems*, pp. 333–334). Other tasks of the Administrative Department were a census and a gathering of intellectual cadres in German areas. One by-product was the formation under KONR of an Academic Council.

Chief of KONR's Military Department was General Trukhin, erstwhile commander of

Dabendorf and of its ROA School. It was Trukhin's earlier clandestine padding of his school's drill section with senior ex-Soviet officers that enabled Vlasov now to declare, in December 1944, that "already the Staff of the Armed Forces has a quite satisfactory number of experienced field officer cadres who passed through combat training" (*Volia Naroda*, December 20, 1944). But KONR's initial statements regarding its military ventures still referred to that phantom army, ROA, and were as vague and unspecific as was the title of its Military Department: Staff of the Armed Forces of the Peoples of Russia. It was not until the end of January 1945 that Vlasov could announce that the Führer had transferred to him the command of the Armed Forces of KONR. Not until a time so desperately critical for Hitler's Germany was the formation of the KONR Army begun.

The Civilian Department of KONR was set up to care for the Soviet nationals under German control who were not in military units: the *Ostarbeiter* and the Soviet prisoners of war. Chief of this department was ex-Soviet Major General D. E. Zakutnyi. Less colorful or central in the Soviet opposition movement than either Vlasov or his other chief associates, Zakutnyi nevertheless through this post assumed a key position. In an interview soon after the establishment of the Civilian Department, Zakutnyi defined his main goals as the equation of the *Ostarbeiter* to other foreign workers and the abolition of the discriminatory *Ost* patch (*Volia Naroda*, December 6, 1944). In addition, a network of local KONR representatives was set up to provide scattered spokesmen and protectors for Soviet nationals in various areas. But the improvement achieved by KONR's Civilian Department was pathetically slow. It was only two months before the final collapse of Germany that KONR was able to announce in *Volia Naroda* of March 8, 1945:

1. The German government, as an outcome of negotiations, has equated the food supply of workers from Russia to the supply of foreign workers from countries friendly to Germany. . .

2. The so-called social tax amounting to approximately 15 percent of the wage of the workers from Russia, is abolished. The wage will in the future . . . be paid out fully the same as to other foreign workers.

3. Workers from Russia are assigned to the most favorable tax group.

4. The Reichsführer SS has issued an order that all who allow unfair treatment of workers from Russia will be punished severely.

Even this eleventh-hour modification was far from complete, making no mention of that hated *Untermenschen* symbol, the *Ost* patch.

The picture was probably hardly more cheerful for the Soviet prisoners of war. The wanton mass deaths of the first war year had been stopped, and minor concessions were granted. But the German authorities continued to resist the pleas of the Soviet opposition movement that Red Army soldiers, upon capture, be given a choice between imprisonment and service in ex-Soviet units fighting the Stalin regime.

The Propaganda Department, the fourth division of the KONR apparatus, competed with the military factor in being of greatest interest to the movement's powerful sponsor, Heinrich Himmler. It was only fitting, therefore, that it should have been headed by the one of all the Vlasov Movement leaders most acceptable to (and accepting of) the Nazi regime. This was Lieutenant General Zhilenkov, the former Soviet commissar. As chief of KONR's Propaganda Department, Zhilenkov was in charge of the KONR press that after Prague replaced *Zaria* and *Dobrovolets*. In addition to the central organ, *Volia Naroda*, the KONR press consisted of a publication for Soviet volunteers in the German Army, *Za Rodinu*. Vlasov also spoke of large cadres of radio and stage actors and specialists, and of an extensive network of propagandists, doubtless trained at Dabendorf, who were also under Zhilenkov's control (*Volia Naroda*, December 20, 1944). In addition, Zhilenkov filled the role of KONR's public-relations specialist. Thus it was he, after the Prague meeting, who conducted the press conference for foreign correspondents. It was he whom KONR dispatched to Slovakia, where he delivered a major address, and was received by top Slovak pro-German leaders (*Volia Naroda*, January 17, 1945). And, when Vlasov formally met with Propaganda Minister Goebbels on February 28, 1945, he was accompanied by Zhilenkov (*Volia Naroda*, March 4, 1945; see also von Oven, *Mit Goebbels bis zum Ende*, II, pp. 254–260).

Despite Zhilenkov's unique cordiality to Hitler's Germany, he issued numerous statements expressive of the movement's independent aspirations. For example: "Invaluable aid was furnished by Germany to the liberation struggle of the peoples of Russia by the fact that it not only offered asylum to these millions of people, but also gave them an opportunity to organize themselves into an independent political force, aimed at the overthrow of the Stalin regime (*Volia Naroda*, November 15, 1944). Probably most, if not all, of Stalin's Soviet opponents within Germany would, at the time, have subscribed to those words.

Another component of the KONR apparatus was the Committee's organizational response to the continuously bitter and unresolved separatist boycott of KONR. At the second session of KONR, on December 17, 1944, approval was given to the establishment, under KONR, of the following National Councils: Russian, Ukrainian, Byelorussian, and those of the Peoples of the Caucasus and of the Peoples of Turkestan. As a corollary of these national councils, there was established the KONR Central Office for Cossack Troops. The KONR communique added that the chairmen of the KONR National Councils would constitute themselves a permanent KONR Commission on National Affairs (*Volia Naroda*, December 20, 1944). Most of the time and energy of the KONR national councils was understandably devoted to one task: alternate negotiations and rivalry with the separatist National Committees remaining outside KONR. Some KONR members of non-Russian origin hoped that the KONR Commission on National Affairs would develop into a second chamber with powers and function parallel to KONR itself. But neither the time available, nor the progress made on the national issue, nor, lastly, the caliber of the leaders involved, made this feasible.

[12] Dr. N., "Po Povodu Tak Nazyvaemogo 'Vlasovskogo Dvizheniia'," pp. 108–109.

## Chapter VIII. The KONR Army

[1] *Volia Naroda*, February 21, 1945.

[2] Gilbert, *Hitler Directs His War*, pp. 147, 148.

[3] *Nazi Conspiracy and Aggression*, VI, p. 677. See also Gilbert, *Hitler Directs His War*, p. 111.

[4] *Volia Naroda*, December 3, 1944.

[5] *Ibid.*, March 8, 1945.

[6] Referring to the pre-VE Day computations by the Operations Section of the KONR Army headquarters, Pozdniakov in one of the seven installments of his series of articles on the end of the KONR Army, lists its total strength as almost 100,000. This total is arrived at by adding to the strength of the First KONR Division (25,000) and the Second KONR Division with units attached to it (13,000) the Von Pannwitz Cossack Corps (45,000–50,000) and General Turkul's Austrian units of the KONR Army (2300–2700). See Pozdniakov, "Poslednie Dni," September 9, 1951.

[7] A telegram sent by Himmler to Vlasov on February 11 stated that in its first battle the KONR Army's Volunteer unit had already shown exemplary courage (*Volia Naroda*, February 15, 1945). The telegram also identified the commander of this detachment, Colonel Sakharov, an adventurous old émigré who had previously participated in one of the earliest Soviet opposition ventures, the RNNA. Sakharov's force was made up of *Ostbattalione* which, upon the issuance of the Prague Manifesto, had expressed the desire to join the KONR Army. The German authorities had retained these units near Stettin, and now ordered them into action before Berlin, in the path of the strongest concentrations of the Red Army surging toward its major goal.

Aside from Himmler's praise of their fortitude, we know little of what actually occurred in this first KONR Army engagement. However, Colonel Sakharov's undertaking occupies a firm place in the postwar mythology of the Vlasov Movement. Legend has it that dozens if not hundreds of Red Army soldiers surrendered daily to this unit, and only to this unit, while it fought on the Eastern Front in those days that were so triumphant for the Red Army as a whole. In his speech to the February 27, 1945 session of KONR, Vlasov himself lent credence to this story. "These are our only proving stones," Vlasov said; "however, now they have clearly proved that our ideas are immortal, that the officers and soldiers of the Red Army, on those sections of the front where our units were, met the officers and soldiers of ROA as blood brothers, and movingly united for the struggle against Bolshevism, for the freedom of their own motherland. Yesterday's officers and soldiers of the Red Army, who got as far as the Oder, today without hesitation crossed over into the ranks of the Russian Army of Liberation and are exhibiting unmatchable examples of conscious heroism. And this at a time when Stalin considers the question of his own victory settled" (*Volia Naroda*, March 8, 1945).

[8] Kazantsev, *Tretia Sila*: Pozdniakov, "Pervaia Pekhotnaia Diviziia."

[9] Thorwald, *Einer von Ihnen war Wlassow*, pp. 31–48.

[10] *New York Times*, May 6, 1945.

[11] Peterman, "Prague's Four Fantastic Days," p. 20.

[12] Dwinger, *General Wlassow*, pp. 353–354.

[13] Rebecca West, *The Meaning of Treason* (New York: Viking, 1947), pp. 109–110.

[14] Thorwald, *Das Ende an der Elbe*, p. 346.

## Chapter IX.  The End of a Tragedy

[1] Thorwald, *Ungeklärte Fälle*, pp. 193–194; Kazantsev, *Tretia Sila*, June 18, 1950, pp. 14–15; Dwinger, *General Wlassow*, pp. 213, 220, 271; Thorwald, *Einer von Ihnen war Wlassow*, pp. 56, 58–59.

[2] Kazantsev, *Tretia Sila*, August 20, 1950, p. 14.

[3] Woodbridge, *UNRRA*, III, p. 423; and International Refugee Organization, *Statistical Report*, pp. 9, 12–13, 20. See also U. S. House of Representatives Report No. 1687, *The Displaced Persons Analytical Bibliography* (Washington, D. C.: Government Printing Office, 1950); and Jacques Vernant and others, *The Refugee in the Post-War World, Preliminary Report of a Survey of the Refugee Problem* (Geneva, 1951).

[4] *Nazi Conspiracy and Aggression*, I, p. 894; *Trial of the Major War Criminals*, XLI, p. 186; Eugene M. Kulischer, "Displaced Persons in the Modern World," *Annals of the American Academy of Political and Social Sciences* (Philadelphia), March 1949, p. 171; Fred Wyle, "Memorandum on Statistical Data on Soviet Displaced Persons," Russian Research Center, Harvard University, March 8, 1952, mimeographed; *Life* (New York), March 24, 1952; and Upravlenie Upolnomochennogo . . . po Delam Repatriatsii, *Otvety*, p. 3.

[5] The new and old emigrations would at present be proximate in size if the post-1917 group was halved between 1937 and 1952 as it is estimated to have been in the preceeding 15-year period. The original over-all size of the old political emigration from Russia has been put at about one million. This estimate, more conservative than earlier ones, is contained in a detailed summary on the subject: Sir John Hope Simpson, *The Refugee Problem, Report of a Survey* (London: Oxford University Press, 1939), Chapter V, "The Russian Emigration." The same work (p. 561) places the 1937 total of "Unassimilated Russian Refugees" at 450,000 (as against 863,000 in 1922). By geographical areas, the following are among the figures given for the same pre-World War II year: Baltic, 23,000; Poland, 80,000; Balkans, 57,600; Central Europe, 15,500; Germany, 45,000; France, 110,000; Far East, 94,000.

[6] Numerous instances of overt animosity in 1945 by advancing Red Army officers

toward German-held and now liberated Soviet citizens are cited by Varshavskii, an old émigré who was then in Germany as a French prisoner of war. See Vladimir Varshavskii, *Sem Let* (Seven Years) (Paris, 1950), pp. 223, 245–246, 251–252, 256, 281.

[7] John R. Deane, *The Strange Alliance, The Story of Our Efforts at Wartime Co-operation with Russia* (New York: Viking, 1947), chap. xi. On Soviet defector resistance to repatriation to the USSR, both from the United States (Fort Dix, New Jersey) and from Germany, see *Stars and Stripes*, European ed., January 20 and 23, 1946; *New York Times*, June 30, 1945 and May 14, 1946.

[8] Deane, *The Strange Alliance*, pp. 186–187.

[9] Marguerite Higgins, "Now the Russians are Fleeing Russia," *Saturday Evening Post* (Philadelphia), June 4, 1949.

[10] Statement by John J. McCloy, U. S. High Commissioner for Germany, in *New York Times*, April 25, 1951.

[11] Pozdniakov, "Pervaia Pekhotnaia Divizia," pp. 42–55.

[12] Kazantsev, *Tretia Sila*, September 3, 1950, p. 15.

[13] \* \* , "Poslednie Dni Generala Vlasova" (The Last Days of General Vlasov), *Rossisskii Demokrat* (Paris), 1948, I. This and the preceding accounts are supplemented by Pozdniakov, "Poslednie Dni," October 7 and October 21, 1951.

[14] Dwinger, *General Wlassow*, pp. 371–376.

[15] Jolis, "When the Red Army Fought Stalin," pp. 31–33.

[16] *Pravda*, Moscow, August 2, 1946.

## Chapter X. Likelihood of Opposition

[1] See a study based on 1949 interviews of Soviet exiles in Germany: Merle Fainsod, "Controls and Tensions in the Soviet System," *American Political Science Review* (New York), June 1950. Two further views on Soviet defection, based on interviews, have been issued to date by the Harvard Russian Research Center: Henry V. Dicks, "Notes on Some Observations of Russian Behavior," November 17, 1950, mimeographed; Alexander Dallin, "Popular Attitudes and Behavior under the German Occupation [of the Soviet Union], 1941–1944, Interim Report" (Project on the Soviet Social System), March 31, 1952, mimeographed.

[2] Rear Admiral Leslie Stevens, "What Makes Russians Patriotic?", *Life* (New York), September 4, 1950, p. 89. See also O. Anisimov, "Sovetskoe Pokolenie" (The Soviet Generation), *Novy Zhurnal* (New York), xxii, 1949.

[3] Alex Inkeles and Raymond A. Bauer, "Portrait of Soviet Russia by Russians," *New York Times Magazine*, November 25, 1951, p. 33; O. Utis, "Generalissimo Stalin and the Art of Government," *Foreign Affairs* (New York), January 1952, pp. 212–213.

[4] C. Wright Mills, *White Collar, The American Middle Classes* (New York: Oxford University Press, 1951); David Riesman, *The Lonely Crowd, A Study of the Changing American Character* (New Haven: Yale University Press, 1940) William H. Whyte, Jr., and the Editors of *Fortune, Is Anybody Listening? How and Why U. S. Business Fumbles When it Talks With Human Beings* (New York: Simon and Schuster, 1952).

[5] George H. Gallup, "What We Don't Know Can Hurt Us," *New York Times Magazine*, November 4, 1951.

[6] Samuel Lubell, *The Future of American Politics* (New York: Harper, 1952); Erich Fromm, *Escape from Freedom* (New York: Rinehart, 1943); Isaiah Berlin, "Political Ideas in the Twentieth Century," *Foreign Affairs* (New York), April, 1950, p. 383.

[7] George Orwell, *Nineteen Eighty-Four* (New York: Harcourt, Brace, 1949).

[8] The long-lasting and burning exile controversy revolved around the émigré concept of "*porazhenchestvo*" (defeatism). This is the view that what happened in 1941 and 1942 was in fact similar to the revolutionary doctrine during the Russo-Japanese War of 1904–1905 and World War I. Then "*porazhenchestvo*" urged the Russian soldiers to

weaken their own side so that its regime would be the sooner overthrown. The émigré controversy following World War II was originated by one of the most striking survivors of the post-1917 Russian emigration, Boris I. Nicolaevsky. Eminent today as a historian-archivist and also as an exile political figure, Nicolaevsky was born in a Ural village in 1887 and in 1903 joined the political movement in which he has been active ever since: the Menshevik wing of the Russian Social Democratic party. After arrests and exile under the Tsarist regime, he was as a member of the Mensheviks' top council during the 1917 revolution. From 1919 until 1921 he served as Director of Archive of the History of the Revolution in Moscow. In 1922 Nicolaevsky was expelled from Russia by the Soviet government and years of exile followed — in Berlin from 1922 to 1933, in Paris from 1933 to 1940, and since then in New York. During these years Nicolaevsky continued to alternate his roles, as a political figure (as one of the editors of the Menshevik Journal, *Sotsialisticheskii Vestnik*) and as a historian-archivist. In the latter role he edited and published the voluminous correspondence of top Russian revolutionary leaders (Plekhanov, Martov, Axelrod, Potresov) as well as biographies of Azef, the famous Russian provocateur, and of Karl Marx. He also served as Representative of the Moscow Marx-Engels Institute from 1927 until 1931, and from 1935 on of the Institute of Social History of the Second (Socialist) International, now in Amsterdam. Nicolaevsky touched off the controversy in 1948, after a tour of Western Germany, by publishing the first two installments of an analysis (not continued since) of the Vlasov Movement. It appeared in the leading exile journal, *Novy Zhurnal*: "Porazhenchestvo 1941–1945 Godov i Gen. A. A. Vlasov" (The Defeatist Movement in 1941–1945 and Gen. A. A. Vlasov), *Novy Zhurnal* (New York), XVIII, XIX (1948).

One of the two émigrés who were first to attack Nicolaevsky was also a Menshevik, Boris L. Dvinov. He did this in the New York daily, *Novoye Russkoye Slovo*, as well as in his book: *Vlasovskoe Dvizhenie v Svete Dokumentov* (The Vlasov Movement in the Light of Documents) (New York: Published by the Author, 1950). Dvinov's disagreement was aimed particularly at the émigré concept of Soviet "*porazhenchestvo*," which had been assumed as axiomatic by most anti-Stalin exiles. Dvinov's denial of its importance was taken as an objectionable and, moreover, an ill-informed attack on the new Soviet emigration itself. Dvinov uses the denial of the importance of "*porazhenchestvo*" to substantiate his over-all polemic against the wartime Vlasov Movement. Specifically, he seeks to prove its unrepresentativeness and its opportunistic initial motivations by emphasizing that actually the majority of the Red Army did *not* surrender, that this majority had the sense to remain anti-Nazi even if it may also have hated Stalin at the same time. Dvinov's dichotomy was between the Red Army majority which perceived Hitler as enemy number one — a favorite phrase of émigré polemics — and Stalin as a lesser evil, and at the other extreme the minority, the Soviet defectors who blundered into conceiving of Stalin as enemy number one and the Nazi system as enemy number two.

The other writer for *Novoye Russkoye Slovo* who, like Dvinov, has recently drawn sharp fire from most compatriots in exile is Ekaterina D. Kuskova. She is the octogenarian old émigré now living in Geneva, who is best remembered as an "Economist" target of Lenin's prerevolutionary attacks. It is Kuskova's contention that most émigrés err in their optimistic estimates of the degree of anti-Stalin disaffection within the USSR. She emphasizes that all societies develop among their members loyalties and identifications that weaken or compete with whatever tendencies toward disaffection there might be.

Up to a certain point, this study has coincided with the views of both Dvinov and Kuskova. But major differences appear in each case, as they do in relation to Nicolaevsky's pro-"*porazhenchestvo*" and pro-Vlasov position. All three writers emphasize the political motivation of Soviet citizens in 1941. This study offers the opposite picture: it was apolitical Inertness that was decisive. This means rejection of both Dvinov's stress on the Red Army's considering Hitler as enemy number one (and therefore fighting on) and Nicolaevsky's contention that it was Stalin who was enemy number one in the eyes of Soviet soldiers (who therefore surrendered by the millions). It also means a rejection of Kuskova's view. She holds the Soviet citizen's acceptance of the Stalin regime to be political as well. This study has held it to stop short of that, in the area of psychological as well as political Inertness.

## Chapter XII. Aspirations of Opposition

[1] *Programnye Polozheniia i Ustav* [1938]: *Skhema Natsionalno-Trudovogo Soiuza* [1944]; *Natsionalno-Trudovoi Soiuz Novogo Pokoleniia, Kurs Natsionalno-Politicheskoi Podgotovk* [1937–1939]. Of interest also is a work by a German Baltic historian, Walter Schubart, *Russia and the West* (New York: Ungar, 1950). Intensely Russian-nationalist in its conclusion, this book was translated into Russian and promoted both during and since World War II by NTS: Walter Schubart, *Evropa i Dusha Vostoka* (Europe and the Soul of the East) (3rd ed., 1947).

[2] In NTS ideology, nationalism was central — intense Russian nationalism. "National statehood is the sole possibility and guarantee of the fulfillment by a nation of the task which it has been predestined to fulfill" (*Kurs*, I, pp. 115–117). In elaborate schemes, the NTS built its nationalism not around the Russian people but the Russian nation (*Kurs*, I, pp. 127–130). The latter concept is conveyed by *all*-Russian instead of Russian, *rossiiskii* instead of *russkii*, emphasizing the NTS view that their nationalism included all components of the Russian nation (or the USSR), rather than only the Russian people proper, the Great Russians. For the latter the NTS reserved a central role, as a nucleus around which the other *rossiskie* peoples grouped themselves (*Skhema*, p. 13). The intensity of this NTS nationalism precluded faith in internationalism.

Also crucial in the NTS position is antirationalism. Throughout its prewar literature, NTS looked with skepticism and contempt upon the philosophy of rationalism that is basic to all of Western society. And NTS heaped similar abuse on the Western institutions in part traceable to philosophical rationalism: liberalism, the parliamentary system, democracy. "We therefore sweep aside liberalism, which leads to despotism by parties, to economic anarchy, and to spiritual emptiness" (*Kurs*, III, p. 15). It was Russia's unique, historical mission to show the world a new type of social order that would remedy the profound defects of modern Western institutions (*Skhema*, pp. 13–14). In this the Russian Orthodox Church was to participate, a shining example of moral purity as contrasted to Western religion (*Kurs*, I, pp. 145–146).

But it is only on the subject of the content of Russia's mission that the ideological orientation of NTS becomes wholly clear. NTS believes that an anti-Stalin revolution is a task for the "authoritarian," the "strong personality," the leader. But in the long run the "solidarist" society would best be led by the elite. Repeated distinctions are made between such a "leading element" and either an aristocracy or an oligarchy. But it is clear that this NTS scheme is directed against the democratism, the rationalistic optimism, and the liberalism of which NTS disapproves so strongly (*Kurs*, I, pp. 52–81). "The selection of the leading element in the long run takes place not so much through the nomination of individuals at elections, as on the basis of the exhibition of their usefulness in practical work" (*Skhema*, pp. 33–35). Indeed, NTS would free the state from political parties and replace them by Mussolini-like corporatism (*Kurs*, III, pp. 15, 89–94). A selected type of candidate could be elected by occupational groups to a corporate national assembly. Into it additional outstanding individuals could be coöpted. "Russia does not need the comedy of parliamentary elections and the falsification of the popular will: it needs a businesslike selection of capable public figures — genuine representatives of the country" (*Skhema*, pp. 41–42).

For recent critical studies of NTS, see Department of State, *NTS — The Russian Solidarist Movement* (External Research Staff, Office of Intelligence Research, Series 3,

No. 76, Washington, D. C., December 10, 1951); Boris L. Dvinov, "Messrs. Solidarists and Company" (American Committee for Free Russia, Inc., New York [1952], mimeographed); and Anatole Goldstein, "The Attitude of Recent Russian Emigrés Toward the Jewish Question" (Institute of Jewish Affairs, World Jewish Congress, New York [1952], mimeographed).

³ *Kurs*, III, pp. 91–100; *Za Rossiiu*, December 1936.

⁴ Aronson, *Pravda o Vlasovtsakh*; Nicolaevsky, "Porazhenchestvo" pp. 242–246.

⁵ Anti-Semitic items were found in *Dobrovolets* for 1943: September 22; October 3, 6; November 3; December 5; *Dobrovolets* for 1944: January 6, 9, 12, 16, 19, 23, 30; February 2, 6, 16, 20, 27; March 5, 22; April 16.

⁶ What is known regarding the position on Jews and anti-Semitism of Vlasov himself? Neither Vlasov's earliest declaration, the September 10, 1942 leaflet appeal nor his famous "Open Letter" contains an anti-Semitic statement or even a reference to Jews. However, three such statements are credited to Vlasov, all during the course of 1943. In June, the Paris émigré newspaper, *Parizhskii Vestnik*, quoted Vlasov as having said: "In the New Russia all of its peoples will be able to live according to their aspirations. But there will be no room there for Jews" (*Parizhskii Vestnik*, June 5, 1943). In the same month, the same paper attributed these words to Vlasov: "Bolshevism had the intention of realizing world revolution, but this revolution served only Jewry, and not the Russian workers, peasants, or intellectuals" (*Parizhskii Vestnik*, June 19, 1943). Lastly, according to two Russian-language newspapers, Vlasov's November 1943 statement on the *Osttruppen* shift contained three separate references to "Judo-Bolshevism" (*Dobrovolets*, November 17, 1943; *Parizhskii Vestnik*, November 27, 1943).

Of the other Vlasovite leaders, Malyshkin is quoted as having made several similar references, as to "a New Russia without Bolsheviks, Jews, and capitalists" (*Parizhskii Vestnik*, July 31, 1943). But by far the most extreme and lengthy anti-Semitic statement by an opposition leader comes, not unexpectedly, from the propaganda chieftain, Zhilenkov. In an extensive interview printed on January 20, 1945, in the Nazi *Vöklischer Beobachter*, Zhilenkov emphasized the power of the Jew: "Let me tell you who knows how to live well in Soviet Russia: the Jew. . . Today the Jews are in the leading positions of the USSR." He also stressed a point frequently made in Vlasovite statements: "These Jews never belonged to the family of the peoples of Russia." But he was the only major opposition leader that we know of to echo the Nazi theme of the world-wide Jewish conspiracy to dominate the world.

Turning to the official pronouncements of the Vlasov Movement, we again find an anti-Semitic strain, but again it is subordinate rather than dominant. No references to Jews are made in either the Smolensk or the Prague Manifesto. In the published outline of the course of lectures given at the Dabendorf School, two of the twenty-eight topics were concerned with the Jewish problem, as were two of the *Dobrovolets* pamphlet's answers to fifty questions.

We do not possess, unfortunately, a complete set of any Vlasovite newspaper. However, from the issues of *Dobrovolets* already cited, the early-stage publication for the *Osttruppen*, about two dozen anti-Semitic items can be found. Two of these were front-page articles; fourteen were on page four. A brief sample of the topics covered reveals a reference to the kikes (*zhidy*) Morgenthau and Litvinov, a comment that Jews are cowards in the Army, another that the Jews dominate the press, and the characterization of Stalin as pro-Jewish. And the banner front-page headline of the May 9, 1943, *Zaria* proclaims: "Death to the kike executioners of the Russian people."

Altogether, the printed record gives ample evidence of anti-Semitism among the Vlasovites. But this is by no means a complete answer to the question of just how anti-Semitic the Vlasov Movement was. Once again we must remark on the unreliability of wartime German-controlled publications. The propaganda apparatus of Hitler's Germany sought constantly, and through every possible means, to inject its own material — much if not most of it anti-Semitic — into the Vlasov press. In regard to the published reports of oral statements, an émigré historian has seconded the testimony of wartime eyewitnesses that not infrequently the printed versions of these addresses were "doctored" by the insertion of anti-Semitic remarks. In a detailed analysis of Malyshkin's Paris speech, he points out that "a New Russia without Bolshevism and capitalists" was perhaps the most often repeated slogan of the Vlasov Movement. Banners bearing this phrase were displayed in the very hall where Malyshkin spoke. Therefore, it seems not unlikely that Malyshkin may indeed merely have reiterated the slogan rather than, as the Nazi-minded *Parizhskii Vestnik* reported, altered it to "Bolsheviks, Jews, and capitalists."

But even if this falsification theory is disregarded, we cannot disregard the fact that the German pressure to embrace this basic Nazi tenet was ceaseless. It was always difficult to resist without jeopardizing the still high hopes of the Soviet defectors of winning major concessions from the German authorities. Thus it is not unlikely that the Vlasovite leaders, unable to omit anti-Semitic references completely, agreed to a minimum amount, along a certain line. This line stressed that the Jews were not a Soviet nationality, and thus not a concern of the "New Russia." Certainly our entire survey of published anti-Semitic references suggests that in both quantity and content the Vlasovite statements do not show a fanatical obsession, or a fundamental emphasis on anti-Semitism, an obsession so typical of Nazism and in Hitler Germany so easy — and so rewarding — to indulge in.

This is not to suggest that there was not indeed considerable anti-Semitism among Soviet defectors, nor that all that was published in this vein can be ascribed solely to German pressure. Not only Zhilenkov, but probably many other Soviet defectors, were *politically* anti-Semitic in that they were resentful of Soviet Jews in high office. Doubtless, too, many of them were prejudiced against Jews in a *social* sense of personal interrelations. For this social type of anti-Semitism, called *bytovoi* in Russian, probably is only relatively less widespread in the USSR than it was in Tsarist Russia. It is, moreover, certain that the Soviet defectors had not escaped the Soviet-bred authoritarian intolerance, or the Inertness that rendered clear, unbiased, independent thinking so difficult. Above all, anti-Semitism was everywhere in the air in Nazi Germany, and to succumb to some of it was almost inevitable. Even such a proudly liberal "open society" as the United States today produces enough free-floating anti-Semitism to spread the contagion far and wide. How infinitely more compelling must have been the outside influences in Hitler Germany, which was officially and fanatically dedicated to the propagation of anti-Semitism!

But to categorize a whole movement as anti-Semitic, it must be demonstrated that anti-Semitism had become a fundamental component of its ideology. And in the case of the Vlasov Movement, this we cannot do. Though it seems probable that many Soviet defectors were ill-equipped psychologically to reject anti-Semitism individually, the movement as a whole did not embrace anti-Semitism as a doctrine.

[7] Dvinov, *Vlasovskoe Dvizhenie*, p. 121.

## Chapter XIII. Soviet Opposition and the United States

[1] Representative official statements on Psychological Warfare may be found in *New York Times*, June 21, 1951, July 8, 1951, March 5, 1952, and March 24, 1952 (President Truman); *New York Times*, March 22, 1951, May 27, 1951, and June 29, 1951 (Secretary of State); *Congressional Record*, June 26, 1951 and *New York Herald Tribune*, November 4, 1951 (United States Congress); *New York Times*, January 30, 1952 (Assistant Secretary of State for Public Affairs); *New York Times*, June 25, 1951 (head of State Department's Voice of America).

[2] *New York Times*, March 5, 1952.

[3] For definitions of Psychological Warfare, see Charles A. H. Thomson, *Overseas Information Service of the United States Government* (Washington, D. C.: Brookings

Institution, 1948), pp. 10–13; Paul M. A. Linebarger, *Psychological Warfare* (Washington, D. C.: Infantry Journal, 1948), p. 40; Daniel Lerner, *Sykewar, Psychological Warfare against Germany, D-Day to VE-Day* (New York: G. W. Stewart, 1949), p. 6.

[4] Bruce Lannes Smith, Harold D. Lasswell, and Ralph D. Casey, *Propaganda, Communication, and Public Opinion, A Comprehensive Guide* (Princeton: Princeton University Press, 1946), pp. 1–2.

[5] For recent general analyses of Psychological Warfare, see Renzo Sereno, "Psychological Warfare, Intelligence, and Insight," in *Personality and Political Crisis*, Alfred H. Stanton and Stewart E. Perry, ed. (Glencoe, Ill.: Free Press, 1951), and *Propaganda in War and Crisis*, Daniel Lerner, ed. (New York: G. W. Stewart, 1951). Psychological Warfare in a World War III between the USSR and the West was touched upon in the widely discussed special issue of *Collier's* (New York), October 27, 1951, "Russia's Defeat and Occupation, 1952–1960."

[6] On the National Security Council, see *United States Government Organization Manual, 1951–52* (Washington, D. C.: Government Printing Office, 1951), p. 63. The relation of the Psychological Strategy Board to the National Security Council and to other U. S. Government agencies is shown in chart in *New York Times*, December 10, 1951.

[7] *New York Times*, February 11, 1952. See also *The Free World's Secret Weapon: The Peoples of Russia* (New York: American Committee for the Liberation of the Peoples of Russia [1952] and William Henry Chamberlin [a founding member of the American Committee], "Russians Against Stalin," *Russian Review* (New York), April 1952.

[8] The question of exiles from the USSR is discussed earlier in this book, on pp. 18, 32, 108–112, 129–130, 157–158, 212–214. In the stream of writing by exiles on their native land, three nonbiographical books stand out: F. Beck and W. Godin, *Russian Purge and the Extraction of Confession* (New York: Viking, 1951); Alexandre Ouralov, *Staline au Pouvoir* (Stalin in Power), (Paris: Les Iles D'Or [1951]); and G. F. Achminow, *Die Macht im Hintergrund* (The Power in the Background), (Grenchen, Germany: Spaten-Verlag, 1951). That such writing tells at least as much about this group as about the USSR is illustrated by the recent exiles' journals — such as *Literaturny Sovremennik* and *Svoboda* in Munich and *Satirikon* in Frankfurt — as well as by the literary and political sections of the two leading old-émigré publications, both appearing in New York: the daily *Novoye Russkoye Slovo* and the quarterly *Novy Zhurnal*. See also the publications of the Institute for the Study of the History and Institutions of the USSR, founded in 1950 by World War II exiles, in Munich, and of the two organizations for former Soviet citizens established in 1951 in New York by the Ford Foundation's East European Fund: the Chekhov Publishing House and the Research Program on the USSR. On the nineteenth century, see Oscar Handlin, *The Uprooted, The Epic Story of the Great Migration that Made the American People* (Boston: Little, Brown, 1952); Alexander Herzen, *My Past and Thoughts* (London: Chatto and Windus, 6 vols., 1924–1927).

[9] *New York Times*, March 12, 1952.

# Sources on the Vlasov Movement

## I. PRIMARY SOURCES

*Biblioteka Propagandista No. 9, Semia i Vospitanie Molodezhi v Germanii* (The Propagandist's Library No. 9, The Family and Education of Youth in Germany), ([Dabendorf]: Published by the Propaganda School of the Russian Army of Liberation, 1943).

Dvinov, B., *Vlasovskoe Dvizhenie V Svete Dokumentov* (The Vlasov Movement in the Light of Documents), (New York: Published by the Author, 1950).

Fischer, George, "General Vlasov's Official Biography," *Russian Review* (New York), October 1949. For the Russian original of the document translated in this article, see V. Osokin.

———, "Vlasov and Hitler," *Journal of Modern History* (Chicago), March 1951.

Gilbert, Felix, ed., *Hitler Directs His War, The Secret Records of His Daily Conferences* (New York: Oxford University Press, 1950).

*Goebbels Diaries, The*, Louis Lochner, ed. (New York: Doubleday, 1948).

Hitler, Adolf, *Mein Kampf* (My Struggle) (Munich: Verlag Franz Eher Nachfolger, 58th ed., 1933).

———, *Mein Kampf* (My Struggle) (New York: Reynal & Hitchcock, 1940), text in English.

International Refugee Organization, *Statistical Report with Four Year Summary* (Geneva: International Refugee Organization, 1951).

Kleist, Peter, *Zwischen Hitler und Stalin, 1939–1945* (Between Hitler and Stalin, 1939–1945) (Bonn: Athenaeum, 1950); contains an appendix with wartime documents.

Köstring, Ernst, "Aufzeichnung über den Besuch des Generals der Kav. Köstring, General der Freiwilligen-Verbände beim Herrn Reichsminister am 28.11.44" (Notes on the Visit of Cavalry General Köstring, General of Volunteer Units, to the Minister [of Occupied Eastern Territories] on November 28, 1944) (unpublished).

Kovach, A., *Ukrainska Vizvolna Borotba i "Vlasovshchina"* (The Ukrainian Struggle for Liberation and the "Vlasov Gang") ([Germany], 1948); contains an appendix with wartime documents.

*Natsionalno-Trudovoi Soiuz Novogo Pokoleniia, Kurs Natsionalno-Politicheskoi Podgotovki* (National Alliance of Russian Solidarists of the New Generation, Course of National Political Training) (Published by NTS): vol. I, *Osnovy Natsionalnogo Mirovozzrenia* (The Foundations of a National World View) (1939); vol. II, not published; vol. III, *Sotsialnaia, Ekonomicheskaia i Politicheskaia Zhizn* (Social, Economic, and Political Life) (Belgrade, 1937); vol. IV, *Istoricheskii Otdel* (Historical Part) (Belgrade, 1938).

*Nazi Conspiracy and Aggression* (Washington: U. S. Government Printing Office, 1946–1948), vols. I-VIII, Supplements A and B.

Nuremberg Trial, unpublished document NG-3534, "Ertzdorf Files," Columbia University Library.

Nuremberg Trial, unpublished document NG-4301, Columbia University Library.

Nuremberg Trial, unpublished document NO-2544, Columbia University Library.

Osokin, V., *Andrei Andreevich Vlasov, Kratkaia Biographia* (A. A. Vlasov, A

Brief Biography) ([Dabendorf]: Published by the Propaganda School of the Russian Army of Liberation, 1944). For an English translation of this pamphlet, see G. Fischer, "General Vlasov's Official Biography."

*Otvety Redaktsii gazety "Dobrovolets" na 50 voprosov* (Answers by the Editors of the Newspaper "Dobrovolets" to 50 Questions) ([Dabendorf], 1944).

*Programnye Polozheniia i Ustav Natsionalno-Trudovogo Soiuza Novogo Pokoleniia* (Program Statutes and By-Laws of National Alliance of Russian Solidarists of the Younger Generation) (Belgrade: Published by NTS, 1938).

Rosenberg, Alfred, *Memoirs of Alfred Rosenberg*, Serge Lang and Ernst von Schenck, eds. (Chicago: Ziff-Davis, 1949).

——, *Der Mythus des 20. Jahrhunderts* (The Myth of the 20th Century) (Munich: Hoheneichen-Verlag, 5th ed., 1930).

Rudnev, D., "Andrei Andreevich Vlasov, Zhiznennyi Put Syna Naroda" (A. A. Vlasov, The Life Path of a Son of the People), *Volia Naroda* [Dabendorf], November 15, 1944.

*Skhema Natsionalno-Trudovogo Soiuza* (The Scheme of the National Alliance of Russian Solidarists) (Preshov, Slovakia: Published by NTS, 1944).

Stalin, I., *O Velikoi Otechestvennoi Voine Sovetskogo Soiuza* (On the Great Patriotic War of the Soviet Union) (Moscow: Gosudarstvennoe Izdatelstvo Politicheskoi Literatury, 5th ed., 1950).

*Trial of Major War Criminals before the International Military Tribunal* (Nuremberg: International Military Tribunal, 1947–1949), vols. I–XLII.

Unpublished German document identified by British classification as "PWD 3 Aug. 44 captured German Document," Hoover Library, Stanford University.

*Untermensch, Der* (Subhuman Being) Heinrich Himmler, ed. (Berlin: Published by the SS, 1942).

Upravlenie Upolnomochennogo Soveta Ministrov Soiuza SSR Po Delam Repatriatsii, *Otvety na Volnuiushchie Voprosy Sovetskikh Grazhdan Nakhodiashchikhsia za Granitsei, na Polozhenii Peremeshchennykh Lits* (Answers to Questions of Interest to Soviet Citizens Located Abroad as Displaced Persons) (Moscow: Office of the Representative on Repatriation Affairs of the Council of Ministers of the USSR, 1949).

Vlasov, Andrei A., Leaflet Appeal, "480 RAB/IX.42," YIWO, Jewish Scientific Institute, New York.

Woodbridge, George, ed., *UNRRA, The History of the United Nations Relief and Rehabilitation Administration* (New York: Columbia University Press, 1950), vols. I–III.

[Zhilenkov, G. N.], "Das ist die UdSSR!" (This Is the USSR!), *Völkischer Beobachter* (Berlin), January 20, 1945.

Wladimirow, W., *Dokumente und Material des Komitees zur Befreiung der Völker Russlands* (Documents and Material of the Committee for the Liberation of the Peoples of Russia) (Berlin, 1944).

*Newspapers*

*Dobrovolets* [Dabendorf], 1943–1944.
*Novoe Slovo* (Berlin), 1940–1944.
*Parizhskii Vestnik* (Paris), 1942–1944.
*Pravda* (Moscow), 1941–1946.

*Volia Naroda* [Dabendorf], 1944–1945.
*Za Rodinu* (Sophia), 1937–1940.
*Za Novuiu Rossiiu* (Sophia), 1933–1937.
*Zaria* [Berlin and Dabendorf], 1943–1944.
*Za Rossiiu* (Sophia and Belgrade), 1932–1939.

II. Secondary Sources

Aronson, Grigorii, *Pravda o Vlasovtsakh, Problemy Novoi Emigratsii* (The Truth About the Vlasovites, Problems of the New Emigration) (New York: Published by the Author, 1950).

Boldyreff, Constantine W., "The Story of One Russian Underground Organization Attempting to Overthrow Stalin," *Look* (New York), October 26, 1948.

Bor-Komarowski, T., *The Secret Army* (New York: Macmillan, 1951).

Buchardt, Friedrich, *Die Behandlung des Russischen Problems während der Zeit des National Sozialistischen Regimes in Deutschland* (The Treatment of the Russian Problem During the National Socialist Regime in Germany) (unpublished, 1945).

Carroll, Wallace, "It Takes a Russian to Beat a Russian," *Life* (New York), December 19, 1949.

Curie, Eve, *Journey Among Warriors* (New York: Doubleday Doran, 1943).

Dvinov, Boris, *Vlasovskoe Dvizhenie V Svete Dokumentov* (The Vlasov Movement in the Light of Documents) (New York: Published by the Author, 1950); in addition to a collection of documents, contains extensive commentary.

Dwinger, Edwin Erich, *General Wlassow, Eine Tragoedie unserer Zeit* (General Vlasov, a Tragedy of Our Time) (Frankfurt: Otto Dikreiter Verlag, 1951).

Fevr, Nicolas, *Solntse Voskhodit na Zapade* (The Sun Rises in the West) (Buenos Aires: Novoe Slovo, 1950).

Fischer, Alfred Joachim, "A Russian Quisling," *Contemporary Review* (London), February 1945.

Fischer, George, *Der Fall Wlassow* (The Vlasov Case) (Berlin: Der Monat, 1951).

——, ed., *Russian Emigré Politics* (New York: East European Fund, 2nd ed., 1951).

Guderian, Heinz, *Erinnerungen eines Soldaten* (Memoirs of a Soldier) (Heidelberg: Kurt Vowinkel Verlag, 1951).

Hilger, Gustav, "Observations on General Vlasov and the So-Called 'Vlasov Action'" (unpublished, 1948).

*J'ai Choisi la Potence, Les Confidences du General Vlasov, Felon Sovietique* (I Chose the Gallows, The Confidences of General Vlasov, Soviet Traitor) (Paris: Editions Univers, 1947).

Jolis, A. E., "When the Red Army Fought Stalin, the Story of Hitler's Red Divisions" (unpublished, 1945).

Kazantsev, A. S., *Tretia Sila, Istoriia Odnoi Popytki* (Third Force, the History of One Attempt), excerpts published in *Possev* (Limburg, Germany), in twenty-three installments, April 25, 1950 to September 24, 1950.

Kerr, Walter, *The Russian Army, Its Men, Its Leaders and Its Battles* (New York: Knopf, 1944).

Kitaev, M., *Russkoe Osvoboditelnoe Dvizhenie* (The Russian Liberation Movement) (unpublished, 1947; supplement in 1949).

Kleist, Peter, *Zwischen Hitler und Stalin, 1939–1945* (Between Hitler and Stalin, 1939–1945) (Bonn: Athenaeum, 1950); includes an appendix of documents.

Köstring, Ernst, "Freiwilligenverbände" (Volunteer Units) (unpublished, 1951).

Kovach, A., *Ukrainska Vizvolna Borotba i "Vlasovshchina"* (The Ukrainian Struggle for Liberation and the "Vlasov Gang") ([Germany], 1948).

Lebed, Mikola, *UPA, Ukrainska Povstanska Armiia* (UPA, Ukrainian Partisan Army) (Published by Press Bureau, Ukrainian Supreme Liberation Council (UHVR) [Germany], 1946).

Michel, Karl, *Es Begann Am Don* (It Began on the Don) (Bern: Verlag Paul Haupt, 1946).

——, *Ost und West, Der Ruf Stauffenbergs* (East and West, the Call of Stauffenberg) (Zurich: Thomas-Verlag, 1947).

N., Dr., "Po Povodu Tak Nazyvaemogo 'Vlasovskogo Dvizheniia'" (On the So-called "Vlasov Movement") *Vozrozhdenie* (Paris), VII, January–February 1950.

*New York Times*, 1941–1952.

Nicolaevsky, B. I., "Porazhenchestvo 1941–1945 Godov i Gen. A. A. Vlasov" (The Defeatist Movement in 1941–1945 and Gen. A. A. Vlasov), *Novy Zhurnal* (New York), XVIII, 1948, and XIX, 1948.

Oven, Wilfred von, *Mit Goebbels bis zum Ende* (With Goebbels to the End) (Buenos Aires: Dürer Verlag, 2nd ed., two vols., 1950).

Peterman, Ivan H., "Prague's Four Fantastic Days," *Saturday Evening Post* (Philadelphia), July 14, 1945.

Petrov, Vladimir, *My Retreat from Russia* (New Haven: Yale University Press, 1950).

Pozdniakov, V., "Pervaia Pekhotnaia Diviziia Vooruzhennykh Sil Komiteta Osvobozhdeniia Narodov Rossii, Po Vospominaniiam Komandira 2-go Polka" (The First Infantry Division of the Armed Forces of the Committee for the Liberation of the Peoples of Russia, Based on the Memoirs of the Commander of the 2nd Regiment) (unpublished, 1949).

——, "Poslednie Dni" (The Last Days), *Golos Naroda* (Munich), series of seven articles from August 5, 1951 to October 21, 1951.

Thorwald, Jurgen, *Das Ende an der Elbe* (The End on the Elbe) (Stuttgart: Steingrüben-Verlag, 1950).

——, *Ungeklärte Fälle* (The Unsolved Cases) (Stuttgart: Steingrüben-Verlag, 1950).

——, *Einer von Ihnen War Wlassow* (One of Them Was Vlasov) (unpublished, November 1951); Scheduled for book-form publication in 1952 by Steingrüben-Verlag, Stuttgart.

*Ukrainian Resistance, The Story of the Ukrainian National Liberation Movement in Modern Times* (New York: Ukrainian Congress Committee of America, 1949).

Volzhanin, "Kto Zykov?" (Who Was Zykov?) *Borba* (Munich), November–December 1950.

[Wlassow, Heide], "Die Tragödie eines Generales," (The Tragedy of a General), *Schweizer Illustrierte Zeitung* (Zurich), January 10, 1951.

"14-oe Noiabria 1944 Goda v Prage" (The 14th of November, 1944 in Prague), *Borba* (Munich), November 1948.

\*\*\*, "Poslednie Dni Generala Vlasova" (The Last Days of General Vlasov), *Rossiiskii Demokrat* (Paris), I, 1948.

## III. ORAL TESTIMONY

*Soviet Exile*

Aldan, Mikhail A.
Artemov, Alexander N.
Bogdanov, A.
Fatali, Abo
Kanatbay, Karis
Karpinsky, Andrei
Kunta, Abdurakhman
Pismennyi, Yuri A.
Pozdniakov, Vladimir V.

Romanov, Evgenii R.
Samygin, Mikhail M.
Shteppa, Konstantin F.
Smirnov, Leonid P.
Solovev, Mikhail S.
Vassilaki, Vladimir P.
Vetlugin, Nikolai V.
Vetukhiv, Mikhail A.
Yakovlev, Boris A.

*Old Emigré*

Baidalakov, Victor M.
Balinov, Shamba
Boldyreff, Constantine W.
Kazantsev, Alexander S.

Kobiashvili, Simon
Kromiadi, Konstantin G.
Magoma, Akhmed-Nabi
Shandruk, Pavlo

*German*

Bräutigam, Otto
Hilger, Gustav

Köstring, Ernst
Strik-Strikfeldt, Wilfried

# INDEX

Page numbers in italics refer to appendixes and footnotes.